Computer-Assisted Language Learning

Context and Conceptualization

MICHAEL LEVY

CLARENDON PRESS · OXFORD
1997

Oxford University Press, Great Clarendon Street, Oxford OX2 6DP
Oxford New York
Athens Auckland Bangkok Bogota Bombay
Buenos Aires Calcutta Cape Town Dar es Salaam
Delhi Florence Hong Kong Istanbul Karachi
Kuala Lumpur Madras Madrid Melbourne
Mexico City Nairobi Paris Singapore
Taipei Tokyo Toronto
and associated companies in
Berlin Ibadan

Oxford is a trade mark of Oxford University Press

Published in the United States
by Oxford University Press Inc., New York

British Library Cataloguing in Publication Data
Data available

Library of Congress Catologing in Publication Data
Computer-assisted language learning : context and
conceptualization / Michael Levy.
Includes bibliographical references.
1. Language and languages—Computer-assisted instruction.   I. Title.
P53.28.L48   1996   418'.00285—dc20   96-35169
ISBN 0-19-823631-X (paperback)
ISBN 0-19-823632-8 (hardback)

10 9 8 7 6 5 4 3 2 1

Typeset by Best-set Typesetter Ltd., Hong Kong
Printed in Great Britain on acid-free paper by
Bookcraft (Bath) Ltd., Midsomer Norton

To my mother and father

Contents

List of illustrations

Figures

Tables

Preface

In writing this book, I have been motivated by three major concerns. Firstly, I have felt a strong desire to understand, and to some extent to circumscribe Computer-Assisted Language Learning (CALL) for the purposes of teaching it. For the last six years I have been coordinating a Master's degree in CALL, first at Bond University and now at the University of Queensland. Under the guidance of my colleagues Professor Andrew Lian and Professor Roland Sussex, I have had to determine the subjects that might go into such a Master's degree, then decide upon their content and appropriate assessment procedures. I have also been required to undertake research supervision at Master's and Ph.D. level. As a result, I need to have an idea of what constitutes CALL, what forces drive it forward, and what needs to be done by students who want to study it.

Secondly, I believe the CALL community needs to build upon what has gone before, rather than be led purely by the capabilities of the latest technological innovation. With the almost monthly appearance of new hardware and software there can be a tendency for those interested in CALL materials development simply to pick up the latest machine or technological option and get to work on a project. If the technology has not been widely distributed, it is rather too easy to impress. Moreover, past work and valuable experience can be ignored or overlooked. It is usual, when commencing research in other fields, to review and extend the work of others, but with CALL the approach can sometimes be a little more cavalier. Over the last three decades, a substantial number of CALL programs have been created. The concepts and principles underpinning the best of these programs do not necessarily become obsolete when the computer that is used to run them is retired. In fact, the valuable knowledge and experience that has accumulated through this work needs to be absorbed and used to inform new projects in the future.

Thirdly, I have been motivated by a desire to understand better the relationship between theory and application. In this, I have been particularly influenced by the collection of papers in Carroll's book

Designing Interaction published in 1991, which looked closely and profoundly at the relationship between psychological theory (basic science) and the practice of Human–Computer Interaction (HCI) design. To me, there are many parallels between the situation described in HCI, and the one prevailing in CALL. Like HCI, CALL authors seek to apply theory in the actual construction of programs, and much remains to be understood about this process. Theory and application in CALL provided the conference theme at the second Canadian CALL Conference in 1993, highlighting the interest in this issue. The union between theory and application is not as strong as it might be in CALL, and for this and other reasons I believe it is worth exploring further.

In addressing these three concerns, descriptive work has, I believe, a crucial role to play at this point in the evolution of CALL. Sufficient work in CALL has now been accomplished to warrant a description, and an assessment of the work completed so far. A description of CALL materials and projects can provide a sense of the whole, a feeling for the scope of CALL, and it can help identify key issues and themes. Some issues or topics may only be of a temporary concern, while others may continue to assert their influence over an extended period of time.

A sense of the whole is imperative because in my view CALL practitioners and researchers have not really assimilated the work that has been done, nor appreciated its relevance for current work, a point also made by Last (1989: 14). Researchers have increasingly narrow specializations, and it is easy to lose sight of the broader picture. Moreover, CALL is interdisciplinary, and as such we need to be aware of developments in related disciplines. Other fields such as instructional design, artificial intelligence, and psychology will undoubtedly also have contributions to make. This is particularly important, I feel, because CALL abounds with one-off projects that are often not described in relation to other similar CALL projects, nor set in the broader context. A description can provide an appreciation of what has been achieved so far, and provide a sensible platform for a discussion of possible directions in the future.

Attempting to situate CALL in relation to such fields and disciplines involves a certain degree of risk. Many boundaries are crossed that in many cases segregate knowledge, and the people and publications that represent it. As a result there is a danger of being accused of superficial treatment of the subjects that are held to contribute to the topic under examination. Nevertheless, for the reasons above, I feel it is worth this risk. Thus, rather than looking at CALL through the lens of a particular theory, field, or discipline from the outside, I am looking at CALL from within, and trying to make sense of it as a body of knowledge in its own right. By describing what people do when they do CALL, and thereby better understanding the processes of CALL materials development and use, I feel we will gain important insights into how CALL practice relates to the various theories and practices that are presently competing with each other to drive CALL forward.

The decision to write a book in this area was not an easy one. As I near completion of this manuscript in February 1996, I know that it will be at least one year before the book is published. Other forms of publishing such as electronic publishing are certainly quicker, and facilitate the dissemination of knowledge and information most effectively. Nevertheless, I feel a book is an appropriate forum for a broad-ranging exploration and description of CALL. Moreover, if CALL is worthy of being considered a field in its own right, then I believe it should contain some invariant qualities, issues that remain pertinent to the theorist and the practitioner over time, notwithstanding the pace with which technology continues to develop.

Acknowledgements

In my work over the last twelve years, I have been fortunate to be able to discuss aspects of CALL with a variety of people, especially in the United Kingdom, North America, and Australia.

In particular, I would like to thank Andrew Lian. Having a profound understanding of the processes of language teaching and learning, and a firm grasp of the strengths and limitations of technology, Andrew Lian has been able to provide expert advice and comment on many occasions.

I am also grateful for the help and encouragement of my colleagues at the Centre for Language Teaching and Research at the University of Queensland, especially Michael Harrington and Roland Sussex, the Director of the Centre.

For the survey component of this work, thanks are also due to the CALL practitioners who agreed to lengthy interviews, and who gave generously of their time and expertise. These individuals include Carol Chapelle, Graham Davies, David Eastment, John Higgins, Tim Johns, Glyn Jones, Frank Otto, and John Underwood. I would like to record my thanks to the 104 CALL practitioners who generously took the time to complete the detailed CALL Survey described in Chapter 5 of the book. Without their assistance this work would not have been possible.

Finally, I would like to acknowledge my debt to all those who read and commented on early drafts of the manuscript. They include Mary-Louise Craven, Graham Davies, James Garton, Alison Green, Stephen Heap, and Peter White. Jiansheng Chen also deserves my thanks for helping with the references. Of course if any errors remain, they are my sole responsibility.

Acknowledgements are made to the following people and publishers from whose texts the extracts below have been taken:

Dix, A., J. Finlay, G. Abowd, and Beale, R. 'Time/space matrix', Figure 13.1 in *Human–Computer Interaction*, published by Prentice Hall in 1993.

Ahmad, K., Corbett, G., Rodgers, M., and Sussex, R., 'A model of the three main factors in CALL (learner, language, computer)',

Figure 1 in *Computers, Language Learning and Language Teaching*, published by Cambridge University Press in 1985.

Nunan, D., *The Learner-Centred Curriculum*, published by Cambridge University Press in 1988.

Carroll, J. M., in J. M. Carroll (ed.), *Designing Interaction: Psychology at the Human–Computer Interface*, published by Cambridge University Press in 1991.

1. Introduction

Computer-Assisted Language Learning (CALL) may be defined as 'the search for and study of applications of the computer in language teaching and learning'. The name is a fairly recent one: the existence of CALL in the academic literature has been recognizable for about the last thirty years. The subject is interdisciplinary in nature, and it has evolved out of early efforts to find ways of using the computer for teaching or for instructional purposes across a wide variety of subject areas, with the weight of knowledge and breadth of application in language learning ultimately resulting in a more specialized field of study.

CALL has been made possible by the invention and subsequent development of the computer. As a result, the nature of CALL at any particular time is, to a large degree, a reflection of the level of development of the technology. In the early days, when developers had access only to large mainframe computers, they needed to know a machine language to program the computer, and they tended towards numerical applications because such computations were more directly compatible with the workings of the computer. In more recent times, computers have become smaller, faster, and easier for the non-specialist to use. Developments in 'user-friendly' human–computer interfaces and higher-level languages and authoring systems insulate the developer from the lower-level workings of the computer, allowing comparatively complex applications to be written with relative ease.

The speed with which technology has developed since the invention of the computer has been both extraordinary and surprisingly sustained. For educators, the rapid and continuing introduction of new technology into education has outpaced the ability of teachers and developers to evaluate it properly. No sooner do we come to terms with one machine and develop some CALL materials for it than another, 'better' machine arrives to replace it. Nevertheless, it would be irresponsible to be led purely by the latest technological breakthrough. Somehow, we must try and make sense of what is going on, in spite of the rate of change, and invent reliable and cost-effective mechanisms for dealing with it.

Set against this background of a rapid, continually evolving technology, there are conceptual and practical problems that all newcomers to CALL encounter in one way or another. For all those who wish to create new CALL materials, either privately or commercially, independently or as a member of a team, even a cursory glance at contemporary CALL activity shows that there are a multitude of approaches.[1] Points of departure range dramatically from top-down approaches centred perhaps upon a theory of language or language learning, or a curriculum specification, while others might develop CALL materials from the bottom up, perhaps by using the computer to address a particular classroom problem. Other points of departure might include a learning strategy, a macroskill, computer conferencing, or an exploration of aspects of the technology itself. Once the point of departure has been clarified, there are immediately practical issues to consider—for example, the selection of the hardware and software development tools for the project. *HyperCard, Authorware, ToolBook,* CALIS, C, and *Visual Basic,* or a mark-up language to enable publishing on the World Wide Web such as the Hypertext or Virtual Reality Mark-up Languages (HTML and VRML), are just a handful of the many options now available.[2]

Given that the way in which CALL is conceptualized can be largely determined by the hardware and software that is used, this initial design choice is a most important one, and it can have a sweeping influence on what is ultimately created. This is a consequence of the development process, where the strengths and limitations of the development environment variously shape and constrain the CALL materials that are produced. The software then has to reach the students and be used on a regular basis. Here there is a twofold problem: on the one hand the equipment might have been superseded by the end of the project; on the other hand, the intended student group might not be able to get access to the materials because the cost of the equipment is prohibitive. If textbook materials prove themselves they may be used for years with good effect; if CALL materials are effective then often they are discarded when the next model of computer comes along—and for no other reason. In the twentieth century, it takes a special kind of courage to continue to use a particular technology once it is considered to be outmoded, even if that technology is more than adequate for the task at hand.

Within this volatile environment, a substantial number of CALL
materials have been produced, especially over the last ten to fifteen
years, and, judging by the number of projects described in the
CALL journals and at conferences, there is no sign that this interest
is about to diminish. Yet it has to be said that CALL remains a
peripheral interest in the language teaching community as a whole,
still largely the domain of the CALL enthusiast, and there is scant
evidence to suggest that CALL has really been absorbed into mainstream thinking, education, and practice.

Of the CALL materials that have been produced, there has been
much criticism, most especially directed at the software produced
by language teachers. In the 1980s particularly, the inferior quality
of CALL materials was blamed on inexperienced language teacher–
authors who may not have known how to make appropriate use of
the medium (Hofmeister and Maggs 1984: 1–19; Weible 1988: 67).
As a result, questions have arisen concerning the most appropriate
role of the language teacher in CALL materials production (Smith
1988: 3; Last 1989: 34). Whilst on the one hand leading writers on
CALL appear to want language teachers to be involved in CALL
(e.g. Farrington 1989: 70; Sussex 1991: 21), at the same time,
somewhat paradoxically, language teachers who have become
CALL authors have received much unfavourable criticism. In this
debate, it should not be forgotten that were it not for the ambitious
pioneering efforts of language teachers in CALL, the whole endeavour might not have got off the ground. Arguably, within the field of
computers and education, especially within humanities computing,
it is teachers in the area of English as a Foreign Language (EFL) and
foreign languages more generally that have been in the vanguard.
For all the false starts and incomplete realizations of CALL, the
1980s were a highly creative decade. More recently, concerns have
appeared to move away from the question of the role of the language teacher in CALL materials development, though concerns are
still expressed about the status of CALL. In this respect, Kohn
suggests that current CALL is lacking because of poor linguistic
modelling, insufficient deployment of natural language processing
techniques, an emphasis on special-purpose rather than general-
purpose technology, and a neglect of the 'human' dimension of
CALL (Kohn 1994: 32).

Although many of these criticisms may well be justified, a lack of
guidelines or standards for the current generation of CALL materi-

als has meant that CALL authors, be they language teachers or otherwise, have no reliable conceptual framework, or yardstick by which to measure their work (Smith 1988: 5; Last 1989: 35). Emerging most strongly in a review of the literature on CALL materials is the lack of a generally accepted theoretical framework that authors can use to guide their work. The absence of 'a standard for the industry', a 'generally agreed set of criteria for the present generation of CALL', or 'guiding principles' is noted by Smith (1988: 3), Last (1989: 35), and Ng and Olivier (1987: 1).

It appears that a clear, general theoretical framework has not emerged for a number of reasons. There is some anecdotal evidence to suggest that materials developers fall into two broad bands in their approach to their work. As early as 1977, for example, in computer-assisted learning Kemmis *et al.* (1977: 391) observed that many developers rely on their intuition as teachers rather than on research on learning. He referred to development being practitioner-led, not research-based. A similar division is noticeable in the field of artificial intelligence, where Ginsberg (1988) maintains that the field is divided between those who are primarily interested in solving problems by formulating theory (formalists), and those who prefer to solve problems by writing programs (proceduralists). A perception of this division has remained and more recently in 1995 it was reiterated in slightly different terms at two CALL Conferences. First, in a keynote address at the EUROCALL Conference in Valencia, McCarty spoke of the path of engineering versus the path of science in CALL (McCarty 1993, 1995), and secondly, at the CALL Conference in Exeter, Sussex, quite independently, contrasted Engineering CALL with Empirical CALL (Sussex 1995). Such divisions are worthy of further investigation and reflection.

Where theory has been used as a point of departure, theoretical sources that have been proposed and used have been diverse, not surprisingly perhaps given the range of CALL activities and the evolving nature of the field. Theories emanating from psychology, especially cognitive psychology and Second Language Acquisition (SLA), are a frequent point of departure (Schneider and Bennion 1984; Doughty 1991; Liou 1994). The theories utilized from psychology are usually drawn from a restricted set thought to be amenable to the CALL context generally. For instance, Doughty (1991) limits her focus to comprehension-based models of SLA because of their suitability for the CALL environment. Other theoretical bases include theories of language (e.g. Demaizière 1991;

Catt 1991) and theories of instruction (England 1989; Lawrason 1988/9). In addition, integrated frameworks have been proposed, such as Hubbard (1992, 1996), or Mitterer *et al.* (1990: 136) who suggest an integrated framework using theories from instructional design, language teaching, language learning, and knowledge of the applicability of the technology. Integrated frameworks recognize the multifaceted nature of CALL materials development.

There is also some evidence to suggest that a number of CALL projects have not been driven directly by theory as such. Although some projects clearly begin with a theoretical orientation, others begin at a lower level of abstraction more immediately determined by conditions governing actual practice and problems arising directly from it. CALL projects of this type as they are described by their authors in the literature include vocational language programs which begin with addressing student needs (Keith and Lafford 1989), *KanjiCard* which uses a specific language problem as a point of departure (Nakajima 1988, 1990) and CLEF, where developing grammar skills is the goal (Paramskas 1989, 1995).

In all, it is clear there are a number of possible theoretical points of departure in CALL, either utilizing a single theory or a mix of theoretical perspectives. It also seems apparent that some CALL projects do not begin with a theory at all, reflecting the comment by Kemmis and his colleagues about work that is practitioner-led as opposed to research-based (Kemmis *et al.* 1977). To help resolve this issue further, we need to have a clearer idea of what CALL authors actually do when they go about designing CALL materials.

Little is known about the conceptual frameworks and working methods of CALL authors at present. Sussex (1991: 26) stresses the importance of investigating the processes of CALL materials production and says:

At the present time rather little work has been done on the question of how teachers become CAL authors: how they objectify their knowledge domains, learning, and teaching; how they conceptualize learning materials and learning modes for transfer to the CAL medium; how they achieve this transfer; how the existence and use of CAL media influence theories of CAL, and vice versa.

By carefully reviewing what has already been done, and by exploring the ways in which CALL is conceptualized, a clearer understanding of theory and practice will emerge. This book attempts to address these areas of concern, not by providing definitive answers, but by shedding light on the nature of the problems. Such a description has the potential to improve our understanding of:

- the scope of CALL and prominent areas of focus within it;
- the theoretical sources and conceptual frameworks of CALL authors;
- the possible weaknesses or gaps between theory and practice.

As yet the scope of CALL is not well defined, and its relationship with other related fields is not clear. For example, some writers see CALL as a sub-domain of Applied Linguistics (e.g. Leech and Candlin 1986: 204), while others challenge this view (e.g. Fox 1986*a*: 235). A description of CALL projects to date, together with the points of departure their authors proclaim, can help situate CALL in relation to cognate fields and disciplines, and provide pointers towards relevant resources, both theoretical and practical.

Given the newness of CALL, when practitioners do search for a theoretical foundation for their work, they are likely to draw on theories from the more established disciplines that surround it. In attempting to make use of these theories, care has to be taken to ensure that the theories are applicable. At this time, it does CALL a great disservice to try and force it into a single epistemology or theoretical framework, especially one that comes from a field where language learning *with the computer* is not foremost in mind. It is tempting to approach the complexities of CALL in this way, of course, because such a strategy provides a well-trodden path for further research and development. But what if the theory does not encompass the unique qualities of learning with the aid of a computer? Ideally, the use of non-CALL theoretical frameworks should only occur if they are sufficiently well articulated and powerful in themselves, and if they are fully applicable to the context of CALL. By reviewing the motivations for CALL materials design, and by describing the CALL programs that have been produced, the relationship between theory and practice can be examined. By describing what CALL authors actually do, their conceptual frameworks and working methods, their personal 'theory' of language teaching and learning can be set against their CALL programs, many of which are now in circulation and can be described and evaluated in their contexts of use. But first a description of what has already been done is needed.

Historical and interdisciplinary perspectives can help provide a context for CALL. An historical perspective can help identify topics and themes that keep reappearing over time, probably with good reason: for example the question of the role of the teacher in CALL. Also, it can help prevent CALL succumbing to the latest technological advance in a way that is blindly accepting. For example, multimedia is much in vogue at present, not only in CALL but right across the educational curriculum. While undoubtedly having much to offer, multimedia is not new—it was available in a primitive form in the TICCIT project in the 1970s, and in a form rather similar to that of today in the Athena Project in the late 1980s, albeit on workstations rather than microcomputers (see Chapter 2). Knowledge of the approaches taken in the design and implementation of these early multimedia programs provides insights for the contemporary multimedia author. A historical view is also helpful in mapping the changing relationship between approaches to language learning and computing. Early in the history of CALL, a highly structured view of language teaching and language learning provided a straightforward path towards materials development on the computer because the principles behind the theory could be easily matched to the qualities of the machine: lock-step drill and practice software was, for example, easy to program. More recently, with the advent of communicative views of language teaching and learning, and with more eclectic approaches to language teaching generally, the relationship between pedagogy and the technology has become more tenuous and more complex.

An interdisciplinary perspective on CALL shows it to be a relatively new field of study that has been subject to the influence of a number of other disciplines. In addition to the fields of computing and language teaching and learning, real or potential influences in the development of CALL have included aspects of psychology, artificial intelligence, computational linguistics, instructional design, and human–computer interaction. Many of these disciplines are relatively new in themselves, having developed significantly since World War II. They each have their own perspective and frame of reference, they often overlap and interrelate, and the extent to which any one discipline should influence the development of CALL has not been determined. At various times, CALL workers have called upon each of these fields to guide their own work in some way, and in Chapter 3 an interdisciplinary perspective gives examples of how these links have been utilized.

Having set forth a context for CALL, the book continues with a description of how CALL authors have conceptualized CALL. In broad terms 'conceptualization' is used as a label to signify the mental picture a CALL author or a teacher has when envisaging the use and role of the computer in CALL. The term is used by Richards and Rodgers (1986: 15) in discussing the evolution of their model of language teaching method. As with a discussion of approaches and methods in language teaching, 'conceptualizaton' would seem the best term to use for a discussion of similar issues in CALL.

It is not immediately obvious how to go about building a picture of how CALL has been conceptualized. On reflection, the strategy finally taken was that used by Hirschheim *et al.* (1990: 22) in ascertaining the impact of microcomputer use in the humanities. That team of researchers used a number of component 'indicators', each considered to represent a key factor that needed to be examined if the phenomenon as a whole were to be understood. The indicators that are held to relate to how CALL is conceptualized are the:

- language teaching and learning philosophy;
- role of the computer;
- point of departure;
- hardware and software;
- role of the teacher (as contributor);
- development process;
- role of the teacher (as author);
- materials developed.

A CALL author's views of language teaching and learning are held to influence how that author conceptualizes CALL, even if the author cannot explain the effects or make them explicit. The role of the computer contributes to the conceptualization in many ways, the most important distinction perhaps being whether the computer's role is directive or non-directive. The point of departure describes the CALL author's declared starting-point for a project.[3] Often given when CALL projects are written up and published, points of departure may range from a theory of language or language learning to a problem recognized by a language teacher in the classroom, and that is considered amenable to a solution via the computer.

The hardware and software, in their capabilities and limitations, are considered variously to shape what is, and what is not possible in a CALL project. The teacher may contribute in a conceptualization of CALL, or the role of the human teacher in the implementation of the program may not be envisaged at all. The development process is included as an indicator because of the way the process may deform or shape the initial conceptualizaton leading to an end-product that may be very different to the one originally conceived. As well as contributing in some way to the conceptualization by contributing to it, the teacher may also be involved in developing CALL materials, that is as a CALL author. The role of the teacher as developer of CALL materials is included because of the ways in which language teachers, through their CALL development work, have contributed to CALL's conceptual frameworks. Finally, a description of the CALL materials that have already been created is included. The CALL materials that are now available provide tangible evidence of the ways in which the use of the computer in language teaching and learning has been conceptualized.

The ways in which CALL authors translate their knowledge and experience of language teaching and learning to the computer and produce CALL materials is necessarily a complex and multifaceted process. The major assumption in this work is that these 'indicators' are valid. At this stage in the development of CALL all that may be said is that the indicators for conceptualization have face validity, and there is a reasonable likelihood that an investigation of these elements will provide insights on how CALL is conceptualized.

The indicators were investigated in both the literature reporting CALL projects and through a survey of CALL practitioners following the work of Stolurow and Cubillos (1983), Ng and Olivier (1987), and Fox *et al.* (1990). The component indicators for conceptualization provide the structural framework for Chapters 4, 5, and 6: the indicators are examined in the literature in Chapter 4 and through the CALL Survey in Chapter 5. The international CALL Survey was conducted in late 1991 and early 1992. A total of 213 questionnaires were distributed and 104 (48.8%) usable responses were returned. The questionnaire was sent to 23 different countries, and key practitioners in CALL from 18 countries replied. The key practitioners were chosen on the basis of having written programs or published in the field of CALL. The vast majority of respondents (i.e. CALL authors) were practising language teachers (97.1%). The questionnaire combined with the information found in the literature gives a comprehensive overview of how CALL has been conceptualized so far.

This book is divided into eight chapters. The first two chapters aim to set CALL in context in order to provide a suitable background for the discussion of CALL's conceptual frameworks. Chapter 2 provides a historical perspective on CALL. This chapter is by no means a full and detailed history of CALL, but rather it is a perspective, a synopsis of the field by decade, in the 1960s and 1970s, in the 1980s, and in the 1990s. For each time period, CALL projects are selected and described which are representative of the thinking and the activity of the period, and themes are introduced that have contemporary relevance. Particular emphasis is placed on some of CALL's more invariant qualities: topics and issues that tend to recur in CALL over time, such as the role of the computer in CALL and the role of the language teacher in relation to it. An exploration of the context of CALL continues in Chapter 3 where an interdisciplinary perspective is provided. In this chapter an attempt is made to establish links between CALL and the disciplines that surround it, and have variously influenced its development. A short description of each of the related disciplines accompanies the account. In this way these two chapters on CALL in context provide a setting for the rest of the book, and introduce many of the themes that are explored in greater detail later on. Chapters 4, 5, and 6 focus in much more detail on how CALL has been conceptualized, that is, how language teachers and CALL authors have envisaged the use of the computer in the realm of language teaching and learning. Using the indicators that are held to influence conceptual frameworks as an organizational framework, Chapter 4 looks at aspects and issues described in the literature on CALL, and Chapter 5 presents the findings of the international CALL Survey. These two chapters approach the topic from different angles, the two approaches complement each other, and each perspective provides a window onto the complex phenomena of conceptualization. The threads of this description are brought together for discussion in Chapter 6, where particular themes are identified and drawn out. These themes do not account for all the ways in which CALL has been conceptualized, but they do represent recognizable patterns that are discernible when CALL is viewed as a whole. Chapter 7 looks at one conceptual framework in particular: the tutor–tool framework. This framework is presented as a potential means of conceptualizing CALL. The framework is valuable in helping users and developers recognize significant features in CALL from the vast array of CALL projects that have occurred to date. Other CALL models and frameworks are accommodated within the tutor–tool framework, and possible refinements to this framework are suggested also. The implications of the tutor–tool framework are considered by showing how the role of the computer, that is, whether it is used as a tutor or as a tool, has profound implications for methodology, integration into the curriculum, evaluation, and the roles of the teacher and the learner. Finally, Chapter 8 on the nature of CALL completes the book. Viewing CALL as a body of work brings to light a number of issues such as the relationship between theory and application, and the effects the computer, and technology more generally, may exert on the surrounding educational environment. Finally, this chapter concludes with some suggestions for the future, reflecting on where the energy and the effort in CALL might most appropriately be directed.

Notes

1. In this book the label 'materials' will be used to encompass the different kinds of materials, software, courseware, programs, packages, and learning environments that are created in CALL. This label is used to emphasize the connection between language learning materials development in general—where the term 'materials' is commonly used—and CALL materials development in particular. Though in some instances materials and learning environments will be distinguished and treated separately, generally learning environments on the computer are included under the materials umbrella. This follows the work of Breen *et al.* (1979: 5) who, in the case of Communicative Language Teaching (CLT), suggest the development of two kinds of materials: *content* materials as sources of data and information; and *process* materials to serve as 'guidelines or frameworks for the learner's use of communicative knowledge and abilities' (Breen *et al.* 1979: 5). Thus, learning environments on the computer are likened to process materials in that they provide frameworks within which learners can use and practice their communicative skills. The notion of materials as guidelines or frameworks for learning is reinforced by Allwright who argues for

    materials to be related to the 'cooperative management of language learning' (Allwright 1981: 5). Learning environments on the computer fit comfortably within this broad definition of materials.

2. A mark-up language such as HTML (the Hypertext Mark-up Language) is a set of instructions that are inserted into a plain text file to enable it to be published on the World Wide Web. The set of instructions, or tags, defines exactly how the Web document is displayed. The tags also enable links to be made between documents. Once on the Web, browsers such as *Netscape* can interpret the file. VRML (Virtual Reality Modelling Language) is an emerging standard for creating three-dimensional spaces and objects that can be transferred easily via the Internet, then viewed by many users at the same time.

3. In the CALL Survey the initial orientation and points of departure are distinguished to accommodate more abstract and more precisely described initial positions (see Ch. 5, Apps. A and B). For example, if a CALL author describes the starting-point in a project rather abstractly, as in 'exploration of a new technology' perhaps, then this would be considered an initial orientation; if 'curriculum specifications' were the starting-point, however—a more concrete beginning—then this would be considered a point of departure. This distinction can only provide a rough approximation, but it was included in the CALL Survey because it allows for different degrees of clarity at the outset.

2.   CALL in context I: a historical perspective

Introduction

Histories of computers and education, and CALL in particular have already been documented elsewhere.[1] This historical review is more selective. It aims to pick out beginnings and significant developments in CALL by focusing on selected CALL projects representative of three time periods, the 1960s and 1970s, the 1980s, and the 1990s. The review aims to highlight the developments and the thinking of each period by introducing suitably representative CALL projects decade by decade. The historical perspective aims to identify some of the less variant qualities of CALL, and particular emphasis is placed on insights or developments made some years ago that still have contemporary relevance. In his recent article on the PLATO project, for instance, Hart describes the legacy of PLATO IV, the most recent incarnation of this ground-breaking educational computing project (1995). In so doing Hart describes some of the lessons learnt from past experience. In the same way, in this chapter through an examination of representative projects, I hope to identify some key themes and issues that remain important today. In this way we can endeavour to build upon what has gone before, notwithstanding the speed with which technology continues to advance. Specifically, the review looks at methodological and technological developments, and associated approaches to evaluation. In addition, for each period a cross-section of two or three projects is described each of which illustrates the kind of activity occurring at that time. Though the projects differ greatly in virtually all aspects—scale, funding, and goals—nevertheless, they illustrate rather well the nature of the activity in the time frame. The projects, which are presented in more or less chronological order, are: for the 1960s and 1970s, the PLATO and TICCIT projects; for the 1980s, *Storyboard*, and the Athena Language Learning Project (ALLP); and for the 1990s, the International Email Tandem Network, the CAMILLE/*France InterActive* Project, and the Oral Language Archive (OLA).

To accompany the project descriptions, sections on evaluation are added for each time period. As well as CALL-specific examples and discussion, work on evaluation from computers and education in general is included also, because of its relevance for CALL and its potential to provide insights. In particular, discussion of work by Yildiz and Atkins (1993) is included as it highlights salient characteristics from media evaluation studies from the 1950s in time periods very similar to ones used here, and because an appreciation of the broader educational computing context helps inform the CALL-specific one.

CALL in the 1960s and 1970s

Background

In the 1950s and early 1960s empiricist theory was predominant in language teaching, a theory described by Stern (1983: 169) as 'pedagogically audiolingualism, psychologically behaviourism, linguistically structuralism'. The principles emanating from these three schools of thought were mutually supportive when applied to language teaching and learning. Derived from the work of Skinner in his influential book *Verbal Behaviour* (1957), the central elements of behaviourism, that of stimulus, response, and reinforcement, had a profound effect on language teaching practice, especially in the widespread introduction and use of the language laboratory. The audiolingual approach to language teaching emerged towards the end of the 1950s in the USA (Richards and Rodgers 1986: 47). The approach emphasized use of the target language in spoken form and students were expected to learn the language through a process of habit-formation, that is, practice. The teacher presented new vocabulary and structures through dialogues which students learned through imitation and repetition. Key structural patterns were extracted from the dialogues and used as the basis for pattern drills: successful responses were positively reinforced (Larsen-Freeman 1986: 43).

Another important influence at the time was programmed instruction. B. F. Skinner was largely instrumental in advancing this movement (Skinner 1954). He advocated the use of teaching machines for individualized instruction which would be responsive to the preferred pace of the learner. Underlying principles included the use of instructional steps or 'frames', and active responses from the learner which would be followed by immediate feedback. According to Kenning and Kenning (1990: 94), programmed instruction particularly influenced the grammatical sequencing that was very much in evidence in early CALL.

In CALL, software developers soon realized that drill and practice exercises advocated in the audiolingual approach were readily programmable on the computer because of their 'systematic and routine character' and 'their lack of open-endedness' (Kenning and Kenning 1990: 53). In the PLATO and TICCIT projects described in the following sections of this chapter, the way in which CALL was conceptualized was drawn, at least in part, from audiolingualism and empiricist theory. It must also be said, however, that both systems have shown themselves capable of adapting to more recent approaches to language teaching, and to more advanced technological options.

The PLATO project

Early Computer-Assisted Instruction (CAI) projects tended to involve the development of large-scale systems, involving team efforts that were well funded. The two most prominent projects, costing approximately five million dollars each, were the PLATO and TICCIT projects, both of which were used to teach foreign languages as well as other subjects.

CALL may be said to have begun with the PLATO (Programmed Logic for Automatic Teaching Operations) Project which was initiated at the University of Illinois in 1960.[2] Don Bitzer, a professor of electrical engineering, was instrumental in creating the first version of the system, PLATO I (Hart 1995). This initial version was modified and improved, and three versions of PLATO were to follow. Through the demonstrable success of PLATO III, a fully functional educational computing system itself, the National Science Foundation provided significant funding for the development of PLATO IV, and it was with this version of PLATO that the critical mass necessary for large-scale development was achieved.

PLATO was designed specifically to provide interactive, self-paced instruction for large numbers of students (Smith and Sherwood 1976: 344). The system had a number of innovative features. It supported communication between users in the form of notes files and 'talk', a kind of restricted email system. Two kinds of notes files facilitated general announcements to all users and the exchange of messages between student and teacher. The 'talk' facility enabled written communication to take place between users who were simultaneously signed on to the system. PLATO also allowed for student records to be maintained for the student's information, the teacher's information, and for research purposes (Chapelle and Jamieson 1984: 14). According to Hart (1995: 28), in 1979 PLATO was able to provide a highly coordinated and sophisticated site management system, one that is still unequalled today with micro-computer networks.

Extensive PLATO-based materials were developed for a number of languages, the most comprehensive being developed by Marty (1981) for French language learners. These materials were comprised of a four-semester series on written French grammar and vocabulary, as well as additional lessons in French linguistics, geography, culture, and several dialogue lessons. General examples of foreign language CALL materials can be found in the areas of reading (including vocabulary), writing (especially lessons in both recognition and production of grammatical patterns), and listening with perhaps the greatest amount in the area of writing (Chapelle and Jamieson 1984: 16–17).

It was recognized from the beginning that PLATO, like today's CALL materials, could not look after all the language learners' needs, especially in the areas of speech production and understanding. The role of PLATO was to cater for 'the more mechanical types of vocabulary and grammar drill, thereby freeing class time for more expressive activities' (Hart 1981: 12). Even at this time the quest for an appropriate role for the computer was being considered, as noted by Marty (1981: 85), who suggested we need to 'determine what computers *can* do and *cannot* do for our profession'.

The PLATO philosophy towards writing instructional materials for language learning within an instructional framework is described by Hart (1981: 7):

There are two basic approaches to authoring CBI. One, which might be termed the 'paradigm' method, provides a set of prefabricated instructional formats (e.g. matching, multiple-choice, paired associate drill); the author's task is then to fit content into these schemata as parameters. The other provides a 'toolbox' of general capabilities which the author can use to

construct whatever instructional design he/she wishes. The latter is much
more powerful, but also requires more of the lesson author. Both procedures have valid uses.

Lesson material for use on the PLATO system was written using the
TUTOR authoring language which Hart describes as a high-level
language which represents the 'toolbox' approach (Hart 1981: 7).[3]
Though more flexible than the paradigm method, TUTOR still
shaped and variously constrained the type of CALL activities that
could be created. It provides a good example of how the hardware
and software tools determine, to a considerable degree, how CALL
is conceptualized. Question-answer-feedback sequences could be
developed easily with TUTOR, reflecting closely the methodology
of the day, but the more the author tried to move away from this
approach, the more difficult the authoring became (Hart 1995: 20).
Substantial efforts were made to invent new designs using TUTOR,
one of which included a text-to-speech system, but Hart (1995: 25)
concludes that refining drill and tutorial designs continued to account for most of the materials development activity. He also adds
that from the CALL point of view the 'greatest frustration' of
PLATO was that developers could only create materials using the
TUTOR language (1995: 36). None the less for the first time,
TUTOR enabled language teachers to become directly involved in
CALL materials production, and considerable efforts were made to
ensure that TUTOR was easy to use for the non-programmer (Hart
1995). Authors of lesson material had extensive on-line help available to them and could call on professional consultants through a
PLATO terminal when required (Smith and Sherwood 1976).
CALL development on the PLATO project was not theory driven.
Most of the development was guided by 'immediate utility', and the
course materials were created by classroom teachers, rather than
researchers (Hart 1995: 29). As a result, Hart notes that, though
the data collection facilities on the system were very powerful, they
were underexploited because of the bias towards immediate use
rather than experimental work (1995: 29).

By the end of the 1970s PLATO had clearly proved itself, with
the system delivering 50,000 student hours of language instruction
in a dozen languages, plus 50,000 hours in other curricula (Hart
1995: 30). It was a ground-breaking project in numerous ways, and
whatever its limitations, it was the first project to engage language

teachers and technical staff in the development of CALL materials in a coordinated way.

The TICCIT project

TICCIT is an acronym for Time-Shared, Interactive, Computer Controlled Information Television and the project was initiated in 1971 at Brigham Young University. This system combined television technology with the computer. Importantly, TICCIT had its own in-built instructional system, and it remains one of the very few computer systems to be devised solely around a specific theory of teaching or learning. Those who advocate theory-driven systems would do well to bear in mind some of the lessons drawn from this project, particularly in regard to the reactions of teachers to the project. In this case the language teacher could contribute to the material content of the lesson, but not to the instructional strategy that was employed to present it. With its capacity to combine text, audio, and video, TICCIT was perhaps the first example of multimedia CAI. So multimedia has been a reality for over twenty years, though admittedly not on computers that were widely available.

TICCIT differs from the PLATO system in that a specific instructional framework, which dictates the actual form of the hardware, software, and courseware, is built into the system. The particular instructional design framework, called Component Display Theory (CDT), was developed by Merrill (1983; 1988). CDT is comprised of three parts: 'a 2-dimensional performance-content classification system, a taxonomy of presentation forms, and a set of prescriptions relating the classification system to the presentation forms' (Merrill 1988: 61). CDT assumes that performance levels are associated with different presentational forms, and that when the correct presentational form is used, student achievement and learning efficiency are increased.

A central tenet of the TICCIT system is learner control (Merrill 1980*b*; Jones 1995: 90). Learner control goes beyond the simple selection of content, to include choice over the presentational form. To facilitate this choice, a specially designed keyboard containing fifteen learner control keys can be used to select the instructional displays. Special keys including keys marked Rule, Example, Practice, Advice, Objective, Easy, Hard, enable the student to have control over both the content and the learning strategies used for study. Merrill (1980*b*: 80) gives a specific example for language learning: a Rule display shows a description of a general rule for pronoun-referent agreement; an Example display gives concise explanation and an example; and a Practice display asks the student to edit a passage which contains pronouns that do not agree in number with their referents. Other keys allow students to get help and to choose difficulty levels.

With the original TICCIT system the instructional design was predetermined. Thus, the author, whilst being able to contribute to *what* material was to be taught (the material content of lessons), could not alter *how* it was to be taught (the instructional strategy), the assumption being that strategy and content are relatively independent of one another (Merrill 1980*b*: 86). Within this framework the language teacher–author does not have to learn a computer authoring language. On the other hand the teacher would have to feel comfortable with the instructional design built into the system, and with control over the material content only. With the more recent microcomputer version of TICCIT, called MicroTICCIT, an authoring system has been developed called ADAPT. Here the designers are less prescriptive and although the 'Rule, Example, Practice' (REP) model is highly recommended, the accompanying documentation assures the potential author that 'the built-in REP model is available as an instructional option and authors are free to use the model, develop their own model, or use no predefined model at any of ADAPT's three authoring levels' (MicroTICCIT manual: 2). Such a position is noteworthy, because traditional instructional design advocates a prescription for instruction (see Chapter 3). With ADAPT, the advice given to the user is much less prescriptive, in fact it is quite the opposite. Prescriptive designs which preclude options in presentational and instructional formats may not be received kindly by materials developers because they demand control not only over content, but also over the way the content is presented as well.

To a certain extent, both PLATO and TICCIT have evolved to accommodate subsequent advances in computer hardware, and the systems exist today on a number of mainframe computers at universities and in the form of MicroTICCIT for microcomputers. It must also be said, given that both systems were conceived in the era of audiolingualism, that both systems showed themselves capable of adapting to more recent approaches to language teaching, as illustrated by their continued use today.

Evaluation

Independent evaluations of these two large CAI projects were conducted by the Education Testing Service: for PLATO by Murphy and Appel (1978) and for TICCIT by Alderman (1978). For PLATO the results showed that the system appealed to both teachers and students, but work on the system had no consistent positive or negative effect on student achievements or attrition rates. In contrast, for TICCIT the results showed there was a significant performance advantage compared to that of students in conventional classes, but student and teacher attitudes were not as positive. A dramatic decrease in course completion rates for TICCIT was also noted, an outcome that may be inherent in self-paced instruction where some students may find difficulty in managing their own instruction. Three important points follow from this study according to Hofmeister and Maggs (1984: 3–10): first, because of wide differences in results, care must be taken in generalizing findings from one CAI project to another; secondly, careful monitoring is critical to assess the reasons for attrition; and thirdly, CAI that teaches as well as a conventional instructor is of value, especially in areas where specialist teachers are unavailable.

For media evaluation studies of this period, Yildiz and Atkins (1993) characterize the major thrust as comparative: the new medium of instruction was compared directly with the traditional medium. Traditional experimental design techniques predominated, marked by random assignment of learners to control and experimental groups, and pre- and post-tests of knowledge to assess learning gains. With these research designs, differences in the treatment of content was minimalized so that the effects of the new technology could be set in high relief. In other words, by keeping the content the same, the delivery modes could be compared, that is the teacher might be compared with the computer. The results of these studies showed little or no difference between the final scores of learners in the two groups. Interestingly, though this conclusion seems to be borne out in the evaluation of PLATO, significant differences were found in the evaluation of the TICCIT Project.

More recently, Pederson argues that comparative studies should 'forever be abandoned' (1988: 125), on the grounds that they 'fall into the trap of attempting to attribute learning gains to the medium itself rather than the way the medium was manipulated to affect achievement' (1988: 104). Of course, there remain political motives for comparative studies. If it can be shown that computer-assisted learning is at least as effective as the human equivalent, if not more so, then substituting a computer for a teacher can be substantiated.

Overall computer applications in teaching and learning in the early 1970s were marked by a period of moderate growth and some disillusion. Despite large investments by the National Science Foundation and the Office of Education in the USA, projects often quickly disintegrated once federal funds expired (Hofmeister and Maggs 1984: 1–15). Although a significant bulk of materials were produced for foreign language education (see Chapelle and Jamieson 1984), the number of schools, colleges, and universities using them remained somewhat limited. This period was dominated by the audiolingual approach to language teaching, but by the 1980s a different view was taking hold.

CALL in the 1980s

Background

In the 1960s and early 1970s developments in CALL were taking place against a background of empiricist theory which provided a well-defined, structured approach to language teaching and learning. However, in the late 1970s these strands that had been woven together so successfully, began to unravel. As a result, instead of the set of optimal prescriptions for language teaching that was used in the 1950s and 1960s, views became more circumspect reflecting the complexity of language teaching and learning and the attributes and needs of the individual learner. Notable amongst the new methods that began to appear in the 1970s were the new humanistic methods such as Community Language Learning (Curran 1976) and Total Physical Response (Asher 1977). Humanistic methods and techniques engaged the whole person, their emotions and feelings, the affective dimension (see Moskowitz 1978: 2). But the most far-reaching approach to language teaching to emerge at this time was Communicative Language Teaching (CLT). Richards and Rodgers characterize CLT as an approach rather than a method which 'aims to (a) make communicative competence the goal of language teaching and (b) develop procedures for the teaching of the four language skills that acknowledge the interdependence of language and communication' (Richards and Rodgers 1986: 66). That said, the communicative approach to language teaching is open to a number of interpretations, and as Long points out, CLT practice has not been derived from the results of SLA research (Howatt 1984: 279; Long 1988: 115). It remains a label that is widely used by language teachers, however, and clearly it has meaning for practitioners.

Whilst significant change was occurring in theories of language, language learning, and language teaching, rapid change was also taking place in computing. In 1973 the microcomputer was invented, the Scelbi 8-H based upon the 8-bit 8008 chip, but it was not until 1975 that computer clubs began to form around the USA (Smarte and Reinhardt 1990: 369). In 1976 Apple Computer was formed and the Apple I released. In the following year the Commodore PET, the Apple II, and the Radio Shack TRS-80 were released and these machines were the first really to make inroads into the population at large in the USA. In 1977 the first serious educational applications appeared (Hofmeister and Maggs 1984: 1–17). It was some years later, however, before the impact of the microcomputer became apparent in the wider educational context, with the introduction of the Apple II in the USA (1977), the Sinclair ZX80 (1980), and the BBC micro in the UK (1982), and in Australia in about 1983 with the introduction of the Apple IIe. At this time the interest in CALL grew dramatically and much software was produced, but without a unified theory supporting its structure and content.

The early 1980s saw a boom in computer-assisted language learning largely due to the introduction of the microcomputer. Introductory books on the topic began to appear, including O'Shea and Self (1983), Kenning and Kenning (1984), Wyatt (1984c), Higgins and Johns (1984), Ahmad *et al.* (1985), Davies and Higgins (1982; 1985), and specialized CALL journals, such as the *CALICO Journal* first appeared (1983).

It was in the early 1980s that the language teacher–programmer became prominent. With the widespread availability of inexpensive microcomputers, often supplied with a version of BASIC, the motivated language teacher could write simple CALL programs. Programming in BASIC for language teachers was encouraged through texts such as Higgins and Johns (1984), Kenning and Kenning (1984), and Davies (1985), which contained fragments of BASIC, or complete programs in the language. Prior to microcomputer CALL, most software development had resulted from well-funded team efforts because of the complexity of the task and limited access to mainframe computers. The programming component of these projects was completed by specialists in the field. Now, in theory at least, language teachers were free to develop their own conceptualization of CALL on the microcomputer, the only major constraint being their programming ability. The range of software written by teacher–programmers at this time was broad. It was often centred around a single activity and examples included text reconstruction, gap-filling, speed-reading, simulation, and vocabulary games (Wyatt 1984*c*; Underwood 1984).

In developing CALL software for the microcomputer in the 1980s, teacher–programmers often chose to learn a high-level programming language such as BASIC to design materials from scratch. Other language teachers produced CALL materials using authoring programs such as *Storyboard*. Two other possible approaches to authoring were the use of authoring systems and authoring languages.

An authoring system that has had a resounding influence across educational computing is *HyperCard*, becoming well known when released for the Macintosh computer in 1987. *HyperCard* is a good example of how long-standing concepts can suddenly find expression and widespread acceptance on the computer, though they have existed for many years. The non-linear approach to text production and consumption was derived from the work of Ted Nelson who first coined the word 'Hypertext' in 1965 (see Nelson 1967, 1981).[4] This work itself was derived from the idea of the 'memex' first outlined by Vannevar Bush in 1945. Other manifestations of the concept include *Notecards* by Xerox PARC, *Intermedia* at Brown University, and *Guide* at the University of Kent, which was the first commercial implementation of hypertext (Cooke and Williams 1993: 80). More recently, of course, the phenomenal growth in the use of hypertext started when the NCSA Mosaic browser was released early in 1993, and the hypertext concept has in part been responsible for the extraordinary growth of the Internet and the World Wide Web ever since.

The language teacher has not only played a role in developing CALL materials, but also in using them effectively with students. Many CALL commentators have stressed the importance of carefully integrating CALL work into the broader curriculum (e.g. Farrington 1986; Hardisty and Windeatt 1989; Garrett 1991). In achieving successful integration, the teacher's role is central, not only in choosing materials to incorporate into the programs, but also in integrating the computer activity into the lesson as a whole (Jones, C. 1986). This point is emphasized in Jones's influential paper 'It's not so much the program, more what you do with it: the importance of methodology in CALL' (Jones, C. 1986). Jones stresses the intelligent combination of class work away from the computer with work on the computer, achieved by coordination and advanced planning by the teacher. Thus, CALL materials are not intended to stand alone, but to be integrated into broader schemes of work (see also Hardisty and Windeatt 1989).

The development of word processing on microcomputers must be mentioned also because of its widespread use in language teaching (Wresch 1984). In 1978 MicroPro announced *WordMaster*, the precursor to *WordStar*, and *Word* and *WordPerfect* for a variety of micros followed in 1983 and 1984 respectively (Smarte and Reinhardt 1990).

Storyboard

A typical example in the authoring program genre of the 1980s is the *Storyboard* program written by John Higgins. *Storyboard* is a text-reconstruction program for the microcomputer where the aim is to reconstruct a text, word by word, using textual clues such as the title, introductory material, and textual clues within the text. The program also falls into the authoring program or authoring package category, in that teachers (or students) can use the authoring facility within the program to write, or author, their own texts which are then incorporated into the program for future use.

Storyboard has an interesting history that gives some indication of how a CALL software program evolves as the concept and the technology develop.[5] The original total text reconstruction idea for a microcomputer probably emanates from Tim Johns at the University of Birmingham, who wrote two programs called *Masker* and *Textbag* that variously exploited the general concept (Davies 1996). Both programs are described in Higgins and Johns's seminal book, *Computers in Language Learning* (1984). John Higgins wrote the original version of *Storyboard* in 1981 for a Sharp CP/M computer and for the Sinclair Spectrum in BASIC (*Eclipse* manual: Higgins 1989: 18). Graham Davies (1996) then worked collaboratively with Johns to produce a version for the Commodore PET and BBC microcomputers. Chris Jones produced an Apple II version at the same time. Early versions of *Storyboard* were published by Wida Software, London in 1982. An agreement with a second publisher, who insisted on certain modifications to make the program more user-friendly, led to a new version of the program called *CopyWrite* which was published in 1984. *Storyboard* itself underwent further modification, and new versions of the program were created for different languages and for different microcomputers. In the mid to late 1980s text reconstruction programs proliferated, with many variations exploiting the same central idea in different ways. They included *Developing Tray*, *TextPlay*, *Storyline*, *Quartext*, *Storycorner*, and a Swedish version called *Memory*. I even had a go myself, and developed a program called *GuessText*. Other programs such as *Fun with Texts* extend the total text reconstruction idea considerably by adding further activities. Versions of *Storyboard* are now available for IBM style (DOS and Windows) and Macintosh computers for English, French, Spanish, and German. To my knowledge, the most recent manifestation of the Storyboard concept, released by Higgins in 1989, is called *Eclipse*. In this version instead of hiding all the text automatically at the start, as did *Storyboard*, the user can choose to mask or display specific word types. In other words, learners instead of beginning the activity with all the words hidden, could now begin with selected categories of words displayed, (e.g. nouns), thus extending the flexibility of the program considerably. Over time the Storyboard idea has been refined and modified, both to exploit the capabilities of new hardware as it evolves, and to ensure that user needs are properly met.

The level of expertise and the amount of time required to create such programs as *Storyboard* was within the reach of individual language teacher–programmers. It is interesting to note, however, that as the 1980s progressed expectations grew, and in more recent versions of the text-reconstruction idea, professional programmers have usually been employed to optimize the workings of the program, and to ensure that the programs are suitably user-friendly and 'bomb-proof'. Last refers to programs like *Storyboard* as first-generation CALL, and text reconstruction, alongside gap-filling, text manipulation, and simulation, provided the basis for many CALL activities created by language teacher–programmers at this time (Last 1989: 47; Scarborough 1988: 301).

Brett (1994) discusses the use and value of text reconstruction programs. He emphasizes the use of authentic material, and suggests that text reconstruction activities are best exploited as one in a series of communicative tasks. The careful integration of CALL work and non-CALL work is apparent in the way Brett organizes the learning environment. Legenhausen and Wolff (1991) assessed the *Storyboard* program more formally, particularly with regard to the learning strategies used by students. They noted six strategy types: frequency strategies, form-oriented strategies, and strategies related to grammatical knowledge, semantic knowledge, textual knowledge, and world knowledge. They conclude that regardless of the particular learning strategy learners employ, the use of *Storyboard* is valuable for promoting language awareness.

The Athena Language Learning Project

While many language teachers were becoming directly involved in creating CALL software for the microcomputer, the tradition of the larger scale project for more sophisticated computers continued, notably through the Athena Project. In 1983, the Massachusetts Institute of Technology (MIT) established Project Athena as an eight-year research program to explore innovative uses of the computer in education. One focus of the project was to create an experimental system for building multimedia learning environments. Within this framework is the Athena Language Learning Project (ALLP), whose aim is the creation of communication-based prototypes for beginning and intermediate courses in French, German, Spanish, Russian, and English as a Second Language (Morgenstern 1986). The Athena Language Learning Project (ALLP) was conceived within the communicative approach to language learning. The educational principles underlying ALLP are described by Murray *et al.* (1989: 98):

Language is seen as a negotiable system of meanings, expressed and inter-
preted via the social interaction of reader and text, or between speakers in
a culturally coded situation rather than as a closed system of formal lexical
and grammatical rule. Accordingly the aim of the materials being developed is not so much mastery of the grammatical and syntactic code as the
ability to use this code to perform certain actions.

Project Athena began in 1983 at MIT with initial funding of $50
million dollars from Digital Equipment Corporation and IBM with
the aim of exploring innovative uses of the computer in education
(Lampe 1988). As of 1988, MIT had 450 computer workstations,
interconnected using a campus-wide network, on various sites
around the institute. Among these workstations is 'a cluster of 32-
bit "Visual Workstation" machines which are capable of combining full-motion digitized colour videodisc, cable television, digital
audio, high resolution graphics and CD-ROM' (Lampe 1988).

Of the many new research initiatives associated with this project,
two are particularly noteworthy. The first is the development of the
MUSE multimedia authoring environment. It uses the basic structure of hypertext and hypermedia systems to provide for extensive
cross-referencing of video, audio, and graphic materials (Lampe
1988). The second important initiative employed in the ALLP is
MIT-based artificial intelligence techniques where the goal is to
'develop a natural language processing system that can intelligently
"guess" meanings intended from minimal clues, and check its understanding with the user' (Murray *et al.* 1989: 98).

An example of an application of these techniques is *No
Recuerdo*, language learning materials for Spanish. *No Recuerdo* is
an interactive video narrative based on a simulation game about an
amnesiac Columbian scientist (Murray 1987: 35). The video provides a series of structured conversations with strong narrative
interest and a topic-based discourse structure (Murray *et al.* 1989:
106). As students explore and try to understand the plot, they query
people in the story by typing questions and commands on the
keyboard. The program uses artificial intelligence techniques to
parse the questions and commands and thereby determine the flow
of the action through the story (Murray *et al.* 1989: 107). The goals
of the program are vocabulary learning in context, reading and
listening comprehension, cultural awareness, and practice with
conversational strategies (Morgenstern 1986: 31).

As the ALLP is intended as a prototype only, it is difficult to
assess the role of the teacher when these materials are in use.

Nevertheless, Morgenstern (1986: 24) asserts that the software will 'certainly not supplant' the teacher–learner relationship, as the materials are designed for use in the language laboratory and in conjunction with classroom activities. It is also significant that language teachers were heavily involved in the ALLP and their areas of interest and expertise were utilized in their development (see Murray 1987: 34). Finally, since the ALLP has not been widely implemented, extensive evaluative studies have not yet been conducted.

The three major projects, the PLATO and TICCIT projects and the ALLP, described in the first part of this chapter, are illustrative of how CALL has been conceptualized in the larger scale projects. In each case many of the innovations of the larger projects have subsequently been modified and implemented on smaller-scale, less expensive technology, particularly microcomputers. Few microcomputer projects have involved approaches not encountered first in relation to the larger projects described here. For example, multimedia applications in language learning, of strong contemporary interest to CALL materials developers, were first explored in the Athena project. Thus, filtering and diffusion effects can be observed over time. Development projects that initially require a specialized group of programmers and highly sophisticated technology, later become feasible for a much wider group of CALL practitioners using machinery that has grown in power and availability in the interim. More recently, multimedia applications such as those explored in the Athena Project are now possible on microcomputers using tools such as *Authorware* (IBM/Mac), *ToolBook* (IBM) and *Director* (Mac). Instead of learning a high-level language, CALL authors have the option of using one of these authoring tools all of which are capable of controlling a range of interconnected media including computers, videodisc, and CD-ROM.

Evaluation

When empiricist theory predominated there appeared to be a perfect match between the qualities of the computer and the requirements of language teaching and learning. With the advent of the communicative approach to language teaching, some writers began to say that CALL methodology was 'out of step' with current ideas on language teaching and learning (Stevens *et al.* 1986: p. xi), that the ideologies conflicted (Smith 1988: 5) and that CALL was not adaptable to modern methodologies (Last 1989: 39). Last commented that, 'The potentiality of the computer appears all the more restricted as a language teacher if you couple that to the fact that communicative competence is now increasingly playing a central role at all levels of language learning' (Last 1989: 37).

Aside from the question of matching methodological demands with technological capabilities, other critics of CALL have directed their attention towards the dominance of the microcomputer and, in some instances, specific brands of microcomputers. For example, in 1989 Last (1989: 32) blamed the static state of the art in CALL in the UK on the market dominance of the BBC microcomputer. Lian also maintains that conceptualizing CALL only within a microcomputer framework is overly restrictive (Lian 1991: 2).

Two major syntheses of research on CALL in the 1980s have been completed by Pederson (1988) and Dunkel (1991*b*). They summarize their findings on effectiveness research on CAI and CALL to date as 'limited' and 'somewhat equivocal' (Dunkel 1991*b*: 24). Of the research on CALL and education generally conducted to 1988, Pederson summarizes the research findings as follows:

1. Meaningful (as opposed to manipulative) CALL practice is both possible and preferable.
2. The way CALL is designed to encourage the development of language learning skills can result in more learning.
3. Learner differences can be documented easily and accurately through computer tally of interactive learning strategies.
4. Learner differences can affect learner strategies, learning gains, and attitude in CALL.
5. Students tend to demonstrate a more positive attitude towards CALL written by their own instructor.
6. Language teachers need to develop strategies for manoeuvering effectively within the culture of the learning laboratory and the educational institution in order to secure needed computer resources.
7. Despite the enthusiasm of language teachers already using CALL, many language teachers are dissatisfied with existing software and desire training on how to integrate CALL into the existing curriculum.

In suggesting research directions for the 1990s, Carol Chapelle (1989*a*) describes how the assumptions underpinning the CALL research question of the 1970s—'Is CALL effective in improving students' second language competence?'—have been invalidated during the intervening period and gives the following justification. Firstly, it is now recognized that the term CALL covers a range of activities, not just one type; next, 'second language competence' is now defined as a complex set of interrelated competencies, making it more difficult to test directly as a result; thirdly, researchers have recognized the importance of studying the processes of learning, causing research that focuses on learning outcomes alone to be inadequate; and finally, individual student characteristics have been shown to have a significant impact on SLA (Chapelle 1989*a*: 7–9).

Trends in evaluation studies from this period in CALL, were reflected in changing attitudes toward evaluation generally. Yildiz and Atkins (1993: 134) note a 'fundamental shift' in the purpose of evaluation studies at this time, from a rather 'naïve' search for a superior teaching machine to a more 'atomistic study' of the characteristics of the new media in relation to key factors associated with learning, the learner, and the learning context. Such approaches to evaluation usually require laboratory-based work. Yildiz and Atkins discuss the 'genuine dilemma' with which all evaluators must contend: whether to aim for high internal validity through laboratory-based methods where variables can be carefully controlled, while running the risk that equivalent results may not be achievable in real classroom settings; or to aim for authentic use, which, while satisfying the need for studies in real contexts, raises the likelihood that the findings cannot be generalized beyond the specific context where the evaluation takes place. For CALL the number of variables involved in evaluating CALL makes it difficult to reach any conclusion on the viability of CALL 'on any concrete and measurable grounds' (see Ahmad *et al.* 1985: 119; Hirvela 1989: 64). Chapelle concludes that research efforts need to recognize the multifaceted nature of CALL activity, the components of language competence, the relevance of the learning process, and the individuality of the learner in order to plan effectiveness research in a suitably precise way. Only then will the research findings be of real value in helping to direct CALL research and development in the future.

CALL in the 1990s

Background

Few would argue that one of the most dramatic and far-reaching technological developments in the 1990s is the Internet, the world-wide 'network of networks'. A decade or so after the introduction of the microcomputer, the Internet has produced another leap forward in terms of greater access to materials, people, and learning environments. The Internet is said to have begun in 1969 as a project of the US Government's Department of Defense, with the aim of providing an electronic communications network capable of surviving a nuclear attack. Like the first CAI project before it, military concerns yet again entrained significant technological innovation.[6] Several brilliant computer engineers were drawn together by the Advance Research Projects Administration (ARPA), and the result was the military network, ARPAnet. Unlike prior systems which worked in a hierarchical way, that is each computer in the system was dependent upon another in order to function properly in the network, this computer network treated every computer within it in the same way, so that if one or more computers were out of action, the system could easily circumvent the problem.

At about the same time that the Internet came into being, local networking in the form of LANs (Local Area Networks) was evolving fast. LANs are usually restricted to one site, or a close group of sites and the computers in the network are physically connected, that is by cable rather than by a satellite or microwave link. A LAN is more or less a closed system; it may exist in a building, or it may constitute the network in a computer laboratory, for example. As LAN technology evolved and the demand grew stronger, rather than connecting to a single large time-sharing computer at each site, users wanted to connect their own local networks to the ARPAnet so that pathways of communication could be extended to the benefit of all concerned. For the various LANs and the ARPAnet to be linked together, each network had to speak the same language. In the process of creating ARPAnet, the Internet Protocol (IP) was developed, and this communication 'language' enabled different networks to talk to each other.[7] The protocol defines how messages are packaged and addressed so that they can be sent and received on the Internet. The IP can be likened to the disc operating system in stand-alone computers. In 1982, the Transmission Control Protocol (TCP) was added, providing a set of protocols (TCP/IP) that is still with us today. These protocols led to the first definitions of an 'internet' as a connected set of networks with TCP/IP as the manager. This network was successful, and other networks, particularly university systems, connected to it. A combination of two or more LANs form a WAN (Wide Area Network). WANs grew in size and complexity. Eventually, it became clear that the system as originally envisaged could not handle all the messages, so in the late 1980s a new network was created, a network that is essentially the same as the present Internet as we know it. The Internet might be considered the ultimate WAN, although it is important to remember that many schools, at least in Australia, are unable to connect their LANs to the Internet because of the expense of the connection.

In the 1990s with the foundations of the Internet secure, more attention has been paid to the development of software that might help users locate and retrieve information. To this end *Gopher*, a menu-based system for exploring the Internet was released in 1991. A further breakthrough was made in 1992 with the release by CERN of the World Wide Web (WWW), a hypertext-based system for finding and accessing Internet resources. Using the WWW requires a browser (sometimes referred to as the application of the 1990s, as the word processor was the application of the 1980s), and the race was on to create one. *Mosaic* was released in 1993, and *Netscape Navigator* (*Netscape*) followed in 1994.

The Internet continues to evolve and develop at an extraordinary rate. As its capacity for passing greater quantities of digital information through its communication channels increases, so does its capacity to handle more text, video and audio material, that is, multimedia materials. The CALL projects in this section make use of the Internet in different ways, or illustrate advances in multimedia, which, like the Internet, has come into its own in the 1990s.

The International Email Tandem Network

The International Email Tandem Network, begun in 1993 by Helmut Brammerts, is described as language learning by computer mediated communication using the Internet (Brammerts 1995). In the Tandem Network, universities from around the world are linked together to enable students to learn languages in tandem via email on a reciprocal basis. The Tandem Network consists of a steadily increasing number of subnets, for instance the Spanish–French subnet, each of which includes a bilingual forum, where participants can engage in discussions and ask each other for advice in either language, and a database, where users can both access and add teaching and learning materials themselves.[8]

The Tandem Network functions via a discussion list on the Internet where a 'posting' goes to all subscribers on the list. The label 'list' or 'listserv' is used because the groups are driven by a special listserv program; they are also under the control of a system administrator who manages the list. In the case of the Tandem Network, two or more coordinators look after each subnet. The coordinators help participants in various ways: they moderate discussion in the forum, and they oversee the development of the database (Brammerts 1995). In the Tandem Network, most of the subnets use a computer at the Department of Computer Linguistics at the University of Trier, but in principle they can be run by any computer.

At the Exeter CALL Conference in 1995, St John and Cash spoke of their experience with the Tandem Network, specifically the German–English subnet, in developing written German via a one-to-one exchange (St John and Cash 1995*a*, 1995*b*). Their talk was unusual in that the two speakers represented the teacher and the student, in this case an English speaker learning German. The student, David Cash, had a reasonable grasp of German (English O-level standard) and was attending an evening course at intermediate level in the conventional way. This study was supplemented by the work undertaken via email. The teaching/learning approach taken in the email interactions emerged very much from the views of the participants on how language learning occurs. The student reported that the construction of a personal dictionary was most helpful, and he described making a conscious effort to try out new expressions. He also reported that the email work stretched him, whereas the course work did not. An interesting strategy used by the teacher was not to correct learner errors directly, but simply to reply with the same expressions in context and in the correct form, a strategy that appeared to work very well. Further advantages of the email exchange noted by the student included the value of a permanent record of what was said, and the frequency with which the interactions could occur: sometimes every day with email as opposed to two hours once a week with the course (St John and Cash 1995*b*).

The use of an email connection in this way raises a number of issues. It points towards language learning beyond the offerings of an institution, and highlights learner, and in fact teacher, autonomy. Interactions may be determined more by individual ideas about how language is learnt, and through mutual negotiation and agreement, rather than ideas more formally received. In this instance, the email work accompanied a formal course of study, but there is no reason for this to be so. Such interactions entrain more informal learner–teacher relationships, where a curriculum, methodology, and techniques are negotiated and determined by the individual participants. Such modes of operation emphasize the emancipatory qualities of technology in bringing more options to the learner to access language learning opportunities, perhaps entirely outside more traditional institution-based environments.

The CAMILLE/*France InterActive* projects

The CAMILLE (Computer-Aided Multimedia Interactive Language Learning) consortium consists of partners from the UK, France, Spain, and the Netherlands, and the goals of the group are to provide beginner courses in Dutch and Spanish, and advanced courses for French (business and industry) and English. The CAMILLE Project, which grew out of *France InterActive*, combines a 'communicative competence' approach to language acquisition with an interactive multimedia environment (Ingraham and Emery 1993: 26; Ingraham 1993: 48; Ingraham *et al.* 1994).[9] The earlier project required the creation of 'a collection of pedagogical and computational strategies' suitable for a computer-mediated learning environment. This collection of strategies has been further extended and refined and is now represented in CAMILLE (Ingraham 1993: 43).

In the CAMILLE Project, the notion of a learning environment is central. The learning environment supports the study of the language, and as a result CAMILLE/*France InterActive* is a learning, rather than a teaching resource. The computing environment provides the learner with tools and information to facilitate the learning of languages (Ingraham 1993: 49, 65). The tools and information include a textbook of learning activities, a grammar, a dictionary with recordings of a native speaker saying the words, audio and video recordings, a book on the culture of the target language, and a notebook.

In order to help the student manage and organize these resources, in CAMILLE the metaphor of the electronic desktop is used. The metaphors that are employed in any conceptualization of CALL are especially helpful, because they provide a means of coming to terms with the unfamiliar, and a mechanism for transferring concepts that are well known and understood to circumstances which are new and uncertain. Metaphors in computing and CALL can range from the book or the desktop to more extravagant conceptualizations, at least in computing terms, such as the globe which we enter and explore and where we can look up or down, in front or behind; this metaphor has been discussed in relation to the creation of three-dimensional virtual worlds on the Internet. Though metaphors can be valuable, in helping us imagine what can and cannot be done in a computing environment, metaphors can impede progress if new technology is tied down to inappropriate metaphors that unnecessarily restrict our vision of what technology can accomplish.

With the desktop metaphor, we envisage perhaps a table top where things can be moved around and organized, and where particular items may be picked up and read. In CAMILLE, on the desktop the learner first encounters a textbook open at the contents page. Surrounding the textbook are icons representing the various tools and resources referred to above. The student may select from the table of contents in the textbook, or alternatively select one of the reference sources. Students are directed in their studies through lessons, which are subdivided into modules and units. The approach is eclectic (Ingraham 1993: 57) and students complete activities ranging from the conventional to the novel, including drills, quizzes, cloze, and role-playing exercises (Ingraham 1993).

The *France InterActive* model, described by Ingraham and Emery in 1991, provides a detailed, well-organized, and perceptive discussion of the multimedia development process with a useful discussion of underlying assumptions and the problems to be overcome. Ingraham and Emery suggest that the development decisions fall into three groups: hardware issues, software issues, and pedagogical issues. Briefly, in the hardware section, they decide to settle for the technology which is the most widely available. In the software section, they begin by testing the suitability of existing authoring packages: none was entirely adequate. The use of a high-level programming language was for a time considered, and then rejected. In the end a compromise position was adopted with the use of a number of compatible authoring systems. The pedagogical issues were treated in more detail and organized as follows:

Overall objectives and structure
  Levels of competence
  Course structure
  Lesson structure
Methodological issues
  Language-learning methods
  CAL methodology
Interface issues
  The televisual environment
  The windows environment
  Screen design
  Hypermedia and linearity
  Autonomy versus control
  Autonomy and self-tuition
Practical considerations
  Authenticity
  Active and passive learning
  Interaction and response

This list illustrates most effectively the number of interrelated areas that have to be considered in the development of a multimedia project if it is to be properly conceptualized and implemented. Higher-level issues such as the theoretical base, the curriculum, methods of language learning, and the role of the learner are encountered in the development process, as are lower-level concerns such as screen design, interaction and response mechanisms, and the design of the user interface. Overall, the list represents a combination of methodological and technological components that somehow have to be integrated into the final package. And all this must occur with a knowledge of the strengths and limitations of the hardware and software that is available at this time.

Multimedia, which began in a primitive form in the TICCIT project, and which was refined on specialized computers in the

ALLP has, in the 1990s, reached critical mass. Instead of requiring expensive purpose-built systems, the current generation of micro-computers, with the associated hardware and software, are now fully capable of supporting multimedia. These generic machines which are widely available mean that projects such as CAMILLE are viable and accessible for a much larger population of teachers and learners. Arguably the next step is to present such materials via a commonly used communications link such as the Internet. Just now, and in the main, transfer of multimedia materials on the Internet is painfully slow. In fact receiving colour pictures can be slow, let alone full-motion colour video sequences. Most projects which utilize multimedia in this way tend towards dedicated and expensive link-ups such as ISDN.[10] Projects such as the Multimedia Teleschool provide a good example of users of this technology for videoconferencing with multimedia.[11] While we can look forward to the capacity and speed of the Internet connections increasing, at present the transfer of video material is slow. The storage and transfer of audio material, however, is more accessible, as we shall see in the description of the next project.

The Oral Language Archive (OLA)

The Oral Language Archive (OLA) was initiated at Carnegie Mellon University in 1994.[12] Its goal is to establish a collection of digitized sound recordings for foreign language learning that is accessible from around the world via the Internet. As well as the sound archive itself, the OLA contains a suite of management tools to enable users to locate and use sound segments easily and flexibly. The recordings are segmented and coded for various at-tributes such as level of formality and complexity. Specifically, Jones (1996) reports that users will be able to search the archive by language, gender of speaker(s), grammar trait (e.g. indirect object pronouns), functions, topic, formality, subject keywords, and lexi-cal difficulty. To make use of these materials, users will only require log-on privileges and, as a resource on the Internet, many users will be able to access the materials simultaneously.

So far, the languages included are French, German, and Japanese, with Russian and Spanish to follow. To avoid copyright problems, the recorded materials are new, and they are based on the Threshold taxonomy developed by J. A. Van Ek for the European Community, which describes topics, functions, and concepts that are relevant for language learners who wish to be able to operate successfully within a new linguistic and cultural environment (Van Ek 1984). The participants in the project expect to travel in order to record speakers in their country of origin. This is considered crucial, if the archive is to satisfy the enormous range of user needs anticipated (Jones 1996).

Much attention has been paid to the structure of the OLA, and participants in the project are making significant efforts to make the materials easily accessible and usable, starting with the Carnegie Mellon Campus, then nationally, then worldwide. In addition to the sounds themselves, a variety of software tools have been constructed to manage and distribute the sounds. An OLA 'browser' will constitute the primary form of access, and users will make their selections through a series of menus. Another software component of the system has been designed to enable sound segments to be extracted and then integrated into an appropriate authoring system for interactive teaching purposes. The authoring systems that the OLA can accommodate so far include *Dasher*, *HyperCard*, *ToolBook*, *WinCALIS*, *Libra* and *SuperMacLang*. In addition, the OLA has been implemented in such a way that it can serve different hardware platforms, and any computer that can access the Internet will be able to access data in the archive. In the future, it is anticipated that video segments as well as audio segments will be available.

Of course, international access to a resource such as the OLA is only made possible by virtue of the Internet. For authors or publishers on the Internet, the potentially vast audience crossing language and cultural boundaries, and the variety of hardware and software configurations that is used suggest that, ideally at least, authors have to respond to needs that reach far beyond the needs of a conventional audience, one that might include all those people who might read the same newspaper or book, or watch the same television programme for example. The Web author or publisher has to project far beyond his or her own cultural and language context to relate successfully to the needs and contexts of the end-user. Of course, an author can blissfully ignore the needs of the end-user, but then runs the risk of never being read. The OLA Project is especially sensitive to the diverse needs of the end-user. The developers have moved to ensure that the materials are well organized, appropriate, and accessible to the potentially large, diverse, and distributed audience for whom they are intended.

Evaluation

The question posed by Chapelle in 1994, 'CALL activities: are they all the same?' is most apposite for the 1990s (Chapelle 1994*b*). With the Internet now available to mainstream educationalists, and with the functionality this remarkable system provides—notably in terms of access to and interactivity with new materials, people, and learning environments beyond the classroom—it is crucial to understand that CALL does not represent one homogeneous type of activity, one that can be described simply in terms of a stable, invariant framework relating computer, learner, and task. In this regard the notion that the question-answer-feedback loop is the *only* viable form of interactional design in CALL has been somewhat difficult to dispatch. For those not presently involved in CALL, including some commercial developers and administrators, this view of the role of the computer and the implied one-to-one relationship between machine and learner can still be found. Of course, the interactional possibilities are far more varied, and indeed sophisticated, than that. This variability has been reflected in the difficulties that have been encountered in providing a workable description of CALL materials. A narrow view of CALL activities has also had repercussions on the approaches that have been taken in evaluation studies where in many cases a didactic teaching model is assumed.

The approach taken to evaluation needs to be sufficiently powerful to capture the essential qualities of the software under review, to successfully distinguish between the qualities that matter and those that do not, and to assess these characteristics in the light of a given set of criteria. Typically, this involves an appreciation of the learner, the theoretical base, and the precise nature of the interactions. Then, evaluation can perform a number of different roles or functions. For instance, it may be a formative evaluation, which Flagg (1990: 1–2) describes as 'the systematic collection of information for the purpose of informing decisions to design and improve the product'. In CALL, Henry and Zerwekh (1994) describe formative evaluation procedures in the development of a Multimedia

Electronic Dictionary for South-East Asian Languages
(MEDSEAL). The evaluation proceeds in an iterative fashion with
end-users intimately involved in the development process. They
describe four principles that underscore their approach:

1. People will always find a way to use things that the designers
   did not anticipate.
2. People will always want or need features that they did not
   know they wanted or needed until they begin to see and use
   the software.
3. Preferences and priorities among users and between developers and users will certainly differ.
4. Important aspects of the way people use the system depend on
   certain software features and structure.

For Henry and Zerwekh the development process is iterative, exploratory, and transformational, and it involves the discovery of
new goals. Formative evaluation techniques can help ensure that
the developers remain in close contact with the users enhancing the
value of the final product.

Yildiz and Atkins suggest we have learned little from the evaluation studies of the past. More needs to be understood about how
courseware design elements can impinge on conceptual understanding, and learner differences and their differential effects on multimedia design. Yildiz and Atkins conclude their discussion of
guidelines for evaluation with the following list of principles for
future studies:

(a) the evaluation design centred on the characteristics of the
    courseware, the students, and the nature of the learning task
    rather than on the underlying technological platform;
(b) analysis of what this type of courseware can do when fully
    exploited that other forms of instruction cannot do, and
    what it signifies for the role of the teacher or instructor;
(c) analysis of the implicit beliefs about how students learn that
    have informed the design of the application: reporting results
    in relation to this theoretical baseline;
(d) a design that includes testing of transfer to real life from
    simulations if this is claimed as a learning outcome;
(e) a description of the learning context in which the application
    is being used including the extent to which the learners are

familiar with computer-based technologies and their attitudes to them;

(f) evaluation of the learning outcomes with different sizes of
learner group and with different methods of integrating the
multimedia application into other learning taking place in
that context;

(g) more attention to conceptual learning and high-order cognitive skills according to the dominant ways of thinking in the
discipline for which the application is intended.

In the 1990s, evaluation is a most complex issue. It is made complex by the speed with which new technologies are introduced, the
range and sophistication of the interactional types that are now
possible, and the lack of time and funding that this final phase in
the development process seems to attract. As it stands now, CALL
represents a matrix of diverse activities, all of which in their many
ways support learning. Such novel approaches may well require
new evaluation techniques to capture the qualities of the new
medium (see Reeves 1992; Reeves and Harmon 1993; Fritze 1994;
Crosby *et al.* 1995). However, in spite of the complexity, evaluation studies are crucial if CALL is not to be entirely technology-
led, and if we are to identify and build upon prior successes.

Summary

Generally speaking, a diffusion effect can be identified in CALL,
where ideas tried out in well-funded, large-scale projects have
spread over a relatively short period of time to the population at
large. Swift diffusion of technological innovation is realized
through the ever increasing power of a computer for a given cost.
Projects which initially require expensive, specialized hardware
soon become available to all those who have access to widely
available generic models of microcomputer. Thus, early multimedia
projects like TICCIT or ALLP are now viable on personal computers. Similarly, long-distance network interactions, like the 'talk'
function in the PLATO Project are now open to a much wider
population than was previously possible, and in a much refined
form. Incidentally, the 'talk' function on PLATO was the most
advanced for its time. I am sure many contemporary CALL authors

would appreciate having consultants available to provide advice within a shared development environment.

Finding an appropriate role for the computer, in the light of the technological options available at any given time, has remained an issue. The comments made by Marty in 1981, determining what computers can and cannot do, is as pertinent now as it was then. Given that change is likely to continue, the role of the computer will need to be continually reassessed over time. Moreover, ascribing a role for the computer has implications for the role of the teacher, and for the ways in which material content and activities are distributed between the two, especially if work conducted at the computer and away from the computer is to be properly integrated.

The PLATO Project also introduced the notion of authoring, a key concept that has remained with us. CALL materials can be developed in such a way that the author or language teacher can enter the content and the preferred instructional design (as in PLATO), or the content only, with the instructional design inviolate (as in TICCIT). This division corresponds to the paradigm and toolbox approaches to authoring described by Hart, and remains a most important distinction. For those who seek to identify the paradigm that will facilitate the prescription of all the elements of a CALL design, TICCIT and its evolution over time should provide a cautionary note. The advice accompanying the recent version of the TICCIT authoring system for the microcomputer, ADAPT, is much less prescriptive than the original, responsive no doubt to the demands of developers who not only want to control the content, but also how that content might be presented. On the other hand, the success of the toolbox approach used in PLATO with its emphasis on materials writing by teachers rests on the ability of teachers to accomplish this task. A crucial difference between TICCIT and PLATO therefore is that in TICCIT the CALL design is under the control of instructional designers who structure the environment for language teachers; in PLATO language teachers are provided with much more control over the design, and are able to determine to a much greater extent exactly how the materials are to be presented.

That TICCIT has been one of the very few systems to be built totally around a specific instructional system has, in my view, profound implications, especially for those who would develop systems centred upon one single view of how language should be taught and learnt. TICCIT still provides a rare example of hardware that has been specifically designed from the very outset with education in mind. The development of the BBC computer is another example, but by and large the hardware comes commercially packaged to the educationalist who is not involved in the machine's design at the initial engineering stages.

Programs written in the 1980s illustrated the imagination and skill of language teacher–programmers as well, perhaps, as their limitations, in the size and complexity of their programs. At this time language teachers had the opportunity to become closely involved in the conceptualization of their programs, and their input needs to be retained at every level in the more team-oriented efforts of the 1990s. Over the last decade authoring programs have become more user-friendly and more powerful, even allowing multimedia interactions to be programmed with relative ease. With more media at the author's disposal, however, a broader range of expertise is needed to bring an initial concept to fruition and on this basis alone it is likely that team projects will predominate. The lone programmer may continue where individuals have a particular talent for programming, and within certain environments such as authoring or publishing on the World Wide Web. However, it is rather unlikely that multimedia projects will be constructed by individuals.

Storyboard is noteworthy because it has managed to endure through the many models of microcomputer that came and went in the 1980s. The program needed to be rewritten for different hardware platforms if it was to survive and, in this instance, it was small enough and useful enough for the rewriting to be worth the effort. Still, there is a tendency to drop CALL materials when the hardware or operating system software is upgraded, a problem that is not faced in more conventional publishing. *Storyboard* and this genre of program, variously called authoring programs, authoring packages, or mini-authoring systems, have drawn attention to the question of the integration of CALL (Jones, C. 1986; Hardisty and Windeatt 1989). These CALL programs are not held to represent the whole learning environment; they are not designed to function independently, or to manage learning on a more prolonged basis. Their success depends very much on the skill with which they are integrated into a lesson or series of lessons, and the language teacher plays a crucial role in the implementation.

As far as evaluation is concerned, early comparative studies that aim to establish the superior method, have given way to more 'atomistic' studies that recognize the complexity of interrelating factors associated with the characteristics of the media, the learner, and the particular learning context.

Innovations continue to be made, and the pace seems to be accelerating. The convergence of once separate media such as video and the computer, or telecommunications technologies and the computer, moves us towards a multi-user, multi-site environment for interaction and learning, stretching far beyond the confines of the traditional computer laboratory. Amidst all this change, issues such as the role of the teacher and computer in CALL, optimal approaches to authoring, effects of the technology on the methodology, integration, and evaluation remain central issues, as they have over the last thirty years.

Notes

1. A useful discussion of the early history of computer-based education, with a cross-section of project descriptions, is given in an introduction to computer-based education published by Digital Equipment Corporation (1983). A short history of CALL from 1965–85 is given by Ahmad *et al.* in chapter 3 of their book (1985). Key projects include the Stanford Project, the PLATO system, work at Dartmouth College on BASIC, the Scientific Language Project (1965–9) and early work with microcomputers. Also programmed instruction, computational linguistics and machine translation are included. Taking a broader perspective, O'Shea and Self (1983) give a good general history of computers in education. The focus is more on the mechanisms used in the programs (e.g. branching programs) and the activity type (e.g. simulations, dialogue systems), although the TICCIT and PLATO projects are also covered. A recent addition on the history of CALL is given in a special issue of the *CALICO Journal* 1995: 12/4. Though sometimes anecdotal and as the editors explain only a partial collection, this journal issue provides a very valuable perspective on the history of CALL in North America.
2. Hart (1995: 37) says that the acronym for PLATO may have been supplied after the event, in answer to those who asked what it stood for. An alternative version suggests PLATO was named after the philosopher.
3. Hart provides an illuminating discussion on the development of the

TUTOR authoring language, especially in describing the interrelation-ship between the needs of the language teacher–authors and the capa-bilities of the authoring approach (Hart 1995: 19–27).

4. Two good introductions to Hypertext are by McKnight *et al.* (1991) and McAleese (1993*a*). The McKnight book traces the derivation of the hypertext concept and describes its history. It looks closely at the nature of reading with hypertext, and describes ways of understanding hypertext in terms of the user, task and information interactions. Navigation issues, creating hypertext, and broader learning and educa-tion issues are also explored. The McAleese-edited collection provides useful perspectives on hypertext. Its two main themes focus on the importance of metaphor for understanding hypertext, and on tech-niques to improve navigation, management, and control. Many of the arguments are supported by quantitative and qualitative research re-sults. There are informative sections on the nature of browsing includ-ing structuring, filtering, planing, and zooming (p. 9), and ways of keeping track of events and a sense of the whole, through 'terrain' and 'street' views (pp. 31, 35, 36), and using hypertext as a mechanism for cognitive mapping (p. 90).

5. I would like to thank Graham Davies for his history of text reconstruc-tion programs.

6. The first use of the computer for instructional purposes was the Whirl-wind Project, unveiled at MIT in 1950, and designed as a flight simulator to train combat pilots. It is noteworthy, therefore, that the first use of the computer for educational purposes was a simula-tion, which substituted for a reality that was potentially costly and dangerous.

7. A protocol, particularly a communications protocol, defines how inter-acting computers package, transmit, and receive information. Stand-ard protocols, such as TCP/IP, are important since protocols that have been widely agreed and accepted can be built into different software packages. This in turn enables computers produced by different manu-facturers to communicate successfully.

8. The following subnets are available: Danish–German; German–Spanish; German–English; German–French; German–Korean; Ger-man–Dutch; German–Japanese; German–Portuguese; German–Swed-ish; English–Spanish; English–French; English–Italian; and Spanish–French.

9. The European Community (EC) supports the CAMILLE consortium, specifically through funding from the LINGUA programme. Accord-ing to Davies (1993: 22), LINGUA supports CALL projects, especially those using multimedia, interactive video, and distance learning tech-niques. LINGUA works in unison with the EC's DELTA (Developing

European Learning through Technological Advance) programme. Whereas LINGUA stresses linguistic and cultural diversity, DELTA focuses more on technology, particularly research and development initiatives involving telecommunications. The Multimedia Teleschool is an example of one of DELTA's key projects. Both LINGUA and DELTA have helped encourage the use of technology in language learning in the 1990s in Europe (see Davies 1993).

10. ISDN (Integrated Services Digital Network) is a digital telephone service where you are given permanent access to a line that physically connects your computer to a giant computer network run by the telephone company. In essence with this service, the telephone lines carry digital rather than analogue signals, such as those that are usually used with computers attached to a modem. A modem converts digital signals that can be read by the computer to analogue signals that can be transmitted over the conventional telephone system and vice versa—with an ISDN line the system is digital throughout. Though relatively expensive, ISDN provides a high-speed connection (a standard 128 kilobits per second (kbps) rather than 28.8 kbps with fast modems). As a result, where information is densely packaged, as in video or multimedia for example, an ISDN line is an advantage because it can facilitate much faster transmission of material.

11. The aim of the Multimedia Teleschool is to provide language learning at a distance via 'virtual study centres' for students from European companies (Fesl 1994: 25). The project was begun in 1992, and it is one of the major projects of the DELTA programme. It is now called Berlitz Online.

12. The project co-directors of the Oral Language Archive are Christopher Jones, Senior Lecturer in French and Director of the Language Learning Resource Centre (e-mail: cjones@cmu.edu), and Matthew McNally, Director of Humanities Computing (e-mail: mattm@cmu.edu).

videodisc materials in CALL. The systems approach emphasizes precise articulation of all the elements in the development process in contrast to approaches that are less precise, and where the process is not broken down into discrete elements. The systems approach is also helpful in providing a means of thinking about the integration of CALL work into the broader curriculum (see Chapter 7). Using an established theory can save time and builds upon what has already been achieved, rather than duplicating theoretical and practical work unnecessarily. Conversely, when a theory has been inappropriately applied to CALL, a clear understanding of why the theory has had a detrimental effect on CALL may be useful in determining more productive directions for research and development in the future. In some circumstances certain aspects of a theory may prove useful, while in others it may not. Here two of the principles underpinning programmed instruction provide an example: the reduction of learning objectives into a small, discrete series of steps, and the provision of immediate feedback. While a CALL author may accept the need for immediate feedback, the reduction of learning into a set of clearly defined steps may be rejected.

CALL workers also need to be aware of developments in disciplines involved in concentrated work on specific, complex problems. Breakthroughs in areas such as natural language processing (NLP) and machine translation would not necessarily emerge in the CALL literature, though arguably they could exert far-reaching effects in the field of CALL. Writers such as Pusack (1983) and Kohn (1994: 32) maintain that one of the most significant blocks in CALL is the computer's limited ability in handling natural language, and, as far as Kohn is concerned, the limited deployment of the NLP technologies that are in fact now available. A greater awareness of such issues in mainstream CALL will ensure that when advances are made, they find their way into CALL materials more generally. With increased cross-fertilization, relevant work in the disciplines and fields surrounding CALL can be incorporated into CALL itself.

Table 3.1 lists the disciplines, theories, or fields that have been held to have had an influence on CALL. For each entry in the table, the writer specifically refers to the discipline, theory, or field as having relevance for CALL, and the reference is given alongside the entry. The items in Table 3.1 may be grouped into five categories: psychology, artificial intelligence, computational linguistics, in-

TABLE 3.1   *Disciplines and fields with relevance to CALL*

Disciplines, theories, and fields	Reference
Applied linguistics	Leech and Candlin (1986); Pennington and Stevens (1992)
Artificial intelligence	Weischedel *et al.* (1978); Last (1987, 1989); Bailin and Levin (1989); Nyns (1989); Chapelle (1989*b*); Bailin (1990); Bloch and Bates (1990); Yazdani (1991*a*, 1991*b*); Lian (1992); Swartz and Yazdani (1991); Chanier (1994)
Cognitive psychology/ science	Sampson (1986); Legenhausen and Wolff (1989*a*); Sussex (1991)
Computational linguistics	Ahmad *et al.* (1985)
Curriculum development	Bedford (1991)
Educational psychology	Garrett (1991)
Educational technology	Liou (1994)
Expert systems	Phillips (1987); Sussex (1991); Lian (1992)
Human–computer interaction	Sussex (1991); Chapelle (1994*a*)
Information processing	Cook (1985)
Instructional design	Lawrason (1988/9); England (1989); Mitterer *et al.* (1990); Liou (1994)
Instructional technology	Garrett (1991)
Language data processing	Sinclair (1986); Johns (1986, 1990*a*, 1990*b*); Tribble (1990*b*); Tribble and Jones (1990); Kohn (1994)
Language teaching methodology	Jones, F. (1991); Hubbard (1992)
Linguistics	Karttunen (1986); Demaizière (1991); Garrett (1991); Catt (1991)
Machine translation	Ahmad *et al.* (1985)
Materials design	Jones, F. (1991)
Natural language processing	Leech (1986); Cook and Fass (1986); Butler (1990); Bailin and Thomson (1988); Mulford (1989); Kohn (1994)
Parsing theory	Markosian and Ager (1983); Farghaly (1989); Sanders and Sanders (1989); Sinyor (1990); Pope (1990); Kohn (1994)
Programmed instruction/ learning	Ahmad *et al.* (1985)

TABLE 3.1   *Continued*

Disciplines, theories, and fields	Reference
Psycholinguistics	Catt (1991)
Second language acquisition	Jamieson and Chapelle (1988); Doughty (1988, 1991); Garrett (1991); Cook (1992); Liou (1994)
Sociolinguistics	Catt (1991)
Systems theory	Bedford (1991); Meskill (1991)

structional technology and design, and human–computer interaction studies. Psychology includes programmed instruction, second language acquisition, and cognitive psychology in which information processing is included. Artificial intelligence covers expert systems as well. Computational linguistics includes machine translation, natural language processing, parsing, and language data processing. Instructional technology and design covers instructional and educational technology, instructional design, and the systems approach. Human–computer interaction concludes the categories. Many of these topics are interdisciplinary in themselves, and as such they may be grouped together in a number of equally convincing ways. The organizational framework used here is by no means the only one. It is used in this chapter as one of the ways of structuring and presenting the knowledge base. Furthermore, in providing an interdisciplinary perspective, I want to emphasize that each section is only intended to provide a sketch of the field. It is drawn from the point of view of someone whose primary interest is in CALL, and from the outside looking in, so to speak. I know that as I cross disciplinary boundaries, and attempt to present each field as it relates to CALL, there will be significant omissions or misinterpretation on my part: for that I must apologize in advance. I see this excursion into interdisciplinary space as a beginning only, and I proceed only with the conviction that there is much to be gained in CALL by extending our understanding of related disciplines, even by a little.

Psychology

Given that CALL is a relatively new field of endeavour, it is not surprising that practitioners borrow from more established fields and disciplines. A discipline that is referred to often, as providing a theoretical base for CALL work, is psychology. Yet although the literature on psychology is very considerable, relatively little work has been conducted within a computer-based environment (Allinson and Hammond 1993: 55). Partly as a result, a growing number of CALL authors, especially in the area of Intelligent CALL (ICALL), as well as utilizing psychological theory take pains to actually test it in a computer-based learning context as well (see Hamburger 1994; Harrington 1994).

Programmed instruction

The two concepts that did most to shape early ideas about the use of the computer in education were the concepts of the teaching machine and programmed instruction (Digital Equipment Corporation 1983). According to the discussion in the DEC publication, the work of a psychologist called Sidney Pressey was especially influential. In the 1920s he built and demonstrated a device that could present multiple-choice questions, then keep a record of student answers. Programmed instruction, arguably the first application of a theory of learning in a computing environment, emerged out of the work of Pressey and others like him. The programmed instruction movement gained considerable momentum in 1954 with the publication of B. F. Skinner's seminal paper, *The Science of Learning and the Art of Teaching* (Skinner 1954; Gagné 1987: 30). It was based on behaviourist theories of learning and laid great emphasis on the positive effects of reinforcement. To provide the requisite reinforcement mechanisms, Skinner advocated the use of 'mechanical and electrical devices' for the efficient reinforcing mechanisms that could be built into them (see Chapter 7 for further discussion). He spoke of 'mechanizing our schools' using teaching machines designed for individualized instruction (Skinner 1954: 97). Programmed instruction was the direct antecedent to computer-assisted instruction (Schoen and Hunt 1977: 72; Osguthorpe and Zhou 1989: 9).

The key principles underlying programmed instruction, implemented in many CAI materials, are summarized in Ahmad *et al.* (1985: 38) and are listed below:

- compartmentalizing learning into small discrete steps or 'frames' (Gagné 1987: 30) in a highly directive way;
- developing applications for more 'programmable' areas of language, for example, morphology, vocabulary, and syntax;
- treating aspects of language in isolation;
- allowing students to work at their own preferred pace;
- providing students with immediate feedback (reinforcement).

In the DEC publication, two main thrusts for programmed instruction are identified. The first, most closely associated with Skinner, emanates from the idea that learning can be broken down into a linear sequence of steps. Each step or frame adds just a little new information, and on this basis proponents maintained that students could complete the work on their own without the aid of a teacher. The second interpretation, most closely associated with the psychologist Crowder, focuses more on the branching mechanisms that the programs include. Through the use of branching the program can provide different pathways through the material. This structure enables different students to be directed along different paths according to their performance on the multiple-choice questions given after each frame; if errors occur remedial material can be provided. According to Kenning and Kenning (1990: 94), programmed instruction particularly influenced the grammatical sequencing that was very much in evidence in early CALL. Grammatical structures can be isolated readily as separate units, and they lend themselves to individual treatment in a linear sequence. This corresponds well with the frame concept and the compartmentalizing of learning. However, by the late 1960s the programmed instruction movement was coming to an end, owing to a lack of evidence of its effectiveness and a negative response by many teachers and students (Gagné 1987: 32).

Second language acquisition

Programmed instruction was a general theory of instruction centred on the teaching process. Since the mid-1960s, there has been a noticeable shift in perspective from a focus on language *teaching* to a focus on language *learning*. This shift has been caused by inconclusive findings from comparative studies of language teaching methods, and changing views on the nature of language and language learning advanced by specialists in psychology and linguistics (Larsen-Freeman and Long 1991: 5). This perspective has brought a renewed focus on the characteristics of the individual learner, learner needs, and learning strategies (Wenden and Rubin 1987; Nunan 1988*b*). As a result, the quantity of research in Second Language Acquisition (SLA) has increased significantly. So far, SLA research has concentrated primarily on explaining the acquisition of morphology and syntax; a little is known about the acquisition of phonology, and much less about the acquisition of lexis and pragmatics (Ellis 1985: 5; Block 1990: 168; Larsen-Freeman and Long 1991: p. xiv).

The view that research on the language acquisition process should direct CALL research and development is evident in the writings of a number of authors. Garrett (1988) argues that the potential of the computer cannot be fully exploited for CALL until decisions about its use are based on insights from theory and research into the language learning process rather than traditional teaching ideas. Doughty asserts that the design of interactive videodisc instructional software 'can only be determined . . . from the perspective of second language acquisition (SLA) theory' (Doughty 1991: 1). Central concerns for theoretical model builders have been the role of the learner, the nature of the language to be acquired, the influence of the learning context, and the cognitive processes involved in language acquisition and use (Doughty 1991: 4).

While advocating in principle the desirability of formulating CAL programs using the relevant theoretical base, Fox (1993) maintains that this is not always easy to do in practice. He suggests that Applied Linguistics, particularly SLA, has offered frameworks for design and in this regard includes the 'creative construction hypothesis, developments in discourse analysis and applications of the product-process distinction, for example in the SLA and learning strategy literatures (Naiman *et al.* 1978; Ellis 1985; McLaughlin 1987; Wenden and Rubin 1987; O'Malley and Chamot 1990; Larsen-Freeman and Long 1991; Spolsky 1989)'. However, Fox (1993: 101) concludes that their value is limited because there is no 'generally accepted theory of SLA to embrace with confidence'.

After extensive work reviewing the findings of SLA research, Ellis's view on the contribution of SLA to second language pedagogy is represented by four positions (Ellis 1994: 686). With regard to the wisdom of applying SLA research to language teaching and learning, Ellis characterizes these positions as ranging from a 'super-cautious "don't apply" to a confident "go ahead and apply"'. Ellis's conclusion continues to reflect this diversity. On the one hand he maintains that there is now 'greater confidence in SLA research and more conviction that its results can inform language pedagogy'; on the other hand he suggests that 'some educationalists might feel that research undertaken by professional researchers will always be of limited value to language teachers' (1994: 689). This diversity of views on the value of applying SLA research to language pedagogy is paralleled by the range of opinions on the value of applying SLA research to tutorial CALL.

While the arguments for using SLA research to guide CALL materials development are compelling, there are profound difficulties in proceeding solely from this perspective. There are 'at least forty "theories", "models", "perspectives", "metaphors", "hypotheses", and "Theoretical claims" in the SLA literature' (Larsen-Freeman and Long 1991: 288; see also Beretta 1991), and, as Garton (1992: 18) observes, 'it is worth remembering that the only example of theory-driven language teaching technology, language labs based on behaviourist inspired audio-lingual methodology, was a disaster'. Given that there are so many models of SLA the question remains as to how to choose between them. Which conceptual framework is most likely to bear fruit in the CALL context? To answer this question, one must look carefully at the specific attributes of this learning environment and then consider which model of SLA most closely matches the capabilities of the hardware and software. For Interactive Videodisc (IVD)—which shares many of the characteristics of multimedia CALL—Doughty (1991: 7) argues convincingly that comprehension-based models of SLA offer the greatest potential to researchers and materials developers. Doughty (1991), in examining the theoretical motivation for interactive videodisc research and development, narrows it down to two comprehension-based models of SLA: the Negotiated Interaction Model of SLA and the Cognitive Processing Model of SLA. Both these models seek to specify further the Input Hypothesis of Monitor Theory advanced by Krashen (Doughty 1991: 6). According to

Doughty the Cognitive Processing Model of SLA emphasizes the schema used for representing and processing information during internalization and retrieval (1991: 8).

Cognitive psychology

During the late 1960s and early 1970s the orientation of psychology began to change from a behaviouristic to a cognitive one, and currently cognitive psychology represents the mainstream perspective (Shuell 1986: 411; Ashcraft 1993). Ulric Neisser, who in 1967 published the classic reference text, *Cognitive Psychology*, offers the following definition: 'Cognitive psychology refers to all processes by which the sensory input is transformed, reduced, elaborated, stored, recovered and used.' According to Best (1989: 10), the topics of cognitive psychology include the study of attention, pattern recognition, memory, language, reading and writing, reasoning and problem-solving. The modern development of the field of cognitive psychology has been strongly influenced by the information processing approach, developments in computer science, especially artificial intelligence, and developments in linguistics, particularly the work of Chomsky (Anderson 1985: 8).

The information processing approach is the common theoretical approach used by cognitive psychologists; it is not a single unified theory, but rather a broad approach to the problems of understanding human knowledge and action (Best 1989: 3). The approach analyses cognitive processes into a sequence of ordered stages; each stage reflects an important step in the processing of cognitive information (Anderson 1985: 1). This approach as it applies to language and language learning is described by Greene (1986: 55) as a linear processing model where linguistic inputs are processed stage by stage hierarchically, and where each stage has to be completed before the next stage begins.

The Cognitive Processing Model described by Doughty emphasizes the mental representation of information and how it is processed during internalization and retrieval. The mental representation is considered to affect how new information is received and processed. An early version of this perspective was given by Bartlett (1932: 201) who used the word schema to describe 'an active organisation of past reactions or past experiences'. Bartlett claimed that when new material is encountered, we try to relate this material with existing schemata. Later Ausubel (1960) spoke of 'advance organizers' which could be used to facilitate learning. More recently the broader term 'script' has been used to describe 'the large-scale semantic and episodic knowledge structures that accumulate in memory and guide our interpretation and comprehension of daily experience' (Ashcraft 1993: 343). The notion of schema, schemata or script is a central concept associated with the cognitive view (Bonner 1988: 4). Gagné and Dick (1983: 279) give the implications of the concept for instruction as:

- new information is stored in previously formed schemata;
- schemata strongly influence recall of previously learned verbal information;
- a schema not only helps retention by providing a framework for storage but also alters the new information by making it fit the schema;
- a schema allows the learner to make inferences to 'fill the gaps';
- schemata are knowledge structures containing verbal (declarative knowledge) and intellectual (procedural knowledge) components;
- students consider evaluation and modification of their schemata as important in their learning.

The constructs of Schema Theory have primarily been applied to the investigation of comprehension. According to Doughty (1991: 9) comprehension consists of three stages: locating a schema that appears to match the linguistic input; finding the elements of the input that correlate to the roles of the schema; and making inferences to cover any gaps that emerge. This process may be especially difficult for second language learners, since they often lack the necessary cultural and linguistic schemata.

The concerns of cognitive psychologists who investigate language focus on how knowledge is represented in language use, and how meanings are communicated and understood (Greene 1986: 20). McLaughlin (1990: 113), in arguing for a cognitive psychological approach to second language teaching, emphasizes 'automaticity and restructuring' in SLA. He maintains that practice improves performance because lower-level skills become automated; however, he also says that increased practice can also cause a temporary reduction in performance as learners reorganize their schema.

McLaughlin also points out that a cognitive psychological perspective can only provide a partial description of the processes of SLA because purely linguistic considerations, such as those that may result from linguistic universals, need to be considered also.

Information processing or cognitive perspectives have been considered by a number of authors in relation to CALL. Cook (1985) discusses the information processing approach as a suitable model of language teaching appropriate for CALL, and Noblitt and Bland (1989) say the perspective is useful in relation to tracking learners as they work through CALL activities. The value of a cognitive perspective of CALL has been suggested or discussed by Sampson (1986), Legenhausen and Wolff (1989*a*) with regard to CALL software evaluation, and by Sussex (1991). Both Cook and Doughty refer to general cognitive theory as a possible model for CALL development. Block (1990) argues that a broader base than pure SLA research is needed for providing explanations of student behaviour in the classroom and that cognitive psychology might offer a valuable framework. Cognitive psychology is also a significant contributing factor to the fields of artificial intelligence and more recently to instructional design, which are both discussed later in this chapter.

Artificial intelligence

Artificial intelligence

The field of artificial intelligence has given rise to much debate, not surprisingly perhaps given the implications of attaching a label like 'intelligence', an intensely human faculty, to an innate object like a machine. Many consider intelligence to be a uniquely human quality. Even given enormous computing power, the question of whether the workings of the human mind are reducible to zeros and ones is a moot point. If clear distinctions between human intelligence and machine intelligence had always been kept clearly in view, there would probably not have been any difficulties, but, in the early days of AI, the field was surrounded by considerable publicity and overly extravagant claims, claims that were not to be substantiated by the actual performance of the systems. Interestingly, Last, in writing his book on artificial intelligence techniques in language learning, described how he began his book by thinking

AI was the way forward for CALL, but ended four years later with a more sombre and realistic view (Last 1989).[1] The problems turned out to be far more complex than first thought.

According to Augarton the term 'artificial intelligence' was first coined by an MIT computer scientist in 1956 (1984: 298). Artificial intelligence (AI) researchers are concerned with developing computer systems that simulate human intelligence using techniques of semantic representation and semantic processing (Bailin and Levin 1989: 4; Mulford 1989: 31). Beyond this general position statement, exactly what AI comprises is debatable. For example, Kearsley (1987: 3) says that AI research spans three different disciplines, computer science, cognitive psychology and educational research, and researchers within the discipline have quite different research goals, terminology, and theoretical frameworks. Alternatively, for Harmon and King (1985: 4), AI can be subdivided into three relatively independent research areas: Natural Language Processing (NLP), robotics, and expert systems. Clearly, as Last correctly asserts, AI is not a single monolithic entity: instead, as Haugeland states, first and foremost AI is an 'idea' that may, or may not, be realized (Last 1989: 50).

Computer programs for learning that employ artificial intelligence techniques are referred to as intelligent tutoring systems (ITS), or intelligent computer-assisted instruction (ICAI). According to Bonner (1988: 10), cognitive psychologists prefer 'ITS', while instructional designers prefer 'ICAI', reflecting especially the way in which ICAI has developed from the application of principles of AI to CAI (Jonassen 1988: 302). Wenger (1987: 3) adds that his preference for ITS reflects the significant shift in research methodology that has occurred: he adds that this shift is not conveyed by simply adding an 'I' to CAI. Wenger goes on to provide a useful contrast between traditional CAI and ITS. He describes the former as 'statically organized receptacles' used to encompass and present the content and the pedagogical knowledge of expert teachers (1987: 4). Though the process of transferring the teacher's pedagogical knowledge into a program can be complex, the essential structure and content of the program is anticipated and captured in advance. In contrast, the purpose of instructional systems that employ artificial intelligence is to 'capture the very knowledge that allows experts to compose an instructional interaction in the first place' (1987: 5). With intelligent tutoring, the knowledge built into the system enables it to respond dynamically to the student as the ITS is used. Rather than pre-defined content and branching routines, an ITS can provide adaptive, individualized instruction as the student moves through the material.

Kohn (1994: 32) argues that the need for ICALL will increase, and that even modest success will have a significant impact. Artificial intelligence is having a growing impact on CALL and there are now at least two bibliographies of the field: an ICALL bibliography (Matthews 1991) and an ICALI bibliography (Bailin *et al.* 1989). Bailin and Levin (1989) present an overview under the aegis of Intelligent Computer-Assisted Language Instruction (ICALI), detailing ICALI as a part of AI research with a description of a number of prototype systems.

Expert systems

Expert systems research is concerned with developing programs that use 'symbolic knowledge to simulate the behaviour of human experts' (Harmon and King 1985: 5). These systems are designed to capture and make accessible the knowledge of an expert, and the method is usually applied when a class of problems is well defined, finite, and clearly describable. Most expert systems are able to explain how they solved a problem, at least in terms of being able to present what rules were used and what mechanism was used to process the rules and arrive at an answer (Jonassen 1988: 300). In essence an expert system consists of a knowledge base and an inference engine: the knowledge base contains the facts and rules that embody the expert's knowledge; the inference engine contains an algorithm for processing the facts and the rules, and through which a conclusion is reached (Harmon 1987: 170).

An expert system approach has been suggested as the basis of a developmental paradigm for CALL (Phillips 1987: 280) and in the context of an intelligent, general purpose environment for language learning (Sussex 1991: 25; Lian 1992: 68). Phillips (1987: 280) examines the notion of the expert system in relation to 'intelligent' CALL and suggests an expert system with 'sophisticated input parsing, and speech recognition and synthesis' that could 'adjust flexibly to the students' responses in open-ended natural language interaction' through a sequence of individualized learning experiences. More specifically, Lian (1992: 68) describes the EXCALIBUR project which consists of a *domain expert system*, a *student model* for each student, a *teaching expert* which contains pedagogical knowledge, a *natural language interface* and a *reasoning system*. The aim of this system is 'to provide learners and course designers/authors with an environment for managing learning activity in a multitude of unpredictable ways' (1992: 67). Such systems, falling into the expert system-based computer-aided learning (EXCAL) category, give a directive role to the computer which manages the learning process in circumstances where the system is able to respond in sensitive and appropriate ways to the needs of the individual learner.

A number of difficulties arise with expert systems, however. First, it is not a trivial problem to make an expert's knowledge explicit. Usually, it is not at all easy to translate knowledge and experience into a set of clearly articulated rules, however large the rule set. Secondly, expert systems operate within a limited, strictly defined domain. While they can operate successfully within such a closed area, the systems are not transportable to other problem domains— for each problem domain you need a new expert system, severely curtailing their usefulness (Last 1989: 127). Thirdly, given the open-enededness of language interactions, where effective communication is the goal, it is likely that a tool that functions best in a closed domain will be limited.

Computational linguistics

Computational linguistics is the study of computing systems for understanding and generating natural languages. Three classes of applications have been pivotal in the development of this field: machine translation, information retrieval, and human–machine interfaces (Grishman 1986: 4). Human–machine interfaces in the context of computational linguistics refer to the use of natural language as a mode of communication between the user and the computer (Grishman 1986: 5) and this is discussed below in natural language processing. Also included in this section is language data processing, specifically the production of concordances and word indexes for literary and linguistic research. This has been a simple, but very successful application of the computer in computational linguistics (Bott 1970: 218; Ahmad *et al.* 1985: 39).

Machine translation

More effort has been put into Machine Translation (MT) than any other area of computational linguistics (Bott 1970: 222). In a comprehensive introduction to the subject, Hutchins (1986: 15) defines MT as 'the application of computers to the translation of texts from one natural language to another'. MT, which was one of the first non-numerical applications of the computer, has been motivated by a number of concerns, both theoretical and practical: for instance, researchers have looked at MT with a view to studying the 'basic mechanisms of language and mind' (1986: 15). On the other hand, research has been driven by the need to read documents in foreign languages and to improve communication between workers in various fields who do not share the same language. Significant funds were directed into MT from about 1950 to the mid-1960s, but early expectations were not fulfilled (Hutchins 1986: 16). A watershed in the development of machine translation came in 1966 with the production of the ALPAC (Automatic Language Processing Advisory Committee) Report (Pierce 1966). One of the objectives of this document was to advise on the status of mechanical translation of foreign languages. Like the pronouncements made for artificial intelligence much was said about the promise of machine translation, but the reality was more prosaic. For scientific texts, a special focus, no automatic translations were satisfactory without having to resort to human post-editing. The committee concluded that it was advantageous to press ahead 'in the name of science', but that in the foreseeable future machine translation was not likely to improve sufficiently to meet the quality standards of the scientific community. Rather, the recommendations encouraged research that would explore means of speeding up human translation with the help of the computer, rather than attempts to create purely machine-based translation techniques. The ALPAC Report had a resounding effect, and ever since the majority of researchers in the field have adopted a more pragmatic approach, and placed more emphasis on humans working with the machine, rather than on producing a fully automatic translation device.

Hutchins (1986: 324) notes the existence of the *pragmatists* and the *perfectionists* in MT: the pragmatists are mainly designers of interactive MT systems that require human–machine collaboration; the perfectionists are those that experiment with AI approaches to MT, approaches that aim to be non-interventionist. According to Hutchins (1986: 324, 325) there is broad agreement in MT on approaches to morphological analysis, dictionary searching routines, and syntactic analysis. It is the area of semantics that remains the greatest difficulty, and problems surface whenever information beyond the sentence being analysed is required. Thus, Hutchins argues that the basic AI position, that some form of 'understanding' of a text is needed in order properly to convey its meaning, is correct (1986: 327). For the present though, the pragmatic approach prevails. A translator's workstation with a word processor, access to machine aids, a multi-level interactive MT system, and a fully automatic MT system is likely to be the preferred system (see Hutchins 1986: 331; Kemble 1991: 51; French 1991: 55). In a recent article Melby (1996: 94) confirms this position and suggests that the pragmatic approach will remain the predominant one until mainstream linguistics manages to advance beyond the domain of morphology and syntax to capture the 'essence' of natural language.

Research in MT has had an influence on CALL in the development of more sophisticated syntactic and semantic representations of language that can be implemented on a computer (Ahmad *et al.* 1985: 43). This has led to more refined forms of human–computer interactions through text and, in tutorial CALL programs, to feedback that is more precisely tuned to the user's input. In addition, bilingual and multilingual dictionaries are now available on disc (e.g. Collins dictionaries) and on CD-ROM (e.g. *Harrap's Multilingual Dictionary*) for microcomputers and in the form of small pocket computers (e.g. the Besta CD-61 that provides translations from English to Mandarin and vice versa). One of the best known translation programs in the CALL field is *Littré/BonAccord* (see Farrington 1986: 199; 1995). The latest version, *BonAccord*, is described as a semi-intelligent translation learning system for PC-compatible computers. It has been designed primarily for intermediate to advanced learners of French. When using *BonAccord*, the learner is presented with a text to translate paragraph by paragraph. After the learner has made an attempt at a translation, it is checked by the program which then blocks unacceptable versions, and comments on predicted errors where they occur. The *TransIt-TIGER* series is another example of an application of MT in CALL. These programs are described as hypertext-based technical translation programs using word processing and related tools. Thus, work in MT is proving of value in a range of CALL applications, particularly by improving the quality of 'understanding' and response to text input, and in helping to provide a diverse range of dictionary tools.

Natural language processing and parsing

Achieving high quality Natural Language Processing (NLP) has been one of the central goals of computational linguists (Farghaly 1989: 236). NLP is primarily concerned with developing computer programs that are able to read, speak, or understand language as people use it in everyday conversation (Harmon and King 1985: 4). Beyond this general description NLP has been defined in a variety of ways (see Beardon *et al.* 1991; Brierley 1991: 71). According to Beardon *et al.* (1991: 11), computational linguistics spans four major problem areas:

- building parsers that take a text and try to analyse it according to some grammar, bearing in mind the problems of ambiguity;
- exploring different kinds of grammar and their suitability for representing the vagaries of natural language;
- exploring ways of representing the meaning of sentences so that, for example, an appropriate response may be made;
- integrating the syntactic and semantic components in terms of an effective control structure.

NLP is accomplished using a special program called a parser which essentially interprets the syntax and, to a limited degree, the semantics of a given phrase or sentence. A useful definition of a natural language parser is given by Farghaly (1989: 237):

The term 'parsing natural languages' refers to computer programs that model the human process of analysing an utterance and passing judgements of grammaticality on the basis of linguistic rules. In addition to the grammar, the parser has to have a procedure such that within finite time and space the program must halt and either accept the input string and output the structure(s) it assigns to the sentence, or reject it for being ill-formed according to the grammar.

According to Brierley (1991: 71), a description of NLP for language teaching should centre on aspects of the field that relate to the analysis of natural language input, and the creation of an appropriate response, which may or may not require the user to be corrected. The application of natural language processing techniques to CALL is advocated by Bailin and Thompson (1988), who describe how NLP is employed in two drill-and-practice CAI programs to teach grammar, and as a direction for the future research and development of CALL (Leech 1986; Cook and Fass 1986). NLP and parsing have been applied to CALL with the aim of improving communication between students and the computer. Pusack (1983: 63) sees sophisticated parsers as essential if CALL is to fully realize its potential. Brierley (1991: 72) assessed the value of NLP techniques for language teaching, and concluded that its role was limited but important, especially in helping advanced learners consolidate grammatical awareness and for students involved in linguistics and translation. Some of the projects which employ parsing techniques to CALL or CAI are described by Markosian and Ager (1983), Farghaly (1989), Sanders and Sanders (1989), Sinyor (1990), and Pope (1990).

Language data processing

Language data processing by computer includes 'identifying word-forms, representing texts, frequency listing, collocational environments, concordancing and producing text analysis statistics for a range of varieties and styles' (Leech and Candlin 1986: 184). The production of concordances and indexes was the earliest text analysis application and a detailed history of automated concordance-making is given in four articles by Burton (1981*a*, 1981*b*, 1981*c*, 1982).[2] Computerized concordancing is proving valuable in the development of CALL. All early concordancing efforts were completed on large mainframe computers (Hockey 1987: 21). Although mainframe machines are still widely used, and necessarily so in the case of large-scale corpora, in the late 1980s a number of concordancing programs became available for the microcomputer, notably *MicroConcord* in 1985, *Micro-OCP* in 1987, and the *Mini-concordancer* in 1989.

The use of concordancing for CALL has been advocated by a number of researchers, notably Johns (1986, 1988, 1990*a*, 1990*b*) and Tribble (1990*a*, 1990*b*). Johns was responsible for the development of *MicroConcord*, a simple, interactive keyword-in-context (KWIC) concordancing program. Rather than seeing the computer as a kind of surrogate teacher, Johns sees the computer as a research tool for both language learners and teachers (1986). Johns has developed this approach into a methodology called 'data-driven learning' which places the language learner into the role of research worker whose learning needs are motivated through access to linguistic data (Johns 1990*a*: 2). Methodologically, Johns advocates two approaches. The first approach leads from a review of the evidence to the observation of patterns and tentative generalizations (inductive); the second begins with a hypothesis and leads to subsequent testing (deductive). There is a strong focus on learners doing their own research through exploration, making predictions, and hypothesis testing. Much is made of the concordancer giving access to primary rather than secondary sources such as dictionaries and grammars. The manual (Scott *et al.* 1993: 9) says concordance programs provide 'a means of checking the accuracy and completeness of the processed secondary sources, dictionaries etc.'. A concordancing approach is very much tied to a particular view of language and language learning, one that focuses on more form-oriented approaches to language learning.

Language data processing has also had an impact on the development of dictionaries and coursebooks for language learners. For example, the Collins–Birmingham University database of authentic text has been used to identify the most useful words and patterns of contemporary English, knowledge which has been used to compile the COBUILD (Collins–Birmingham University International Language Database) Dictionary and the COBUILD English series for learners of English (see Sinclair 1987, 1988; Willis and Willis 1988).

Instructional technology and design

Instructional technology

In 1977, Schoen and Hunt (1977: 69) asserted that instructional technology had reached the status of a new field of academic endeavour. Programmed instruction can be considered to be the first instructional technology because it was the first system of instruction based on a theory of learning (Seels 1989: 11). Although there is no universally accepted definition of instructional, or educational, technology, most definitions can be classified into two types: the first equates instructional technology with certain media, often called *audiovisual devices*; the second describes instructional technology as a process, often called the *systems approach* (Gagné 1987: 11).[3] The audiovisual devices or media familiar to language teachers include the tape recorder, video player, language laboratory, and the computer. Over the last three decades research has been carried out in the use of filmstrips, radio, television, tape recorders, overhead projectors, and, of course, computers (Stern 1983: 444).

The systems approach looks at the various elements of the teaching environment as a purposeful whole, or 'system' (Stern 1983: 444). In other words, the teacher, the students, and the materials are considered with regard to how they function collectively rather than separately, and always in relation to the whole. In fact, the system concept argues that elements of a system can *only* be conceptualized meaningfully if they are viewed as part of the whole. Meister (1991: 12) states:

> The system movement is first and foremost a philosophical point of view— a belief and a method arising out of that belief. Mattesich (1982) has traced it back to concepts expressed in the philosophies of Lao-Tse, Heraclitus, Leibniz, Vico and Marx. Van Gigch (1974) emphasised Hegel to whom the following ideas are attributed: (a) The whole is more than the sum of its parts; (b) The whole determines the nature of its parts; (c) The parts cannot be understood if considered in isolation from the whole; (d) The parts are dynamically interrelated or interdependent.

Clearly it is possible to break entities into component parts, but system theory would say that the action of the parts cannot adequately explain how those variables function when they are part of the whole. A systems approach as the basis of a methodology for CALL has been suggested by Bedford (1991) and, as the basis for an approach to interactive videodisc courseware design, by Meskill (1991).

Instructional design

Instructional design evolved out of educational technology and the systems approach with a view to understanding and improving methods of instruction (Reigeluth 1983*a*: 7, 1983*b*; Seels 1989: 11; Jonassen 1988).[4] The product of instructional design is often described as an 'architect's blueprint' which is a prescription for what the instruction should look like (Reigeluth 1983*a*: 7; Jonassen 1988: p. xvi). The blueprint may be unique, or it may be presented in a form that is generalizable, enabling it to be reused for the design of many instructional programs. It is *prescriptive* because the primary goal of the blueprint is to specify the optimal methods of instruction (Reigeluth 1983*a*: 21; Scandura 1983: 216). An instructional design is always formulated on the basis of an instructional design theory: thus it is always oriented towards instruction rather than learning, and it must be formed around a theory, rather than models or principles (Reigeluth 1983*a*; Jonassen 1988: p. xx). Instructional design is eclectic in nature, and it integrates the ideas of a number of areas such as behavioural psychology, cognitive psychology, adult learning, systems theory, and media technology (Bonner 1988). Jonassen (1988) specifically excludes such design issues as screen design, graphics, the user interface, and human factors from Instructional Design because, although they are most certainly important components in the design process, they remain outside the parameters of the discipline (cf. Human–Computer Interaction).

The basic assumptions of instructional design are described by Gagné *et al.* (1988: 4) as:

- aimed at aiding the learning of the individual;
- organized such that it has immediate and long-term phases;
- systematically designed;
- conducted by means of a systems approach;
- designed on the basis of our knowledge of how students learn.

A fundamental characteristic of those working within the instructional design framework is that the design process is systematic. Typically the design is broken down into a series of steps, although the actual sequence and number are variable. Examples of the elements and the flow in the instructional design process are given by Andrews and Goodson (1980), Kemp (1985), Bonner (1988: 5), Gagné *et al.* (1988: 15), Roblyer (1988: 14) and Lawrason (1988/9: 33).

Two further characteristics of the traditional instructional design framework are worth noting. First, 'it is heretical to . . . begin with

assumptions about which medium to use in designing instruction'
(Jonassen 1985: 8, 16). According to Jonassen far too much work
begins with an analysis of the capabilities of the technology. In the
Andrews and Goodson instructional model, for example, 'media
selection' is step 8 out of a total of 9. Secondly, in most traditional
instructional design frameworks, teachers do not design or develop
their own materials: instead they are given materials, or they select
materials, that they integrate into their lesson plans (Gagné *et al.*
1988: 29).

Lawrason (1988/9), England (1989), and Mitterer *et al.* (1990)
note the value of instructional design techniques for CALL.
Lawrason considers whether instructional design is a legitimate
tool for use in language learning laboratories and in the development of CALL, and concludes that ID techniques provide useful
tools for assessing, developing, and implementing new technologies
and resources in the learning laboratory (Lawrason 1988/9: 31).
England feels that applying the principles of instructional design
will improve the quality of CALL software, especially in the context
of language 'content specialists' working with instructional designers. Meskill (1991) appeals to the systems approach and the
methods of instructional design to outline a precisely articulated
approach to the design of CALL videodiscs.

Finally, cognitive psychology, as well as influencing CALL more
directly, as discussed in the psychology section above, is exerting
considerable influence on the theory and research base of instructional design (Bonner 1988). Cognitive psychologists object to this
prescriptive part of instructional design and the lack of emphasis on
the active and constructive role of the learner (Bonner 1988: 9).
Specifically, Wittrock (1979: 5) states that a cognitive approach to
instruction implies, for example, more of a focus on how a teaching
style affects the learner's attention, motivation, and understanding,
which in turn influences behaviour, rather than how a teaching
style influences student behaviour directly. Thus, the emphasis
is more on the learner's cognitive processes than behavioural
outcomes.

Human–computer interaction

Over the last decade there has been a shift in focus from simply
making programming applications work successfully towards rec-

ognizing the real needs and perceptual abilities of computer users, and designing applications with these characteristics foremost in mind.[5] In the late 1970s and early 1980s, the status of CALL hardware and software was such that CALL authors had little choice but to adapt to the demands of the computer, demands that could be highly idiosyncratic, if not outright capricious. For example authoring tools, which were in their infancy, often required special instructions to perform the most mundane functions. Program design also tended to be very pedantic, so that a missed full stop or semicolon might result in the program not working. Furthermore, if the program did not work the debugging tools that were made available were primitive: one was more likely to receive the message 'Error 42' after the program was run, rather than any constructive advice on the nature of the problem, or where exactly it was located. The level of sophistication of CALL authoring tools was limited and the range of activities that could be produced with them restricted, a situation that led many language teachers to resort to programming the computer themselves. In the 1990s, good design and ease of use have become paramount—technology should be adapted to our needs, not the reverse. No longer should it be necessary for students or teachers to have to memorize arbitrary relationships between action commands and the computer's response. It should not be necessary, for instance, to have to remember that pressing the Alt and J keys will give you access to the main menu: instead it should be clear and intuitive from what is presented to the user on screen what has to be done to direct the computer to perform a particular action. Now the focus is on design that is sensitive to the needs of users, and the cognitive principles that lead to more intuitive computer systems. The discipline of Human–Computer Interaction (HCI) addresses such concerns, and has been partly responsible for this change in focus.

In contrast to other fields of endeavour that explore how humans work with tools and machines such as 'human factors', 'ergonomics', and earlier 'man–machine studies', HCI restricts its field of view to the computer. In the sense that it focuses on one class of machine, it has a narrower focus than these other fields, although it explores technical design aspects to a much greater degree. According to Card (1993: p. xi), the existence of HCI as a professional community dates from about 1982, the date of a seminal conference on human factors in the USA, and the time when personal computers were really beginning to make an impression on the wider community. Like many of the disciplines discussed in this chapter, HCI has been shaped by some of the more established disciplines that surround it, including psychology, computer science, and sociology (Dix *et al.* 1993: p. xiii). HCI has now matured to a point where initial moves are being made to 'codify' the field (Card 1993: p. xi). In other words, HCI professionals are working on making their models, theories, and frameworks as explicit as possible so that the field may advance beyond practices which are based upon intuition, best practice, or trial and error. In this way vague notions such as 'user-friendliness' or 'ease of use' can be specified and tested precisely in order to identify the elements that contribute to positive or negative reactions to the computer in a given context. There is an emphasis on understanding users, their needs and the nature of the tasks they have to complete with the computer.

A particular interest in HCI work, reflecting the shift in focus from computer to user, is beginning to emerge in CALL. For example, the theme of the 1994 CALICO Conference was 'Human Factors', and the presentations included principles and guidelines and many examples of high-quality design in the CALL context. Authors such as Sussex (1991) and Chapelle (1994*a*) have referred to the significance of HCI data in designing CALL programs.

Of the writers on CALL, Chapelle (1994*a*) argues that HCI research can help to answer pedagogical and psycholinguistic questions about SLA as it relates to the CALL context. For a full understanding of Chapelle's position, which is carefully constructed from first principles in HCI, SLA, and CALL, readers are advised to read the paper in full. Here, only a brief synopsis can be given, which cannot do justice to the logical development of the original.

The first question concerns what HCI data can be used for. In the first instance, HCI data can be used to determine whether software use has instructional benefits; in the second case, HCI data can provide information on learners' developing language and strategies. In order to carry out such work, Chapelle develops the idea of the 'CALL text' that contains 'behavioural and linguistic data' and 'process and product characteristics of language use in context' (1994*a*: 54). Taking an interactionalist perspective of SLA as a theoretical base, Chapelle describes key learner factors and key contextual factors that would enable the SLA researcher to construct suitable hypotheses. Within the interactionalist model, SLA researchers have hypothesized the value of three aspects of interactions: 1) the nature of the input to the learner; 2) the learner's interaction with the input, and 3) the output the learner produces. By analysing the features of the CALL texts and relating them to the features required for language acquisition to occur within this perspective of SLA, researchers can begin to identify the elements that contribute to positive CALL contexts—evidence that may subsequently be used in the design of CALL programs.

Summary

CALL, as an interdisciplinary area of study, has been shaped to a large degree by developments in other disciplines and, of course, the development of technology itself. Many of the difficulties faced by CALL practitioners have been encountered by those working in other areas also. To understand CALL and to circumscribe its field of view, therefore, it helps to appreciate the interplay of CALL with other, contributing disciplines.

This overview has looked at the influences on CALL of psychology, artificial intelligence, computational linguistics, instructional technology and design, and human–computer interaction studies. If one considers cognitive psychology and second language acquisition research as major contemporary concerns emanating from psychology, then all of these disciplines that are having an influence on CALL may be said to have emerged since the last world war, and that attribute, of course, applies to CALL itself. While each of these fields of endeavour has its own particular focus and frame of reference, their newness and broadly defined research agendas may well lead to areas of overlap. Further, while the fields may well overlap, there is no guarantee that workers in each area will be fully aware of developments in others. In fact, with the proliferation of professional journals and conferences that relate quite specifically to a given field, there is a likelihood that researchers may function only within their own domain, remaining unaware of relevant and potentially important developments in others.

The principal avenues of effect on CALL and between the disciplines are illustrated in Figure 3.1. By no means does the diagram indicate all the paths of interconnection between CALL and related disciplines, but it does attempt to set forth some of the key links referred to in the literature on CALL (see Table 3.1). Figure 3.1 is also constructed from a CALL perspective. Of note in the figure is the close association between artificial intelligence (AI) and computational linguistics, and AI and cognitive psychology. The emergence of cognitive science is further evidence of the interrelatedness of this area. Cognitive psychology is also having a significant impact on workers in the field of instructional design.

Over the last forty years, researchers working in psychology, and chiefly involved with programmed instruction, second language acquisition, or cognitive psychology, have provided many models for CALL. Models have been drawn from theories of learning, or theories of teaching, and opinions on the most appropriate source for theory development in CALL differ widely. Integrated theoretical frameworks for CALL have also been suggested (see Mitterer *et al.* 1990).

In addition to psychology, the field of Artificial Intelligence (AI) has had an impact on CALL. Specialist areas within the bounds of AI that concern language, such as ICALL, are developing steadily and a bibliography of the field has now been completed (see Matthews 1991). As earlier discussed, although the influence of this area on CALL has so far been limited, it has the potential to alter significantly the nature of CALL, especially with regard to the

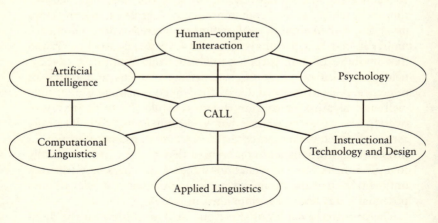

Figure 3.1   *CALL and related disciplines*

nature of the human–computer interface. Work in AI in this area is complemented by work in the emerging field of Human–Computer Interaction. HCI studies bring to CALL a focus on the design of interactive systems with user characteristics and needs paramount, and it includes discussion of the design aspects of menu selection systems, command languages, and interaction styles. With an emphasis on grounding decisions on research findings as well as best practice, it aims to provide a clear and coherent basis for design decisions. Knowledge from this domain can help provide CALL authors with a sense of the range of design options and the implications inherent in each of them. Finally, computational linguistics, particularly machine translation and language data processing, is important to workers in CALL. Like AI, though machine translation has had a limited impact to date, it could make a significant impact in the future. Language data processing has already greatly influenced CALL, especially in the use of concordancing techniques in the language classroom and in the production of textbooks for language learning (see Sinclair 1986; 1988).

Overall, it is clear that the field of CALL is difficult to circumscribe with any degree of precision. Providing a well-defined field of view for CALL may well be unattainable given the breadth and rapidly changing nature of the area. Other work may develop to a point where it suddenly exerts very significant pressures on directions in CALL; one example might be voice synthesis and recognition once the technology matures to a point where it is able to be utilized by the population at large on widely available microcomputers. At this stage definition may be less critical than acknowledging and understanding the effects of other disciplines that explicitly or implicitly contribute to CALL, in their capacities to provide models or otherwise enrich aspects of CALL development. Such an awareness helps to ensure that expert knowledge is used when it is available and experiments are not replicated across different disciplines. Work in these areas is often of mutual benefit and CALL practitioners in particular need to be keenly aware of what is being done. This brings to a close the discussion of CALL in its historical and interdisciplinary perspectives. We now look in more detail at how CALL has been conceptualized, beginning with the acronyms that have emerged to describe the use of the computer in language teaching and learning.

Notes

1. Last (1989) provides a useful introduction to artificial intelligence techniques in language learning addressed to non-specialists and CALL authors. It looks at AI from the point of view of CALL and evaluates its progress and relevance. It includes an historical perspective, both for CALL, and for AI, and it includes many examples of programs that utilize AI techniques in some way, such as expert systems.
2. A concordance is a collection of all the occurrences of a word in a text, or set of texts, with each incidence of the word shown in context. The size of the context can vary. In a Key-Word in Context (KWIC) concordance, the concordance is usually presented with each instance of the keyword displayed one under the other in the centre of each line.
3. Meister (1991) provides a concise and perceptive overview and history of the systems approach, especially helpful in understanding how the core image of a 'system' is understood.
4. The volume edited by Jonassen (1988) provides a comprehensive introduction to instructional designs on the microcomputer. It provides a number of exemplars of how instructional design theories are applied to contemporary computer technology. The book is intended for practising developers, and the examples are built using the process and discipline of instructional design. Of particular interest with regard to the TICCIT project is Merrill's contribution. He discusses the implications of Component Display Theory for instructional design, and provides a number of illuminating examples which show how the theory can be applied directly.
5. Dix *et al.* provide an excellent introduction in their book, *Human–Computer Interaction* (1993). It covers the foundations by exploring the qualities and characteristics of humans and computers, first separately and then in combination. Paradigms, models, and principles are discussed that underpin design practice. A section on advanced topics looks at various forms of CmC and discusses related issues and implications, both technical and social. Multi-sensory systems introduce cutting-edge research issues such as handwriting and gesture recognition, and computer vision. A good complement to the Dix publication, which focuses more on the art than the science of HCI, is edited by Laurel, *The Art of Human–Computer Interface Design* (1990). This collection of articles reflects on the nature of HCI and its metaphors. It includes tools and techniques for creative design, and new metaphors for the human–computer interface. Further books of particular value are Shneiderman (1987), which covers strategies for effective human–computer interaction, and Gordon (1994) on systematic design. These books cover the design of static and dynamic screens, menus, text,

interaction and feedback, colour, backgrounds, foregrounds, and general strategies and techniques for meeting human characteristics and needs. Gordon also presents valuable guidelines for performing user testing and evaluation.

4. Conceptualization I: the CALL literature

Introduction

What goes through a CALL author's mind when contemplating the creation of new CALL materials and learning environments? Is the starting-point, a conception of how learners might benefit through communicating internationally, as with the International Email Tandem Network? Is the initial focus the creation of a resource that can be accessed and used from remote locations, as with the Oral Language Archive or is the point of departure a desire to meet specific learner needs outside and beyond normal class contact time? The points of departure vary enormously as does the path to implementation. Some advocate starting with a particular theoretical position, while others begin with curriculum specifications, or a recognized language-learning problem that appears amenable to a computer solution. It is still unclear how CALL authors make their decisions when they design a new piece of software, or orchestrate a particular CALL environment to facilitate learning. Yet even without a broadly accepted framework large quantities of CALL materials continue to be produced.

Chapter 4 begins an exploration of how CALL has been conceptualized. As described in the introduction, a conceptualization of CALL is assumed to be informed by a philosophy of language teaching and learning, which may or may not be stated explicitly; a role for the computer and the teacher; a specific point of departure; and the hardware and software that is used. Further insight into how CALL has been conceptualized is accomplished by considering the processes of development, the teacher's role in developing CALL materials, and the ways in which they have been described. A conceptualization of CALL is an abstract notion that may go beyond a description of any particular set of CALL materials, though a description of the CALL materials will shed light on the author's conceptualization. In other words, the conceptualization is reflected in the CALL materials developed, but it is not necessarily entirely contained within them. CALL materials that may appear different to the end-user may in fact fit comfortably within the same conceptual framework. The conceptualization concerns the total language learning environment within which the CALL materials are used; therefore, matters of implementation and the role of the teacher in the actual use of the materials, that is, the role of the teacher as contributor, must be included in addition to describing the CALL materials as they exist on the computer or computers. Thus, a conceptualization of CALL depends not only on the CALL materials themselves, but also upon how they are used.

Conceptualization

The acronyms

Computers in education

CAL, CAI, ICAL, ITS, CBI, CALL, TELL, CBE, CMI, CELL—there is certainly no shortage of acronyms for the field. Since these are the broad terms in which practitioners have chosen to describe their work, it is appropriate to begin with a closer look at the acronyms. Adhering to the book's philosophy of providing a broader context wherever possible, we will begin with the acronyms used in education and training generally, before focusing on the instance of CALL in particular.

The generic terms used here are CAL (Computer-Assisted Learning) for the general case, and CALL (Computer-Assisted Language Learning) for the specific one. This follows the suggestion of Wyatt (1984c: 4) who recommended using CALL to emphasize the whole range of possible roles that the computer can play. The question of whether CALL is the most appropriate term, or whether one of the newer terms such as CELL or TELL are preferable, is taken up later.

Commonly used acronyms for computers in education across the disciplines are:

CAI   (Computer-Assisted Instruction)
CAL   (Computer-Assisted Learning)
CML   (Computer-Managed Learning)
CMI   (Computer-Managed Instruction)
CBE   (Computer-Based Education)
CBI   (Computer-Based Instruction)
ICAI (Intelligent Computer-Assisted Instruction)

ITS   (Intelligent Tutoring Systems)
CmC   (Computer-mediated Communication)

Occasionally preferences are determined by geographical location: for example, Ahmad *et al.* note the preference in the USA for CAI, emphasizing the instructional focus, whereas CAL is more common in the UK where learning is the preferred label.

CBE/CBI Of the general terms, CBE and its alias CBI are perhaps the most inclusive terms and cover 'nearly everything that students can do to learn via computers: study programming; practice the application of concepts; use word processors to write essays; design graphics; gather and manipulate data with spreadsheets, databases, or statistical programs' (Pusack 1988: 15). According to Ahmad *et al.* (1985: 3), CBI 'suggests that the computer has a more fundamental role in the education process than in CAI'. When the word 'based' is part of the acronym we are looking at a very central, all-encompassing role for the computer.

CML or CMI delegates the management of learning to the computer. Here the computer acts as a guide to a course of study and covers work away from the computer as well as that occurring on the machine. Typically, the computer administers tests, marks them, and uses the results to work out student profiles which are stored for future reference (Kenning and Kenning 1984: 162). According to Ahmad *et al.* (1985: 3), CMI explicitly assigns 'a more active and controlling role to the computer'. Like the computer-based approaches, the managerial role of the computer is a highly directive one; however, the focus has changed from the 'what' to the 'how'. In other words, with computer-*based* approaches the focus is on the type and scope of the material to be included; with computer-*managed* approaches the key element is the way in which the interactions between computer and human are orchestrated, then recorded.

CAI and CAL Ahmad *et al.* (1985: 2) say that the words 'aided' or 'assisted' are significant, and highlight the computer's 'subservient, auxiliary role' and the function of the computer as 'merely a part of the total learning experience'. This feature highlights one of the starkest contrasts among the acronyms: the division between the all-encompassing role of the computer expressed in terms such as

CBE; and the less directive, less intrusive role indicated in terms such as CAL.

CAI All the acronyms are open to varied interpretation, but CAI has been particularly troublesome in this respect. Given the origins of CAI in programmed learning concepts and the recent, broader definition of CAI that is now more commonly accepted, a distinction is often made between 'traditional CAI', to describe the earlier approaches, and simply CAI for the more recent ones (Pusack 1988: 14). In traditional CAI, according to Barker and Yeates (1985: 364), computers are used 'to guide the user through a prescribed course of learning and testing. The computer assumes the role of teacher, asking questions and assessing the user's responses'. Originally CAI meant tutorial and drill and practice programs, and the computer supplanted the teacher (see Wyatt 1984c: 4).

ICAL/ITS With the terms ICAL and ITS, the focus shifts again, from the role of the computer to the special qualities of the program. The modern field of ICAI or ITS uses artificial intelligence techniques in a variety of ways (see Chapter 2 for more detail). These include, for example, building a model of what the student knows at any particular time and then providing the appropriate instruction accordingly. Or it might involve the use of natural language processing to provide for the use of natural, or close to natural, language interaction between computer and student (Brierley 1991). Contemporary roles for the computer in the ICAI domain are described by Kearsley (1987: 5), who identifies five major paradigms for research and development: mixed initiative dialogues, coaches, diagnostic tutors, microworlds, and articulate expert systems.

CmC is concerned with communication between two or more participants via a computer. It is used generically in the social sciences to cover email, bulletin boards, discussion lists, and computer conferencing, both text-based and video-based.[1] Dana Paramskas (1993: 126) equates CmC with the term 'Telematics' in Europe. In an article on email and the writing instructor for teaching, Hawisher and Moran (1993) lament the lack of a pedagogy in this area, and say that although writings on CmC are prolific in fields like Communications, Management, and Distance Education, there is little to be found in first language composition. The same may be said of foreign or second language writing. Work has been done on the effects of the word processor on writing and on the effects of hypertext and hypermedia on writing and thinking, but there is little so far on the effects of CmC. The use of the term 'mediated' is also used by Hefzallah (1990) who discusses different kinds of computer-mediated interactions. One of the few references to CmC for CALL purposes has been by Leppänen and Kalaja (1995) who discuss the use of computer conferencing in language learning. Overall, however, like first language composition studies, there has been little use of this particular acronym in discussion of CALL so far.

Computers in language learning

In the field of CALL there are also a number of acronyms, some an extension of acronyms for the education set already given.

CALL   Computer-Assisted Language Learning
CAI   Computer-Assisted Instruction
ICALL   Intelligent Computer-Assisted Language Learning
CELL   Computer-Enhanced Language Learning
TELL   Technology-Enhanced Language Learning

Each term suggests a particular focus which tries to encapsulate the use of the computer in language learning, sometimes emphasizing special qualities of the program as in ICALL, sometimes suggesting an improved way of learning as in TELL, and sometimes indicating the role of the computer as in CALL.

CAI or CALL The geographical dimension arises in the definition of CAI and CALL as shown by the two groups of authors contributing to the two special issues of the journal, *System*. The first issue in 1984 (Wyatt 1984*a*), representing a largely North American view, exclusively used the acronym CAI (with the exception of just one article in which the term CAL was used). The second issue in 1986, representing 'a more European view' (Higgins 1986*a*: 14), exclusively used the term CALL.

Wyatt, a North American CALL practitioner, acknowledges the difficulty with terminology in his book *Computers and ESL*, published in 1984, and says:

The term 'computer-assisted instruction' itself is suggestive of only one role for the computer, exemplified in drill-and-practice and tutorial materials. For this reason, it was generally agreed at the CAI symposium . . . to adopt the alternative designation CALL: computer assisted language learning. Throughout this book, therefore, the term CALL will be used to emphasize the whole range of possible roles that the computer can play. (1984*c*: 4)

Similarly, Underwood recognizes the same confusion in terminology and uses the label CALL as a result (1984: 38). Here CALL is used as the general term to cover all roles of the computer in language learning. When CAI is used, it refers to tutorial and drill-and-practice programs and it is regarded as a separate instructional practice.

ICALL The addition of 'intelligent' to an acronym indicates the same shift in focus in CALL as it does in the general case. In contrast to ICAI or ITS, in ICALL specific issues associated with learning a language are addressed. There is more of an emphasis on modelling the language and the language learner with a view to creating an environment on the computer that is conducive to language learning. A number of researchers use ICALL systems to model theories of second language acquisition. Learner responses can be traced in a variety of ways to collect data that can be used to help substantiate the theoretical model. A comprehensive bibliography on ICALL is now available (Matthews 1991).

CELL and TELL are relatively new acronyms. As far as I am aware CELL was first coined around 1988 by Professor Andrew Lian with the view that a new emphasis in the field was needed. CELL emphasizes the use of the computer to make language learning better or more effective. With CELL, no judgement is made as to the kind of programs or materials used. The word 'enhanced' is also used in the TELL acronym. This term has become widely known through the TELL Consortium based at the Centre for Modern Languages at the University of Hull in the UK. The move from 'computer' to 'technology' shows a broadening out of the field and a feeling that a computer is just a part of the many technologies that are being used in language learning today.

My own preference is for the acronym CALL, hence its use in the title of the book. There are three reasons why I believe the term still to be helpful. First, CALL was chosen by Wyatt in 1984 to emphasize the whole range of possible roles the computer could play in language learning. CALL is an established term, as is ICALL, and in spite of more recently introduced acronyms, CALL maintains its forward momentum through books (e.g. Pennington 1996), conferences, and journals, notably *ReCALL*, *CALL*, *On-CALL*, and CALICO, excepting the North American use of instruction rather than learning in CALICO. Secondly, the computer as assistant or aid remains a very useful perspective: in particular the computer can assist in teaching and in providing resources that would not otherwise be available. Words like 'technology' or 'enhanced' have greater coverage, and that is their strength, but one could argue that they lack focus as a consequence. Thirdly, I am reminded of the motto of Sun Microsystems a few years ago: 'The network is the computer'. By conceptualizing the whole network as the computer, CALL at once incorporates one of the most important developments of the 1990s, the Internet. Computers are still at the centre of it all, and at the end of it all, you might say, because after all is said and done the student sees and sits in front of a computer. Having said that, the label 'mediated' strikes me as very helpful too. The use of this term focuses attention on the effects of the tool on the task. It suggests, implicitly, that through mediating the communication the computer exerts an effect on it in some way. If there were no effects it would not be necessary to talk about CmC. This perspective is a useful one for CALL also as we shall see in Chapter 8.

In sum, the acronyms are helpful in painting the broad picture. They indicate broad directions, and particularly the division between an all-encompassing role for the computer and a less central, more auxiliary one. They show an opposition between the more directive, controlling role of the computer in contrast to the one that is neutral. These roles for the computer have clear implications for the roles of the teacher, if the roles of the computer and the teacher are going to complement one another. Overall, the acronyms are useful in marking a particular role, or a particular focus in the work that is taking place.

But finer resolution using the acronyms is problematic, and that is why in my opinion the question of which particular acronym should be the preferred one is a relatively minor issue that need not be pursued too far. The acronyms each cover too broad a range of activities. Although they give an *indication* of the possible roles of the computer, their value is limited because there is little agreement about their meaning—what is CAL to one teacher may be CBI to another. The inverse is true also. Not only may one technique be represented by many acronyms, but also one acronym may encompass widely differing techniques, especially as one traverses time and place. A closer correspondence between terminology and technique would be most helpful and it is time for these terms to be applied with a little more precision, a point we will return to later in the book.

The role of the computer

The acronyms provide one window onto how CALL is conceptualized; in 1980 Robert Taylor provided another. He suggested the tutor, tool, and tutee roles for the computer as a helpful framework for understanding computer use in education. Taylor describes these roles as follows:

To function as a *tutor* in some subject, the computer must be programmed by 'experts' in programming and in that subject . . . The computer presents some subject material, the student responds, the computer evaluates the response, and from the results of the evaluation, determines what to present next. At its least, the computer keeps complete records of each student being tutored . . .

To function as a *tool*, the computer need only have some useful capability programmed into it such as statistical analysis, super calculation, or word processing. The learner can then use it to help them in a variety of subjects . . .

To use the computer as *tutee* is to tutor the computer; for that, the student or teacher doing the tutoring must learn to program, to talk to the computer in a language that it understands.

Essentially, the difference between the computer tutor and the computer tool is quite simple: the tutor *evaluates* the student input in some way, the tool does not. Compared with the computer tutor, with the tutee the direction of control between the computer and the user is reversed. For the computer tutee, the teacher or student tutors, or teaches, the computer to be either a tutor or a tool. This framework has been described as 'perhaps the most useful and lasting' (Jonassen 1988: p. xii). Any framework that remains useful for over a decade in the rapidly changing world of computing is worthy of attention.

While recent computer tutors are highly sophisticated, the roots of the tradition that places the computer in the role of tutor lie in behaviourism and programmed instruction. The tutor role of the computer includes CAI and CMI, and other early, rather rudimentary CAI computer–student interactions, such as those associated with programmed learning. More recent and more sophisticated interactions available in ICAI and ITS also fall within the tutor tradition. A role for the computer as a tool has been widely discussed in general and in relation to CALL (Weizenbaum 1984: 17; Brierley and Kemble 1991). This role for the computer is a fundamental one. It is the basis for the computer's widespread acceptance and use, and in the sense that the computer is an example of a tool used to augment human capabilities, it has had a long history (Phillips 1987: 282). Modern computer tools include application programs such as word processor, database and spreadsheet programs, and communication tools under the umbrella CmC. In CALL they include the word processor again, concordancers, email, text-based and video-based computer conferencing, mono- and multilingual dictionaries, and language databases or archives of various kinds such as the OLA.

The distinction between the instructional or teaching focus as opposed to the learning focus flows through the acronyms and the roles. The tutor and tool are evident in the models developed by many of these writers, made clear in the use of words such as 'assisted', 'aided', 'managed', or 'tutoring' in the acronyms. Similarly, the directive and non-directive roles of the computer, as illustrated through the acronyms and the tutor and tool roles proposed by Taylor, can easily be identified. So thinking about the roles of the computer is one means of gaining access to a better understanding of how CALL authors conceptualize their work, especially at the macro level. Stepping closer, the points of departure declared by CALL authors in their projects provide another point of entry.

Points of departure

Not surprisingly perhaps, given the essential neutrality of the computer as a tool, the approaches taken to the design of CALL programs have been diverse. Using the literature on CALL projects, this section looks first at general approaches to development, then it describes specific points of departure as they are recorded by the authors in their projects.

A number of practitioners have outlined their preferred approach in general terms. In designing effective language learning environments for the computer, Mitterer *et al.* (1990: 136) argue that for CALL materials to be developed effectively a theory of instructional design, a theory of language teaching, and a theory of language learning must be integrated with a knowledge of how the technology is best applied. Hubbard (1992) suggests a methodological framework for the development of CALL courseware based upon a description of a teaching method (Richards and Rodgers 1986: 28). This framework focuses on identifying the key elements in the development process and their interdependencies.

Alternatively, an approach to language learning may be the starting-point. In the case of Communicative Language Teaching, for example, Underwood (1984: 52) provides thirteen premises for communicative CALL software which describe in detail the characteristics that communicative CALL programs would be expected to have. Within the communicative context, Kecskés and Agócs present three important requirements for CALL program design: 'concentration on meaning rather than form; the use of authoring techniques; and the adjusting of the program to the needs of teachers and learners' (Kecskés and Agócs 1989*b*: 64).

Doughty and Cook assert that models of second language acquisition should form the basis of CALL research and development (Doughty 1991: 1; Cook 1992: 21). So far, these models for CALL have been untested, and it is not clear whether such models are powerful enough, detailed enough, or are sufficiently applicable to actively direct CALL development. Even if they are limited in this respect, however, they will most certainly help to provide explanations of why certain kinds of interactions are successful.

Framing a CALL program principally in terms of a theory of language learning is only one of the avenues taken by developers. Table 4.1 shows the points of departure for CALL together with more information on the type of program and the key references. The programs listed are those where a description of the initial orientation of the developers was documented in the literature. Furthermore, programs are listed on a representative basis so that a program would be excluded if it were conceptualized in a very similar way to a more representative example already given.

TABLE 4.1   *Program descriptions and references*

Program	Points of departure	Type	Reference
ALICE	Multimedia workbench for ICAI	Collections of text, audio, and video corpora	Levin *et al.* 1991: 27
Athena	Communicative Language Learning	Simulations, structured conversations	Murray *et al.* 1989: 98
France InterActive/ CAMILLE	Hypermedia and model of 'communicative competence'	Multimedia language courses	Ingraham and Emery 1991: 321; 1993: 26
Choicemaster	An exercise type	Multiple choice	Jones and Fortescue 1987: 10–11
CLEF	Practice and feedback for grammar skills	Tutor for grammar	Paramskas 1989: 333; 1995
Communicating	Research on communicative strategies	Videodisc material linking classroom language with real world tasks	Mah 1990: 214
CompLex	Vocabulary instruction and research tool	ITS facilitating acquisition of L2 vocabulary	Harrington 1994
FLUENT	Conversational practice with a computer partner	Intelligent tutoring system	Hamburger 1994
Hopalong	Reading skill development	A computer reading pacer	Higgins and Wallace 1989: 389
Kanjicard	Specific problem for Japanese learners	Self-instructional software for ideographic scripts	Nakajima 1988; 1990: 143
Kanji City	Exploring hypermedia	Simulation for exploration of real-life environment	Ashworth and Stelovsky 1989: 27
KITES Project	Authentic communication at a distance	E-mail, videoconferencing	Teichmann 1994

TABLE 4.1   *Continued*

Program	Points of departure	Type	Reference
LEXI-CAL	Vocabulary acquisition	Authoring system for learning lexical items in French and English	Kidd 1990: 69
LINGER	AI paradigm with knowledge of pedagogical principles	ICALL system for French vocab. and grammar	Yazdani 1991*a*: 107
Littré/ BonAccord	Translation, Curriculum requirements	Mini-expert system	Farrington 1986: 200
Miniprof	Instruction for elementary French	Intelligent tutor with parsing, diagnosis, and tutoring	Labrie and Singh 1991: 9
Montevidisco	Theory of SLA, individualized instruction videodisc	Conversational simulations	Schneider and Bennion 1984: 41–3
Multimedia Teleschool	Distance learning internationally	Multimedia, computer conferencing	Fesl 1994
Oral Language Archive	Worldwide access to digitized sound for a number of languages	Archive of digitized sound with management tools	Jones 1996, forthcoming
PLATO	Interactive, self-paced instruction for large numbers of students	Largely drill and practice	Smith and Sherwood 1976: 344; Hart 1981: 2, 12
Remote Technical Assistant	Student conferencing and student–teacher interactions	Conferencing software for the Internet	Blake 1995
SL-Lists	Cross-cultural discussion and writing practice	Nine discussion 'lists'	Robb 1995
Spion	Natural Language Processing	Adventure game	Molla *et al.* 1988; Sanders and Sanders 1995

TABLE 4.1   *Continued*

Program	Points of departure	Type	Reference
STOBI	Understanding relation between form and meaning	Text-based system using 'intelligent' text generator	Kecskés and Agócs 1989*b*: 53
Storyboard/ Eclipse	Reading skill development	Elaborated cloze	Higgins 1989: 18
Tandem Network	Pen Pals Project utilizing language pairs	E-mail subscription 'list'	St John and Cash 1995
TICCIT	Theory of instruction, educational applications	Component Display Theory	Merrill 1988: 61–6
Venture-reader	Development of reading skills and vocab. within a single environment	Extensive environment of linked reading-based activities	Clarke 1989*a*: 28

The points of departure for the programs listed include theories of instruction, theories of learning, curriculum imperatives, experiments with a new technology, exercise types, learning problems, language skills and the delivery of materials to a large number of students. The diversity in points of departure and type is quite remarkable, and it is testimony to the enormous flexibility of the computer and the range of problems that practitioners wish to address. In understanding how the conceptualization is shaped further, the next section looks at hardware and software, with a separate section on the Internet.

Hardware and software: authoring

Both the choice of computer hardware and computer software can contribute to the formation of an author's conceptualization of CALL (Mackay 1988; Lian 1991). Software authoring tools give the CALL author the scope to design and write original CALL materials, although within a given framework. Mackay maintains that an authoring system reflects an educational philosophy to the extent that, 'A quick glance at the screen is often sufficient to determine which authoring language was used to create which course' (Mackay 1988: 329). Any authoring system carries a certain conceptualization of CALL that is inherent in its presentational scheme and in the range of options that it offers the author, particularly with the interaction options that it makes available. Only the most flexible option, the high-level programming language, is relatively free of such constraints. Anything less than a high-level programming language carries with it predetermined structures. Such constraints have the effect of filtering the author's initial conceptualization.

Usually some compromise has to be reached between the original conceptualization and the final implementation because of intrinsic limitations in the hardware or software, or simply because the complexity of the programming required to create a certain functionality is beyond reach: contemporary limitations on voice recognition and natural language processing exemplify this point. Hardware and software considerations, therefore, are going to have some effect on the nature of any CALL materials produced, beyond that planned for at the outset.

With hardware the CALL author's primary decision is whether to work within the constraints of existing hardware, or to 'stretch' the capabilities of the hardware so that it may more nearly approximate the author's requirements. In discussing this issue, Morgenstern (1986: 23) says too many CALL programs are 'technology driven', an approach which 'concentrates on the features of the goal system which seem particularly appropriate for the technology to address. Unfortunately, these features may or may not be the most important, merely the most accessible.' In an alternative approach, one that is 'goal driven', Morgenstern suggests 'adapting and deforming' the technology to meet 'significant aspects of the goal system' (1986: 23).

A good example of stretching existing hardware technology to meet certain goals is the TICCIT project described in Chapter 2. Beginning with a particular instructional design framework, 'Component Display Theory', specific items of hardware were specially developed. Instead of employing a standard style keyboard, a specially adapted keyboard was designed, featuring a set of function keys derived from the design framework. Thus, standard equipment was 'adapted and deformed' to meet particular goals. Under most circumstances, however, and often due to lack of sufficient funds, CALL authors rely on existing, commercially available hardware components.

The most widely available microcomputers are those usually used for CALL, notwithstanding any other considerations, such as specific capabilities that might make a computer particularly useful for CALL applications (see Ariew 1984: 43; Last 1989: 32). Last maintains that the development of CALL in the UK was negatively affected by the introduction of the BBC microcomputer, a computer purchased by many schools and colleges. As a result of the BBC's widespread acceptance, software development and publication was directed towards it. Although this helped CALL get started, Last believes it led to stagnation because of the limited power of the machine (Last 1989: 32). In the early to mid-1980s the same may have been said about the Apple II microcomputer in the USA. Ariew describes how the hardware for a CALL project in French was chosen on the basis of 'the most available' machine, the Apple II having 'the largest hardware base in the field of secondary education' at the time of writing (Ariew 1984: 43). More recently, of course, varieties of the IBM PC and Macintosh microcomputers have superseded the BBC and the Apple II as the most popular microcomputers in education.

Authoring software or authoring tools allow new materials to be written for the computer (Haukom and Malone 1987: 102). Such software gives the CALL author the scope to design and write original CALL materials, although the degree of author control varies considerably. The extent to which the author becomes involved in the authoring process is determined by the authoring approach (Underwood 1984: 82). Traditionally in the CALL literature, three approaches to the writing of materials for the computer have been described (Underwood 1984: 82; Kenning and Kenning 1984: 13; Pennington 1989*a*: 17). In addition to these three approaches, there is sufficient justification for a fourth category, namely authoring programs, a subcategory of authoring systems, and this category is included here also. An item of authoring software may have attributes associated with more than one approach (see Sussex 1991). While recognizing the problem of definition, these categories remain convenient for descriptive purposes.

In the early to mid-1980s it was used to describe a template system capable of providing a structure or framework for CALL, but not the material content itself (see Holmes 1984*a*: 22;

Underwood 1984: 90). In more recent years authoring systems have become more powerful and more flexible although authoring systems still retain 'templates' in the form of pre-defined structures or objects and a discrete and limited range of interaction possibilities. Thus, *Authorware* can be described as an authoring system. This is consistent with the program documentation (see *Authorware Tutorial*: p. v), because of the pre-defined structures and objects supplied and the limited range of response types that may be used in the development of CALL materials.

Authoring systems can be broadly divided into general systems and systems designed specifically for language learning. More recent examples in the former category are *Authorware* and cT. In the latter category are *Dasher* (Pusack 1983), *MacLang* (Frommer 1989) and CALIS (Computer-Assisted Language Instruction System). Examples in the earlier category tend to be used across disciplines, especially in training applications. Although they often lack sophisticated text processing, versions are usually available across a number of hardware platforms; for example, both *Authorware* and cT are available in Macintosh and IBM versions. On the other hand, specialized authoring systems for language learning can accommodate a wide variety of language scripts (e.g. CALIS can handle eighteen different language scripts) and the answer-processing techniques are relatively sophisticated.

The early authoring systems provided one of the easiest ways for the teacher to construct CALL programs (Ahmad *et al.* 1985: 25). On the other hand, the range of activities available in the earlier authoring systems was strictly limited (Underwood 1984: 91; Holmes 1984*a*: 27) and they precluded 'any really original use of the resources of the computer' (Kenning and Kenning 1984: 12). The more recent authoring systems provide more flexibility but they are also more complex to learn and use. At the same time such systems still have shortcomings in the range and sophistication of the response types available.

Authoring programs, sometimes called authoring packages (Davies 1986; Jones 1986) or mini-authoring systems (Kenner 1988*b*: 1), tend to be smaller scale and more language-learning specific than authoring systems, but like the earlier authoring systems the program provides a template or framework for the content. This category of programs is usually formed around a language-learning activity, often in the form of a game. These include text reconstruction (e.g. *Storyboard*), gap-filling (e.g. *Gapmaster*), crossword (e.g. *Crossword Magic*), spelling (e.g. *Word Attack*), and simulation (e.g. *Fast Food*). In authoring these programs the teacher has to add the content which is then incorporated into the game. Authoring programs, like authoring systems, shield the author from having to program the computer. The disadvantage is that they can be restrictive because the author is limited to the framework provided by the program (Davies 1986: 15).

An authoring language, or author language, is a highly specialized programming language that enables teachers with relatively little computing experience to produce CALL materials (Kenning and Kenning 1984: 187; Pennington 1989*b*: 17). These languages generally have built-in subroutines for program functions that are required regularly. One of the best-known authoring languages is PILOT (Programmed Inquiry, Learning, Or Teaching) which was deliberately developed as a simplified programming language that was most suited to tutorial and drill and practice (Wyatt 1984*c*: 40). However, for more complex interactions the limitations of authoring languages such as PILOT are soon encountered (Ahmad *et al.* 1985: 99; Underwood 1984: 90; Kenning and Kenning 1984: 13; Higgins and Johns 1984: 102). In the 1990s discussion of the authoring language approach to authoring has been rare, and given the time needed to learn such languages, and the kind of interactions that can be constructed with them, perhaps it is not worth the effort.

Computer languages lie on a continuum that ranges from lists of computer instructions written in a machine code (a low-level language) to languages that are more oriented towards the human user and therefore easier to learn and use (a high-level language) (Ahmad *et al.* 1985: 84). Some high-level languages are general purpose (e.g. BASIC) while others have been designed for a specific purpose (e.g. ICON), a high-level programming language for text analysis (Griswold 1990). LISP and *Prolog* have been used extensively for research on natural languages (Pennington 1989*b*: 17).

The first generation of microcomputers was sold with a version of BASIC (Beginners' All Purpose Symbolic Instruction Code). The language was first developed at Dartmouth College in 1963, with the first microcomputer version in 1975 (Smarte and Reinhardt 1990: 371). In the early 1980s especially, it was the most widespread general purpose programming language. In 1983 Wyatt estimated that 80 per cent of educational software had been written in BASIC (Wyatt 1983: 16) and as late as 1989 Pennington stated that BASIC was the most common language for CALL programming on microcomputers (Pennington 1989*b*: 16).

Although criticized as a development language for educational software (Phillips 1983: 6; Last 1989: 13, 34, 113), its widespread use enabled CALL authors to share programs and expertise in that language. One can point to creditable achievements within it such as Kenning and Kenning's *A Vous la France!* (1986) and Farrington's *Littré* (1987). Many books and articles in the early 1980s included complete programs, or fragments of programs, in BASIC (Kenning and Kenning 1983; Higgins and Johns 1984; Dalgish 1985; Ahmad *et al.* 1985), and there was at least one book solely dedicated to helping language teachers learn the language (Davies 1985). The generic nature of this language, the fact that it was often provided free of charge with new machines, and its widespread use enabled a sharing of programs and expertise amongst developers that has not been seen on the same scale since. The only exception might be considered to be *HyperCard* which is supported through magazines such as *The Stack Exchange, Educational Hypermedia Programs for the Apple II and Macintosh*, which go some way towards encouraging the sharing and exchange of materials produced using *HyperCard* (see Lampert 1993).

In sum, high-level programming languages offer the user complete control over what the program does (Underwood 1984: 82). Relative to the other approaches to authoring, however, such languages are more difficult for the potential author to learn, and it can take a considerable amount of time to produce a useful program (Underwood 1984: 83).

Recently, as authoring tools have become more versatile and powerful, the earlier divisions between the different types of tool have become harder to identify. Now, typically, an authoring tool allows a number of levels of operation depending on the needs of the author. For example, *HyperCard* has five levels of operation: browsing, typing, painting, authoring, and scripting, which is like programming. At the browsing level, the user is free to explore the program, but no changes are permitted. On the other hand at the scripting level, full editing features are available including the use of the scripting language, *HyperTalk*.

With new advances in multimedia, authoring systems designers have shown sensitivity to the need to manage integrated multimedia technologies for applications which combine a wide array of peripheral devices and design options. Typically, such systems may be used to create multimedia applications incorporating text, graphics, sound, animation, and video, and a considerable number have emerged with this in view: *HyperStudio, Authority Multimedia, Multimedia ToolBook, MacroMedia Director*, and so on. Used with sophisticated utilities for handling 'time-based' data such as *QuickTime* these systems become a very powerful authoring tool for multimedia purposes (Walsh 1992: 76). Such authoring systems have greatly expanded the ways in which CALL may be conceptualized. In the context of CD-I (Compact disc-interactive), Canter *et al.* argue that an effective authoring system should be able to: 'take graphics, text, music, and computer code segments from several sources; it has an animation score that is represented graphically . . . ; it provides real-time feedback to the designer and is fast and easy to use; and it incorporates a complete authoring language for specifying interactivity' (1987: 150). Recent multimedia products such as *Visual Basic* also show that programming languages such as BASIC can undergo substantial change in a way that ensures their usefulness when new media options become available.

Another possible avenue of CAL authoring development involves artificial intelligence techniques (Phillips 1987: 280; Sussex 1991: 23; Lian 1992: 68). So far such systems have not reached the stage of offering an authoring component (Bailin and Levin 1989: 10; Sussex 1991: 23), a fact noted in the area of Intelligent Computer-Assisted Instruction (ICAI) where few authoring tools exist as they do for conventional CAI; there is no reason, however, why such tools could not be developed (Kearsley 1988: 381). With regard to high-level language programming, Yazdani (1984: 7) and Farrington (1989: 68) predict a move towards more sophisticated programming techniques associated with Intelligent Tutoring Systems (ITS) using *Prolog* or LISP. At the same time it is noteworthy that no intelligent language teaching system is in regular, everyday use by students as yet (Farrington 1989: 69).

The most recent generic authoring or publishing option that has become available is the one that allows materials to be produced for the World Wide Web. Mark-up languages such as HTML or VRML enable users to create pages on the Web. Early Web publishing required the user to learn how to manipulate a set of instructions to put the Web document into the correct format—potential authors usually had to be familiar with twenty to thirty HTML elements. Creative presentation work still requires the designer to resort to HTML coding, especially for creating background images, or for troubleshooting. However, new add-on facilities to word processing and desk-top publishing packages are helping to automate the process of conversion from conventional file to Web document, and such tools are likely to increase in capacity and sophistication.

In the discussion so far of course, work on stand-alone microcomputers has been the main focus. As Lian notes, there has been a tendency for CALL practitioners to conceptualize CALL only in terms of 'a small single-user, single-tasking microprocessor-based machine' and this view is unnecessarily restrictive (Lian 1991: 2). Lian envisions the use of 'high-powered workstations as a delivery medium (SUN, Microvax) all connected to one another and to centralized software distribution facilities through transparent high-speed networks' (Lian 1991: 6). This brings us to a discussion of the Internet—the worldwide 'network of networks'—a communication system that is revolutionizing the ways in which practitioners conceptualize CALL.

Email and the Internet

The Internet is an extraordinarily dynamic entity that is evolving continually, and it is an understatement to say that it is difficult to characterize simply. Likewise the ways in which email is employed in language teaching and learning are numerous and multifaceted. What follows is an attempt to identify some of the key features of these communication systems, and to discuss them in as much as they have a bearing on how CALL authors and language teachers conceptualize CALL.

Collections of materials or archives can be stored conveniently at local sites for worldwide access. The materials may simply be viewed, or they may be downloaded via the Internet, as would be the case with listening materials in the Oral Language Archive, for example. Material collections may be of a textual, audio, and visual kind, or a subset therein. Examples of these collections relevant to CALL are: online newspapers in many languages providing up-to-

date news from around the world; audio, video, or multimedia
materials; text corpora such as *CobuildDirect*, now available as an
online service; or databases containing information on many topics.
McNab (1991) quoting Hewer (1989) suggests two ways of utilizing remote databases: using bibliographic databases to track down
references and software applications; and using full-text and reference databases which can be incorporated, either partially or entirely, in CALL applications, performing a dictionary or
text-analysis function, for instance. Email discussion lists such as
TESL-L also facilitate access to archives. The TESL-L archives
include numerous files and documents for ESL contributed by
members of the list from around the world (see Warschauer 1995:
24; appendix D for subscription details).

Not only can email and the Internet be used to access resources,
they may also be used to enable communication between individuals and groups, either locally or at a distance. Under the broad
heading of Computer-mediated Communication, mechanisms for
interaction include email, bulletin boards, discussion lists, Internet
Relay Chat, and computer conferencing systems. To help distinguish between these forms of communication and the systems that
support them, it is helpful to use a time/space matrix devised by Dix
et al. (1993) and shown in Figure 4.1.

Different names are sometimes given to the titles along each axis.
The geographical dimension can be divided into *co-located* (same
place), and *remote* (different place); the time axis can be divided
into *synchronous* (same time), and *asynchronous* (different time)
(Dix *et al.* 1993: 425). The situation is not quite as straightforward
as this: for example slight delays in transmission, as in an international telephone call, can complicate these simple distinctions, but

	Same place	Different place
Same time	face-to-face conversation	telephone
Different time	post-it note	letter

FIGURE 4.1   *Time/space matrix*

nevertheless, the matrix provides a helpful background for the discussion. Thus, on the one hand, email, newsgroups, discussion lists are text-based forms of asynchronous remote communication. On the other hand, Internet Relay Chat and desktop video-conferencing are examples of synchronous remote communication.

Of these CmC systems, electronic mail has so far been the most pervasive in language teaching and learning (see Austin and Mendlick 1993; Goodwin *et al.* 1993; Hawisher and Moran 1993; Davis and Ye-Ling 1994/5; Kroonenberg 1994/5; Leppänen and Kalaja 1995; Warschauer 1995). Important pedagogical advantages are described by Kalaja and Leppänen (1994: 89) who praise email for increasing student participation, enabling the students to perform a range of roles in relation to their personal goals, and for encouraging students to concern themselves with maintaining social relationships within the group. From the student's point of view, Warschauer (1995: 2) adds that email provides for real, authentic communication and independent learning; from the teacher's point of view it enriches teachers' experiences because colleagues are able to share new ideas and materials more easily.

Of the reported types of email interaction, pen pal projects are one of the most frequent. Typically, communication takes place between students in different countries, second language learners corresponding with their native speakers, sometimes on a reciprocal basis. Recently, more structured forms of email interaction are being encouraged through collaborative work, especially joint projects (Barson *et al.* 1993; Sauer 1994). A good example is described by Davis and Ye-Ling (1994/5) who have collaborated over the last four years in an exchange program linking undergraduate students at Taiwan's National Kaohsiung Normal University with similar students at the University of North Carolina in the USA. The aims of this project are to provide students with a real context for improving their writing across cultural boundaries.

Students may interact with each other, or with the teacher. For Leppänen and Kalaja (1995: 27) a tutor collaborates with students who use computer conferencing via email as a 'forum' for classroom discussions, and as a means of gaining expertise using process writing techniques. Here the teacher may play a more direct and active role in the email interactions taking place, although in most cases, the goal is for the level of teacher involvement to steadily diminish so that students focus on interacting with each other rather than the teacher. There are a number of examples of student–teacher interactions via email, with the teacher's role ranging from instructor to guide and facilitator (Neuwirth *et al.* 1988; Goodwin *et al.* 1993; Hoffman 1994; Blake 1995). Goodwin *et al.* provide instruction in composition, culture, and research skills across international borders using email. One of the features of Blake's Remote Technical Assistant (RTA) is to provide students with individualized online help while they do course-related work outside of class. Hoffman reports on four teachers providing email feedback to English L2 writers in technical communication courses.

Another form of CmC proceeds via discussion lists where a message, or 'posting', goes to all subscribers on the list. Bedell (1994) reviews a substantial range of Bitnet and Internet lists for language learning. It can be useful to create special lists for language learners and Robb (1995) describes a range of lists for EFL and ESL students. These student lists were established in 1994 to provide 'a forum for cross-cultural discussion and written practice for college, university, and adult students in English language programs around the world'. Currently, there are nine student lists covering business and economics, learning english, current events, the cinema, music, science, technology and computers, and sports. The differences between email and discussion lists will probably blur over time, although significant differences for participants, especially in who controls what, always need to be borne in mind (Dix *et al.* 1993: 429).

Email and lists operate via software that facilitates communication via email in a relatively unstructured way. It is left to the user to sort messages and to keep track of incoming messages. With a computer conferencing system, however, which is still asynchronous, the user is provided with a more structured environment for managing the interactions taking place. Conferencing systems are especially designed to facilitate goal-oriented group interaction (Craven 1995*a*). Craven (1995*b*) describes the use of the *FirstClass* text-based conferencing system which has a tablet of buttons to help students follow the thread of a discussion between members of a group over time. While the system may be connected to the Internet to allow mail to be sent and received from outside, *FirstClass* is essentially a self-contained set-up using a LAN.

For the most part, email, lists, and conferencing systems such as

FirstClass operate in different time frames, that is they are asynchronous. However, synchronous systems are also available comprising textual, audio, and video material that can be transmitted and read in real time. One of the simplest forms of interaction in this manner is the Internet Relay Chat (IRC) which allows people to converse with each other via a keyboard simultaneously. The screen is split in half, the top half usually showing the typed message to be sent, and the bottom half showing the reply. Most real time discussion software works in the same way. Commonly used examples of IRC are the UNIX 'talk' program, or the VAX 'phone' system. In language teaching and learning, the RTA can be used in a 'chat' mode engendering discussion and collaborative projects outside the classroom. In addition, and given sufficient bandwidth, videoconferencing software on computer, such as *CU-SeeMe*, provides a conferencing environment capable of managing text, audio, and video in real time.[2] Projects involving the teaching of languages using videoconferencing and detailed evaluation of such learning systems are described by Teichmann (1994), and Hiraga and Fujii (1994).

In addition to extending access to more materials and to more people, email and the Internet has enabled new learning environments to be created. These learning environments may be place dependent, as with video conferencing, for example, or place independent, as with IRC chat. They range from simulations which utilize the web of connections that make up the Internet (see Klobusicky-Mailänder 1990), to virtual worlds where students can roam around and interact with each other, and their virtual environment.[3] Turner and Pohio (1995) describe the use of text-based virtual reality in the language classroom. They report on the use of MOOs, often associated also with MUDs and MUSHes, and these are described by Krol (1994) as follows:

MUD (Multi-User Dungeon): a group of role-playing games modelled on the original 'Dungeons and Dragons' games. MUDs have been used as conferencing tools and educational aids. MUDs are less complex than other types of interactive online games.
MUSH (Multi-User Shared Hallucination): similar to a MUD but tends to require the use of symbols for certain commands, making it more difficult to manage for the inexperienced.

MOO (MUD Object Oriented): similar to a MUD, but different in that users can help build the environment.

In an ESL/EFL context, one of the best-known virtual worlds of this kind is the schMOOze University, which provides a target language environment for real time discussion between learners of that language around the world. Unlike IRC, which is essentially an open party line, MOOs are characterized by a particular interest, a shared language interest for instance (Warschauer 1995). Currently, MOOs exist for French, Spanish, English, Italian, and German and their number is growing steadily.

Overall, email and the Internet facilitate a suite of wholly new forms of interaction between individuals and groups, locally and at a distance. Teachers and students now have access to materials or archives, fellow colleagues, and students that were hitherto inaccessible or unavailable. As a result, new forms of learning using the computer, either directly or as a support, can be conceptualized in CALL for the first time.

The role of the teacher (as contributor)

The role of the teacher in the actual implementation of CALL depends very much on the extent to which the teacher has been envisioned as having a significant role to play. The teacher may have a minimal role, or be excluded altogether, if the CALL materials have been conceived as a self-contained, stand-alone package; alternatively, the teacher may play a pivotal role in the actual delivery of the materials. By way of illustration compare Ahmad's model (1985: 45) describing the three main components of CALL, learner, language, and computer and their interrelationship, with Farrington's 'Triangular mode' (1986: 199) which relates teacher, class, and computer in Figure 4.2.

The focal points in the Ahmad model of CALL are the learner, the language, and the computer and their paired interrelationships. The authors suggest that CALL development must be based on satisfactory models of these elements, and particular attention is paid to the complexity of natural language and the problems this poses for CALL programs (Ahmad *et al.* 1985: 49). Though the role of the computer described here is mainly of the tutorial type, the authors discuss simulations, generative programs, and heuristic programs as well (1985: 62). The role of the teacher is not entered

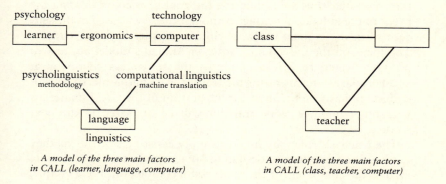

The Ahmad model

The Farrington model

A model of the three main factors
in CALL (learner, language, computer)

A model of the three main factors
in CALL (class, teacher, computer)

FIGURE 4.2   *Two models of CALL*

into however, with the exception of certain ergonomic considerations over which the teacher may have some control. Rather, the emphasis is on the importance of improving the models of the learner, language, and computer with the computer as tutor or 'helpful teacher' as the primary goal (1985: 62). The teacher is shown to have only a minor role in this conception of CALL.

Farrington's model reflects the use of the computer as tool rather than tutor and, with a less central role assigned to the computer, the teacher's role becomes more significant. The series of programs discussed in Farrington's study were found to be most effective when the teacher managed the learning (1986: 198). The package described by Farrington is called *Littré*, a set of programs aimed at helping students translate between English and French. There are no questions or anticipated answers, correct or incorrect, in the program (1986: 200). Instead *Littré* is used to encourage learners to interrogate the system in order to find out what translations are possible. The most common and effective use of the program was with small groups, with the teacher playing a central role in managing the interaction with the computer program.

The two examples show how different the role of the teacher can be depending upon the conceptualization of CALL. In the tutor role the role of the teacher is peripheral, in the tool role it is often critical. Of interest also, is the way in which the Ahmad approach focuses on developing an accurate model of the individual learner, whereas in Farrington's example the whole class is interacting with the computer, thus subordinating the goal of accommodating the needs of the individual learner. Although *Littré* was used in the self-access centre, its main use was with the teacher in the classroom. The focus on the individual learner in Ahmad's model appears to be more suited to private study in the self-access centre or at another place convenient for the learner. Farrington places considerable emphasis on the need for integration of the CALL materials with non-computer work and this will be discussed in the next section.

The teacher's role may involve simply assisting students as they work at the computer, or designing broader tasks that in some way involve the computer for their successful completion. For example, on the one hand, consider the French tutor, *Miniprof*, which 'models the behaviour of a human instructor' (Labrie and Singh 1991: 23) and the LINGER program which contains 'knowledge of pedagogical principles' (Yazdani 1991*a*: 107). On the other hand, observe Jordan (1988: 142) who marks three areas that should be considered in a 'teacher-based' approach for designers of CALL programs: 'taking advantage of the teacher's presence; facilitating use by teacher and students-authoring facilities; using the computer for visual presentations'. Clearly these are two very different realizations of CALL. One approach aims to replace the teacher at least temporarily; the other aims to make use of the teacher, the CALL program actually having been formulated with the premise that a teacher is present.

The notion of the computer as tutor or substitute teacher has proved tenacious. One of the offshoots of this idea is the use of the computer to 'free' the teacher from the 'more tiresome labours' of language teaching (Skinner 1954: 96). Many writers since Skinner have referred to the use of the computer for *freeing* the teacher from the more mundane aspects of language teaching. The teacher is 'freed' from: 'constraints imposed by heavy teaching schedules . . . especially drill and revision sessions, to which it [the computer] is well-suited' (Ahmad *et al.* 1985: 5); 'the more onerous aspects of language teaching' (Bailin and Levin 1989: 4); from a repetitive kind of tuition (Kenning and Kenning 1990: 56); and 'the routine and predictable parts of foreign language teaching' (Geens 1981: 46). Thus freed, the teacher has more time for: 'creative and imaginative teaching in those parts of the course where teacher–student contact is more necessary' (Ahmad *et al.* 1985: 5); 'intensive oral work' (Benwell 1986: 4); 'communicative activities' (Kenning and Kenning 1990: 56); and 'more effective personal contact with the class group' (Last 1989: 39). Morgenstern (1986: 24) comments on this notion of the computer 'freeing' the teacher to engage in communication activities and argues that such a view 'is valid only in a rather ideal situation (where the teacher is inventive, resourceful and can improvise dialogue in the target language)'. One might add that it also depends on how well the computer can fulfil its side of the bargain, that is, how effective it really is as a substitute teacher. This view of the computer does, however, imply a division of labour whereby we have to decide what aspects of language learning are best dealt with by the computer, and what elements are best covered by the human teacher.

This review of how CALL authors conceptualize their work has been approached through examining a number of indicators. So far we have looked at points of departure, the role of the computer and teacher, and hardware and software, including email and the Internet. We now turn to the development process, the role of the teacher as author—as opposed to contributor—and descriptive taxonomies for CALL materials.

When the workings of the Internet are considered, it is difficult to see how the teacher might be freed in any way. The Internet, while providing more learning opportunities for the student, requires the teacher to know more and to do more in order to facilitate interactions in this environment.

The teacher's role is clearly recognizable in organizing and facilitating collaborative projects internationally, and ensuring that project guidelines, or tasks are clear, and the technology works to support their completion (Klobusicky-Mailänder 1990; Austin and Mendlick 1993; Barson *et al.* 1993). In linking classes for long-distance collaboration, Davis and Ye-Ling (1994/5) speak of the *organizational* challenges, in the timing of interactions between different institutions with different campus calendars and class schedules, and *curricular* challenges, in course design and integration. In opening up further channels of communication between teacher and student via email extra demands are made on the teacher in providing additional feedback on student assignments (see Hoffman 1994; Blake 1995). The roles of the teacher in such circumstances are many, and the demands correspondingly high.

The development process

Unlike materials developers operating within an instructional design framework, where components and stages in the process are specified in detail, the literature in the CALL context indicates that developers are less specific about the precise steps to be followed. By way of example, Higgins (1985) contrasts the approaches of the computer specialist and the language teacher–programmer. Higgins asserts that the specialist distinguishes four stages in the process of creating new software, namely analysis, design, coding, and debugging. The language teacher is responsible for stage one, the teacher and the computer specialist for stage two, and a programmer working independently, for stages three and four. Higgins argues that the specialist approach, with clearly defined roles, leads to greater efficiency, but can also lead to lack of flexibility when 'highly individual needs or unusual applications are called for' (Higgins 1985: 69).

In contrast, there are examples of highly articulated models of the development process. Keith and Lafford (1989: 125) give an overview of the development process in designing software for vocational language programs. The process is divided into three stages labelled the pre-design phase, the design phase, and the post-design phase and each contains the following elements:

The **pre-design phase** comprises the question of time commitment, choice of programming modality, staffing of the project, needs assessment, survey of available courseware, and planning for overall content of the courseware. The **design phase** consists of creating or compiling subject material, programming the lessons . . . and making decisions about various aspects of the program . . . The **post-design** phase requires field testing of the completed lessons, revising or modifying the developed lessons based on the results of field-testing, writing user documentation, disseminating the finished product, and integration of the software into classroom activities.

Meskill (1991) adopts a similar stance in outlining a systematic approach to CALL videodisc design, an approach adapted from the systems approach used in instructional design. Eight elements in the design process are identified. The elements are not 'hierarchical' but 'circular' and the emphasis is on 'modifying, rethinking, redefining, rewriting until all these highly interdependent considerations fit together and satisfy one another's definitions and requirements'

(1991: 54). Hubbard (1992: 42), in specifying a framework for CALL materials development, focuses on *identifying* the requisite components of materials design and the relationships between them; unlike Meskill, Hubbard does not specify any particular sequence to be followed in manipulating the components through the development process.

The approaches to the development process, therefore, are variable. CALL practitioners include those that follow a systematic process with a discrete, well-articulated series of stages, and also those who adhere to a non-linear process, often by incrementally improving on an initial prototype utilizing feedback from users. The Meskill example also shows that processes are followed that fit somewhere in between the highly structured approach and the one that is relatively unstructured. Finally, Hubbard does not describe a process at all, but rather focuses on identifying the components of a design and their interrelationships.

The role of the teacher (as author)

Language teachers generally have a choice between using commercially produced materials, either as they stand or adapted, or creating their own materials from scratch. Often the role of the teacher as author of materials arises because existing, commercially produced materials are in some way deficient. Of the materials produced with commercial aims, the 'textbook' is the prime example, and it is instructive to digress for a moment and characterize the main features of a typical textbook.

Textbooks have the advantage that they are written by experienced writers who have trialled the materials before publication. The books are conceived as a whole, based upon an explicit philosophy of language teaching and learning, and are often accompanied by workbooks, teacher's guides, cassette tapes, and so on. They are usually organized or sequenced according to a set of criteria, for example, a sequence of grammatical structures, themes, notions, functions or tasks, or a combination thereof, and often include cyclic repetition. Commercial materials for a wider audience tend to undergo thorough testing and evaluation before publication, and usually they involve teams of writers and editors with the concomitant cross-checks. On the other hand, commercial materials such as the textbook are often destined for an audience that remains remote to the authors. Specific, local learner characteristics at the location where the textbook will be used are unknown, and generalized predictions about the intended audience have to be made (Dubin and Olshtain 1986: 169). Making such predictions is difficult, especially when materials, such as general language learning textbooks, are intended to be distributed internationally. Also, the specific curriculum and syllabus within which the materials will have to function are further unknowns. As a result, the relationship between textbooks and teachers has been a 'rather a fraught one' (Sheldon 1987: 1). The complexity of language learning and its sensitivity to the learning context and the individual learner means that 'a pre-packaged set of decisions embodied in teaching materials' is unlikely to satisfy the needs of all teachers and learners within the range of the target audience set by the textbook writers (Allwright 1981: 9). Other problematic aspects of the textbook include vague information about target learners, grammatical explanations that take terminological and linguistic knowledge for granted, and ancillary workbooks that are poorly designed (Sheldon 1987: 3). Nunan concludes, 'In general, a range of materials which can be exploited in a variety of ways is more useful than a comprehensive package' (Nunan 1988*b*: 99).

With growing interest in the learner-centred curriculum, and the increased sensitivity of the teacher to learner needs, where there is an option the language teacher has come to rely less on the commercially produced textbook. It is likely and desirable that at least some adaptation and development of materials should take place. Block (1991: 213) suggests that teachers should produce materials of their own, at least part of the time, for three reasons: teachers can contextualize language appropriately for their students and their learning context; they can ensure the timeliness of their materials; and they can provide a *personal touch*, which is often well received by students. The role of the language teacher as materials writer is an established one, and it is not surprising that language teachers have wanted to create materials in the context of CALL.

The possible teacher roles in CALL are usefully summarized by Hertz (1987: 183) who describes four levels of computer literacy for language teachers, with levels 2, 3, and 4 involving authoring in some form:

level 1: the computer-using teacher;
level 2: the non-programming author of courseware content;
level 3: the user of authoring systems;
level 4: the teacher–programmer.

At the first level, teachers have basic computer operating skills and the ability to use and evaluate language learning software. At this level, the teacher is not involved in CALL materials writing at all. At the second level, teachers are able to author the content of the CALL materials, but they do not have any programming expertise. At the third level, teachers are familiar with an authoring system and can use it to develop their own materials. Finally, at the fourth level the teacher can program a computer in some way. This discussion will focus on the working methods associated with levels 3 and 4, especially in terms of the degree of expertise of the developer and the degree of flexibility of the authoring tool.

At level 3, the authoring system or program level, the structure of the program is determined in advance. The structure is often built around a question type, for example, multiple-choice, or an activity type such as cloze exercise. The user can insert content into the program and this may mean supplying questions, answers, feedback for correct and incorrect answers, or a text upon which the activity or game can operate. The value of these programs depends upon the applicability of the question type or activity, the relevance of the content, and the way in which the program is used. A case has been made for the integration of such CALL programs into the wider scheme of language work, with the language teacher playing a significant role in organizing and facilitating the presentation of the teaching and learning materials (see G. Jones 1986; C. Jones 1986).

Once the decision has been made to use an authoring system or program, the teacher selects the appropriate content on the basis of student needs. The materials content is relatively straightforward to put on to the computer and this is the main advantage of operating at this level. The materials developer does not need to know a programming language and is guided through the authoring process step by step. The materials developer must select, adapt or create the content, and relate this material to other work away from the computer. The material may then be used in the classroom or in self-access mode, although Chris Jones suggests that classroom use with a teacher present has beneficial effects. This approach can lead to fragmentation if computer work and non-computer work are not carefully coordinated.

The fourth option is for the language teacher to learn to program the computer in some way. Teacher–programmers have received a considerable amount of criticism notably by Phillips (1983: 6), Self (1985, chap. 19) and Last (1989: 13, 34, 113). The thrust of their argument is that the materials produced by language teachers are of poor quality because of inadequate programming skills, adherence to low-powered microcomputers, and the use of computer languages of insufficient power and sophistication. Other writers, though less critical of teacher–programmers, advise against teachers learning a programming language. Programming is potentially a distraction from attending to methodology and the learning process and it can inhibit the development of professional software (Legenhausen and Wolff 1987: 170).

Schaefermeyer (1990: 15) says that, rather than expecting many teachers to *produce* software, the focus should be on ways of *using* software. A similar point is made by Clarke (1989*a*: 29) who advises against teachers learning languages such as BASIC; the time is better spent providing program specifications for a professional programmer. Finally, Pusack (1988: 19) states that 'language teachers should author software but they should not program it', although teachers should still have a basic understanding of elementary programming techniques.

Operating at level 4 entails considerable knowledge and skill in that the developer must be able to use a programming language. This level does provide the freedom, within the bounds of the hardware environment and the software tools, to develop materials in diverse and original ways. It is here that the developer must originate a conceptualization of CALL and formulate an approach to the process of developing a computer program. It is also at this level that the language teacher is most likely to require specialized expert help from outside the discipline.

Describing CALL materials

Before turning to CALL materials in particular, it is helpful to look at general issues arising in the development of language learning materials. The broader view gives insights into the specific instance of CALL, and any unique attributes of CALL materials can be more easily isolated. The broader view is all the more important because CALL is scarcely treated in the literature on language learning materials, and general principles of materials production are seldom covered in the CALL literature. Furthermore, there are clear advantages in viewing CALL at the materials level, rather than higher levels, such as the curriculum or syllabus design levels. Materials are tangible and they are open to comparison and evaluation (Sheldon 1987: 38). Moreover, a discussion at the materials level is highly relevant for the language teacher who often operates at the materials level. Although in an idealized model language teachers would derive their materials from a syllabus, in practice teachers may not use a syllabus or it may be unknown to them (Dubin and Olshtain 1986: 167).

Candlin and Breen's definition of materials is used to refer to 'any published or unpublished data in any medium or collection of media used for the purpose of language teaching and learning' (1979: 4). The range of materials available to teachers today is extremely diverse in form, content, and mode of delivery. Materials include textbooks, teacher guides, workbooks, audio tapes, video tapes and videodiscs, test banks, tape scripts, readers, and CALL programs amongst others (Ariew 1988: 42). Materials can be genuine, authentic, or pedagogic (Beeching 1982: 17; Richardson and Scinicariello 1989: 52), published or commercially produced for a wider audience, or locally produced for a smaller audience (Dubin and Olshtain 1986: 168; S. Otto 1989: 24). Materials may be designed to be stand alone, to replace the teacher, or as is more usually the case, they may be designed for use with the teacher (Richards and Rodgers 1986: 25).

Bolitho (1990: 23) discusses the role of materials, focusing chiefly on the textbook in relation to the roles of the teacher and the learners, and notes how the role of materials has been redefined with the acceptance of the communicative approach. Traditionally, the textbook was the preoccupation of teachers and learners and, as a result, the textbook materials had to cover the entire syllabus. The new role for the textbook within the communicative approach is less central: Wright suggests that teaching materials are now 'only a means to an end' (1987: 76). Although teachers understand this new role for the textbook, Bolitho observes that problems can arise because learners often still regard the textbook in the traditional way.

A number of basic principles have been advanced for communicative materials design. Breen *et al.* (1979: 1) suggest the following principles:

- materials will be concerned with language as communication;
- materials design will be more concerned with the teaching–learning process than with the content for teaching and learning;
- materials will encourage learners to communicate.

In this context Breen *et al.* suggest the development of two kinds of materials: *content* materials as sources of data and information; and *process* materials to serve as 'guidelines or frameworks for the *learner's use of communicative knowledge and abilities*' (Breen *et al.* 1979: 5). The notion of materials as guidelines or frameworks is reinforced by Allwright who argues for materials to relate to the 'cooperative management of language learning' (Allwright 1981: 5).

CALL materials share many of the characteristics of non-CALL materials. Like all language learning materials, CALL materials can be authentic or pedagogic, commercially produced for a wide, perhaps unknown audience, or locally produced for a smaller, known audience. Somewhat negative attitudes towards commercially produced materials are evident in both cases. Also language teacher interest in writing materials that meet specific learner needs is apparent across the board—see Eltis and Low (1985) and Jones and Fortescue (1987), for example.

On the other hand, there are differences between CALL and non-CALL materials and, as Kenning and Kenning (1990: 81) point out, these differences are largely due to the diverse capabilities of the medium. The characteristics of the computer, such as its interactive function, its large storage capacity, and its ability to show or hide information at a given time lead to materials that are inconceivable, or simply impractical, otherwise.

CALL materials have been produced that address all the language skills (Pennington 1989*b*), although speaking and listening have proved the most complex to deal with on the computer (Hope *et al.* 1984: 48; Ahmad *et al.* 1985: 104; Ariew and Frommer 1987: 182). CALL materials have been developed for mainframe computers (e.g. PLATO), workstations (e.g. ALLP), and microcomputers

and for many types of computer within each category. Furthermore, CALL materials have been developed for computers in combination with other media, using the computer to control and
manage the attached media devices, as in interactive video and
interactive audio. Materials have been designed to teach or tutor
students through, for instance, Intelligent Tutoring Systems, or
with the aim of providing a useful tool, as in word processing or
concordancing. Individual, pair work, and group activities have
been designed for CALL (Higgins and Johns 1984: 36) and
authoring programs and dedicated programs are available (Jones
and Fortescue 1987: 4). Moreover, this does not include variables
that exist outside the domain of the program itself, that is those
concerned with the actual implementation: for example, whether a
pair of students are working on the program and are interacting
with each other as well as with the computer, or whether the
program is being used for a whole-class presentation.

Not only are CALL materials kinetic and multidimensional, they
are also mediated by the computer screen and a sound channel,
which means that only a small component of the whole can be seen
or heard at any one time. Unlike a book, where a sense of the whole
can be rather easily assimilated—by holding the book, by viewing
the contents, and by flicking through the pages—with CALL materials the whole picture is much more elusive. On one run of the
program, only a tiny proportion of the material in the program may
be seen or heard. CALL materials may also be constructed that
utilize networks of computers, learners, and teachers interacting at
a distance, synchronously or asynchronously. Clearly conceptualizing CALL materials is much more complex than conceptualizing
traditional text-based materials. Consequently it is no wonder that
devising a means for adequately describing the particular defining
characteristics of CALL materials has proved somewhat elusive.

Descriptions of software categories tend not to be mutually exclusive and an item of software might fall into a number of categories simultaneously, depending on what particular characteristic is
the focal point. This should not be surprising given the interactive
and dynamic nature of CALL materials and the nature of the
descriptive vocabulary generally used to describe them, a vocabulary developed to describe printed rather than computer-mediated
materials. By way of example, a number of program taxonomies
are given in Table 4.2: these groupings are typical of the way in
which CALL materials have been classified.

There are many kinds of overlap between the categories, and the particular viewpoint taken will determine the descriptor. In the listings below, for instance, a CALL activity might easily have characteristics that would cause it to be labelled an exploratory program, a simulation, a problem solving activity, or a game. If it was played at a distance, or in cyberspace, it could fall into Rüschoff's Communication category also.

Nevertheless, typologies have been attempted, notably by Kemmis *et al.* (1977) for CAL, and Phillips (1985*a*) and Hubbard (1992; 1996) for CALL. These attempts have been cumulative in the sense that each typology has built, at least in part, upon the one before. The first typology uses learning paradigms to distinguish between CAL programs. On the basis of an extensive evaluation of ten different CAL projects conducted in the UK from 1973–7, Hooper and Kemmis *et al.* suggested three, possibly four, learning paradigms appropriate for CAL (Hooper 1977: 167; Kemmis *et al.* 1977: 23). The first is the instructional paradigm which covers such traditional activities as drill and practice and adaptive tutorial programs. The second paradigm is labelled revelatory and describes learning by exploration and discovery, as in a simulation program. The third paradigm, called conjectural, emphasizes active knowledge manipulation and hypothesis testing. The last more tentative paradigm is called emancipatory. CAL activities that fall within this

TABLE 4.2   *CALL taxonomies*

Higgins and Johns (1984: 36)	Ariew and Frommer (1987: 179)	Brücher (1993: 8)	Rüschoff (1993: 11)
Programmed learning	Drill and practice	Production	Exploratory exercises
Games	Contextualized activities	Reproduction	Data-processing
Exploratory	Tutorials	Reconstruction	Information
Simulations	Simulations	Rearrangement	• gathering
Text reconstruction	Games	Simulation	• processing
Drill and practice	Tools	Databank	Communication
		Completion	
		Multiple choice	
		Matching	
		Transformation	

paradigm are those that enhance 'authentic labour' which may be instrumental to valued learning, but is not valued for its own sake (Kemmis *et al.* 1977: 28). For a discussion of these paradigms in relation to models of grammar teaching see Higgins (1986*b*: 35).

The typology developed by Phillips (1985*a*) for CALL is largely based upon a careful consideration of the characteristics of CALL programs available on microcomputers at that time. Phillips's survey of programs identified seven possible categories of analysis for CALL programs: activity type, learning style, learner focus, program focus, language difficulty, program difficulty, and classroom management. The activity types used by Phillips are very similar to those given on the previous page. For learning style, Phillips uses five different types of learning described in the experiment conducted by Kemmis *et al.*, namely recognition, recall, comprehension, experimental learning, and constructive understanding. The other categories are similarly divided into a number of elements. By selecting elements in pairs from the seven categories, Phillips is able to form a series of two-dimensional matrices that he uses to determine logical possibilities for the development of CALL materials.

Hubbard's methodological framework, which incorporates the categories devised by Phillips, utilizes a model of language teaching method conceived by Richards and Rodgers (1986: 28). This model is hierarchical, and comprises three levels, Approach, Design, and Procedure (see Chapter 6 for a fuller discussion of this model). Table 4.3 shows the components of Hubbard's version of this network model for CALL with the components at each level.

At the level of Design, Hubbard incorporates six of Phillips's seven categories (the exception is activity type which Hubbard situates at the Procedure level) and adds learner variables, syllabus, content, hardware considerations, and programming language considerations.

The frameworks suggested by Kemmis *et al.*, Phillips, and Hubbard represent attempts to identify the essential attributes of CALL programs and the relationship between them. According to Hubbard (1992: 42), a properly constructed framework provides: a metalanguage for discussion; a useful structure to conceptualize materials development and research; and an 'integrated set of evaluation criteria'. Much further work needs to be conducted on developing a descriptive language for CALL materials that reflects their characteristics satisfactorily. However, given the dynamic na-

TABLE 4.3   *Components in Hubbard's methodological model*

Approach	Design	Procedure
Linguistic assumptions	Learning style	Activity type
Learning assumptions	Program focus	Presentational scheme
Language teaching approach	Learner focus	Input judging
Computer delivery system	Classroom management	Feedback
Approach-based criteria	Program difficulty	Control options
	Language difficulty	Help options
	Learner variables	Screen layout
	Syllabus	
	Content	
	Hardware considerations	
	Prog. lang. considerations	

ture of CALL materials, a new language for description may be required, and a description may then only be possible through using the computer to create a dynamic model (see Swartz and Russell 1989).

Summary

By viewing the complex idea of conceptualization from various angles, the descriptive review given in this chapter has highlighted a number of points. At the broadest level, distinct roles for the computer emerge: the all-encompassing managerial role and the auxiliary role, where the computer is used as an aid or as an assistant. These roles are reflected in the acronyms that have been used to describe computer use in education generally, and in CALL in particular. The more directive, controlling role of the tutor, to act as a substitute teacher, perhaps, can be contrasted with the non-directive, passive role of the tool, to provide a workspace for the completion of tasks. These two roles have to be conceptualized not only in terms of single-user, single-site conditions, but in multi-user, multi-site conditions made available via the Internet. Added to this basic polarity, other acronyms focus on the intelligent computer and the computer as mediator. Attaching the 'Intelligence' label to a machine focuses attention on our desire to attach human qualities to innate objects, that is, anthropomorphism. Such labels can cloud critical differences in the nature of human and machine intelligence. It can lead to a misplaced confidence in the ability of a machine to act intelligently in diverse situations. As a result, more control may be delegated to the computer over the learner than is justified by its real capabilities. The CmC acronym focuses attention on the computer as mediator, or 'go-between', and highlights the fact that the computer is not necessarily a transparent medium. In other words communication mediated by a computer such as email or videoconferencing will be shaped and variously affected by the qualities of the machine. Thus, CmC will have its own characteristics that will probably differ from other forms of communication, such as direct human–human communication. For example, in videoconferencing the nature of the workspace, shyness in front of the camera, or slight delays in transmission make this form of communication unique. To be employed effectively such effects will need to be identified and understood.

The strengths and limitations of the specific technologies being used inevitably shape any conceptualization of CALL, even though we may think there is a smooth and unadulterated transition from initial concept to final implementation. The complex and multi-dimensional nature of CALL materials has become apparent by looking at the many categories that have been used to describe the materials, and by recognizing the difficulty that commentators have encountered when attempting to create a satisfactory classification system. CALL materials have much in common with non-CALL materials, but there are also significant differences because of the dynamic nature of CALL. The problem is compounded by the fact that the same materials may be used in many different ways, so that ideally any description has to extend beyond what is happening on the computer. Though frameworks that have successively built upon one another have been provided by Kemmis *et al.*, Phillips, and Hubbard, a sufficiently powerful description language that effectively captures the unique defining qualities of CALL materials has yet to be formulated.

By looking at the points of departure we have seen just how diverse the approaches to computer use are in language learning. Top-down approaches, bottom-up approaches, and those that lie somewhere in between have all been noted, showing the inventiveness of the designers and the incredible flexibility of the computer. Finally, the role of the teacher in the conceptualization showed that authors tend to fall into one of two categories: for one group the language teacher is an integral part of the conceptualization and the teacher's presence is essential for effective implementation; for the other group, the teacher is not a primary concern in the conceptual framework.

The teacher's role as materials writer in CALL is an important one that has emerged through a desire to meet curricula and learner requirements at a local level. Commercial materials such as textbooks can rarely accomplish this, as their goal is to reach a wide, geographically dispersed audience that can preclude them from meeting the specific needs of a clearly defined local group. For CALL, teacher–authors can engage in materials development at three levels from author of courseware content to teacher–programmer. Their choice will likely depend upon time available, level of expertise, and specific requirements. Development processes range between those that are highly structured to those that are cyclic and ill-defined.

The next chapter looks at what a group of key CALL practitioners said about conceptualizing CALL in response to an international survey. The angle of attack has changed again with this group giving a personalized and, in many cases, more detailed view of CALL concepts. These findings may then be combined with those from the literature to provide a larger pool of data to support the arguments in the ensuing discussion.

Notes

1. A substantial amount of research is being undertaken in CmC across disciplines in the social sciences. Journals which feature articles on the topic are *Management Science*; *Behaviour and Information Technology*; *Human–Communication Research*; and *Organizational Behaviour*; *Human Decision Processes*.
2. *CU-SeeMe* is an example of a video conferencing system for transmitting live video via the Internet. Available for the Macintosh and Windows platforms, *CU-SeeMe* can help facilitate two-party and multiparty video conferences. The development of *CU-SeeMe* began in 1992 at Cornell University (CU-SeeMe Development Team 1996).
3. Here a virtual world is taken to mean a simulation of some description,

supported by a single computer or a network of computers. Such simulations may be text-based or video-based, and they may be explored by an individual or a number of individuals interacting simultaneously and remotely (see Papert's microworld (1982) and MOOs).

5. Conceptualization II: the CALL Survey

Introduction

Using the literature alone as a source of information for a description of CALL is, of itself, rather limited. In particular, information relating to the indicators is often fragmented. The indicators, it will be remembered, are the elements that are held to inform the key issues for understanding CALL's conceptual frameworks. While for some CALL projects, descriptions in the literature and other documentary sources are detailed and comprehensive, in others the descriptions are only partial, and information on one or more of the indicators is incomplete or missing. To complement the findings from the literature, therefore, a detailed CALL Survey was undertaken. The CALL Survey is able to provide a catalogue of responses to specific questions that relate directly to the indicators that underpin conceptual frameworks. This conveniently complements the findings from the literature where opinions are more isolated, and relate to widely differing frames of reference.[1] This combined approach—the literature review and the CALL Survey—was a strategy also adopted by Stolurow and Cubillos (1983), Ng and Olivier (1987), and Fox *et al.* (1990), and it provides a more complete and detailed picture than one drawn from a survey alone. Fox *et al.* also conducted consultations and discussions with experts and subject specialists to derive a more complete assessment (1990: 5), a strategy that is also used here. In this way findings in the literature can be compared with those from the CALL Survey so that a cross-referencing is possible, giving increased weight to salient features emerging from both sources.

The vast majority of participants were language teachers, and as a group they represent a substantial amount of knowledge and expertise in the field. After establishing the respondents' teaching and CALL experience, the CALL Survey looked at the ways in which authors conceptualize CALL, by inquiring about their philosophies of teaching and learning, both independently and in relation to CALL. Their views on the roles of the computer were collected, first in general, and then specifically in relation to classroom and self-access modes of operation. The scope of CALL was canvassed to help determine what fields and disciplines might fall within its domain, or relate closely to it. Initial orientation as well as points of departure was included in the CALL survey to provide for a broader, less precise initial conceptualization of CALL (see Chapter 1, Note 3). Otherwise the pattern of enquiry in the CALL Survey follows that described earlier in relation to the CALL literature; the same organizational structure is used in Chapter 5 as in Chapter 4 in presenting the findings where tables, bar charts, and simple statistics are used. In each section a question number reference is given on the right-hand side of the line containing the section title. This refers to the question in the CALL Survey from which the findings were drawn; the reader may wish to consult the original questionnaire in this regard (see Appendix A).[2]

The CALL Survey

The key practitioners for the CALL Survey were predominantly drawn from those involved in adult language education, especially universities. The key practitioners are known through their publications in the academic literature, conference participation, or the CALL materials they have produced and distributed. The assumption, therefore, is that the individuals who are involved in CALL materials development principally work in the adult language education sector. CALL authors in such sectors as secondary education or those in the commercial world were not canvassed initially. The period for collecting completed CALL Survey responses was terminated at the end of March 1991.

The distribution of the questionnaire was guided by the following parameters:

Country: International (23 countries)
Language: ESL, EFL, Modern languages
Students: Adult
Institution: Universities, colleges of higher and further education, private language schools
Audience: Key CALL practitioners, not necessarily language teachers

'Purposeful' and 'snowball' sampling techniques were employed. Purposeful sampling rather than random sampling was used, so that the knowledge and expertise of key practitioners could be examined. This was complemented by snowball sampling which enabled one key respondent to recommend another. The initial sample of key practitioners was constructed from:

- primary contacts established through the literature, the *On-CALL* journal, and colleagues in Australia and overseas;
- editors and key contributors of journals, including the *CALICO Journal* (CALICO Advisory Board and special interest group Chairpersons—negotiated with the then Executive Director of CALICO), *CAELL Journal* (Editorial Board and key contributors), *Computer-Assisted Language Learning Journal* (General and Associate Editors and selected members of the advisory board), *System* (Editor and Assistant Editors and key contributors);
- the editor and information officer of the newsletter *ReCALL*;
- contact names and addresses from each interviewee;
- authors and editors of books on CALL;
- selected authors of articles in journals on CALL;
- information in *Computers in Applied Linguistics and Language Teaching* by Udo Jung (1988a) which describes CALL activities in eleven countries and gives the names and addresses of all the contributors;
- other books which gave names and addresses of contributors such as *Computers and Modern Language Studies* (Cameron *et al.* 1986) that has a listing of contributors who represent views on CALL especially associated with Modern Languages rather than ESL and who were outside my sphere of UK contacts.

The respondents   (Q. 1.1, Q. 1.3.1, 1.3.2)

A total of 213 questionnaires were distributed and 104 (48.8%) usable responses were returned. Of the 104 questionnaires completed, 20 formed part of the pilot study. The questionnaire was sent to 23 different countries and practitioners from 18 countries replied (see Appendix C, Fig. C.1). The first five, in order of precedence, were from the UK, the USA, Australia, Canada, and Germany. The vast majority of respondents (i.e. CALL authors) were practising language teachers (97.1%). English was by far the most common language taught, followed by French, and German equally. The language knowledge and teaching experience of respondents was extensive. The mean number of years spent language teaching by participants in the survey was 17.6 years. The respondents to the CALL Survey were affiliated predominantly to universities, followed by colleges of higher education, private language schools and high schools equally, and polytechnics (see Appendix C, Fig. C.3).

Given the way in which respondents to the survey were selected, it is not surprising that their knowledge and expertise in CALL is considerable. Two questions attempted to gauge the level of this

TABLE 5.1 *Time CALL interest began by time language teaching began*

1950s		1960s	
1950s	0	1950s	0
1960s	1	1960s	1
1970s	0	1970s	9
1980–3	1	1980–3	11
1984–6	1	1984–6	9
1987–90	0	1987–90	0
	3		30
1970s		**1980–3**	
1950s	0	1950s	0
1960s	0	1960s	0
1970s	8	1970s	0
1980–3	24	1980–3	5
1984–6	10	1984–6	7
1987–90	1	1987–90	3
	43		15
1984–6		**1987–1990**	
1950s	0	1950s	0
1960s	0	1960s	0
1970s	0	1970s	0
1980–3	0	1980–3	0
1984–6	2	1984–6	0
1987–90	0	1987–90	2
	2		2

Note: Sample size of 95.

expertise: the first asked those surveyed to assess their level of expertise using five categories; and the second required respondents to enter the number of years together with their level of involvement in CALL. In the first case the majority of respondents marked the two categories that represented the highest level of expertise. The second question on the number of years and level of involvement in CALL had three parts and the mean scores were calculated for each of them. For 'observing the development or implementation of CALL' the mean score was 8.1 years; for 'directly participating in the implementation (or delivery) of CALL' the equivalent score was 6.7 years; and for 'developing CALL materials' the mean score was 6.0 years exactly. Collectively, this represents very considerable experience in CALL. Given the similarly extensive language teaching and learning experience described already, this group of practitioners represents a highly experienced cross-section of language teachers involved in CALL.

Respondents were also asked when, and under what circumstances, they first became interested in CALL and the findings are given on the previous page. In Table 5.1, by utilizing the results of question 1.1.5, the findings are presented in clusters so that the time a respondent's CALL interest began, might be tabulated against the time the respondent began language teaching.

For respondents who began their language teaching in the 1950s, 1960s, and 1970s the impact of the microcomputer, which became widespread in the period 1980 to 1983, is clear.

Conceptualization

Teaching philosophy, methods and approaches   (Q. 1.2.2)

The communicative approach is the current preferred philosophy of language teaching and learning as Figure 5.1 illustrates.[3] Although the label 'communicative' has been open to a number of different interpretations, there is some agreement as to its central features. Task-based learning may accompany a communicative approach to language teaching or, since it is essentially a neutral construct, it may be used with more form-focused approaches also. In all 15.4 per cent of respondents registered only communicative language teaching and task-based learning.

The eclecticism of language teachers is immediately apparent from the results, both when viewed as individuals and as a group. Altogether, 95.2 per cent of respondents recorded two or more categories, and 35.6 per cent of respondents marked four or more categories from the list. Considered as a whole, in addition to the sixteen methods and approaches provided in the questionnaire, respondents added a further five approaches: data-driven learning, discovery learning, autonomous or self-directed learning, investigative approaches, and total immersion. Of those involved 7.7 per cent specifically stated that their approach was 'eclectic'.

In spite of the prevalence of communicative approaches and task-based learning, CALL Survey respondents also showed support for the more formal, traditional approaches such as formal grammar instruction, situational language teaching, and cognitive code learning. Data-driven learning was the only new approach cited by respondents as a direct result of the attributes of the computer. In other words, this approach has been conceived with the computer in mind; it would be extremely time-consuming to implement this approach, and to use the techniques involved, without the capabilities of the computer.

Teaching/learning philosophy and CALL   (Q. 1.4.7)

How a CALL author's language teaching and learning philosophy affects the way in which CALL materials are developed, is a com-

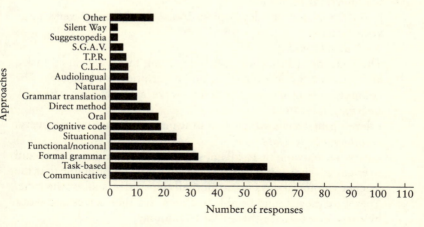

FIGURE 5.1   *Teaching approaches (n = 104)*

plex question and the ways in which answers were formulated were diverse.[4] This applied particularly to the author's chosen frame of reference. While it was not possible to quantify the number of responses in each case, a list of clearly identifiable frames of reference were detected and a list, together with illustrative examples in each, is given.

View of language teaching/learning
I have tried from the beginning to (a) use language in context, (b) deal with complete sentences or larger units, (c) make the activity meaningful, and (d) give the student meaningful and useful feedback.

Learner needs, the curriculum
I would always start from the basis of the learner's needs, the curriculum, and so on—never from the computer, which would have to fit in with the former.

Investigations into hardware and software
I tend to take a very pragmatic, rather than theoretical view. When I see an application, such as an interactive audio or video, where the computer can make a real contribution to learning, I explore it.

Computer as teacher
It has a central role. I try to project myself as a teacher into the machines.

Computer as tool
I am interested in developing tools for learning very large vocabularies.

Task development
The concept of tasks is helpful—enabling tasks, rehearsal tasks, and the need for access to data and descriptions of language. The computer fits in nicely in different ways with different tasks.

Learning paradigm
I develop materials which encourage exploration and discovery.

Complement to class
I use what is available to fill gaps in what can be done in class and to enhance what can be done in class, that is, on principle that the teacher cannot always be around all the students all of the time. Therefore they should be able to choose for themselves and work by themselves—with the aid of technology.

Language practice
I believe that students, especially at the lower levels, need as much practice as they can get, and the computer can provide well for certain kinds of practice.

Beyond these frames of reference, four trends among the responses can be identified. The first relates to how an author articulates and translates the principles of Communicative Language Teaching (CLT) into CALL practice; the second refers to the degree of prominence given to the language teaching/learning philosophy in materials development; the third concerns the roles ascribed to the computer; and the fourth relates to a sense of the dangers of being led by the technology rather than the methodology.

Philosophy into practice

The dominant approach in contemporary language teaching is the communicative approach. This approach is open to a number of different interpretations, and this question sought to investigate further. Many respondents chose to answer this question by describing attributes of their language teaching philosophy pertinent to CALL materials development, often using vocabulary associated with CLT:

- 1. I try to make the language *content* of CALL exercises realistic, if not actually authentic.
  2. I do activities in which the computer sets problem-solving tasks.
  3. I do not expect the program to do everything; the learner and/or the teacher have to make crucial choices.
- I have tried from the beginning to (a) use language in context, (b) deal with complete sentences or larger units, (c) make the activity meaningful, and (d) give the student meaningful and useful feedback.
- The CALL materials I produce aim to promote oral participation and communication outside the classroom and aim also to encourage students to take an active part in language learning rather than play a passive role.

In articulating their philosophy, respondents referred to learner needs on 9 occasions, language learning tasks 7 times, language practice in 6 instances, and motivation 5 times. Other focal points mentioned were language content (3), an eclectic approach (3), language in context (2), autonomous learning (2), and integration of CALL into the broader curriculum (2).

Prominence of philosophy

The second set of responses concerned the degree of prominence given to an author's language teaching/learning philosophy. Some participants in the survey considered this philosophy all important while others, though accepting that the author's philosophy must be taken into account, felt that other factors also needed to be considered. The following entries provide a cross-section of the responses on the degree to which the key practitioner's teaching/learning philosophy determines their approach to CALL materials development:

- It totally decides what will be done.
- It is very important. I developed a methodology for the design of CALL materials that takes it into account.
- My philosophy of language learning/teaching, while important in affecting choices in how I use computers and develop software, is not totally determinative. I have found that I sometimes am led to do some things because of the computer capability or student felt needs that I would not do otherwise.
- I attempt to bring together the computer application, instructional design theory and a teaching methodology.

Computer role

Thirdly, a number of respondents chose to answer this question by ascribing a role to the computer, primarily the tutor or tool roles. Examples of this type of response are as follows:

- My current interest is to use the computer as a focus of interest and facilitator of student learning. I see the computer as a mediator between teacher and learner through which students assume ownership of rules, advice, comments about their writing.
- I consider CALL materials as complements to classroom instruction mainly. This approach decides on what type of exercises I find useful in a particular teaching situation.
- It has a central role. I try to project myself as a teacher into the machines.

- CALL materials can be of two types: tool for developing classroom materials (e.g. W.P., Crossword Magic); self-access or teacher-mediated materials which must take methodology into account.

Dangers of technology

Finally, some CALL authors remarked that their views on teaching and learning help prevent them from being technology-led:

- It forms a basis to ensure that one does not get too carried away with technological possibilities. Not everything that *can* be done *must* be done!
- Probably it restricts my development ('this is impossible to codify linguistically, therefore do not even try it on the computer').
- I think that mainly it keeps me from doing easy things that are tempting (and probably marketable) but that I disapprove of, for example, single sentence product sentence combining exercises. It makes me lean toward content-based activities and multimedia.

Taken together, the answers to this question illustrate more specifically the frames of reference authors use when attempting to describe how their language teaching and learning philosophy shapes their CALL work. The ways respondents chose to answer this question varied enormously and, for communicative language teachers at least, this reflects some of the complexity and the ambiguity inherent in actually developing a CALL program within a communicative framework.

Roles for the computer   (Q. 1.2.1)

Of the roles for the computer in CALL shown in Figure 5.2, the most striking feature is the broad division between the directive and largely non-directive roles of the computer. Non-directive roles are amongst the most frequent responses. In contrast, unequivocally directive roles for the computer, as in a manager of tasks, an expert system, or a surrogate teacher, are cited less frequently with the computer actually taking the place of the teacher the least frequent of all. Roles that may be considered directive or non-directive, according to the program and its use in relation to classroom-

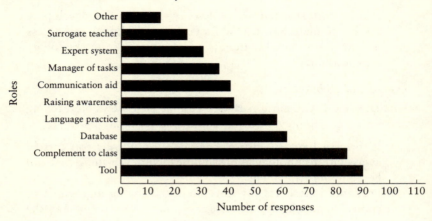

FIGURE 5.2   *Roles of the computer (n = 104)*

based, teacher-led events, such as complementing classroom instruction and providing language practice, also rate well.

The most fundamental role of the computer, the computer as
tool, is the most frequently recorded response in the CALL Survey.
Furthermore, in addition to the roles suggested in the questionnaire, a further seven distinct roles were given by respondents and
they are as follows: a control device for audio and video; a means
of recycling authentic texts; a help system; a manager of people and
users; a stimulus for speaking; a vehicle for discovery learning or
language exploration; and a translating machine.

In all 55.8 per cent of respondents registered a role for the
computer as a useful provider of mechanical language practice.
This particular role for the computer was the most frequently
recorded within the context of the self-access mode. The roles of the
computer as they relate to location, namely the self-access mode,
the classroom, or both are illustrated in Figure 5.3, and the three
categories are mutually exclusive. Only for language practice and
for the computer as expert system did respondents clearly advocate
the use of the computer in the self-access mode over the other
alternatives.

However, the most noticeable feature in relating roles to location
is that respondents saw each role for the computer as appropriate
in *both* the self-access mode and the classroom. In seven out of nine
cases both the self-access mode *and* the classroom were marked as

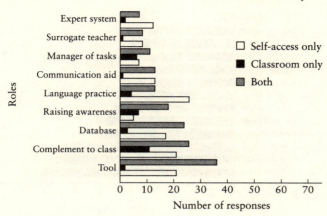

FIGURE 5.3 *Computer roles for self-access and classroom (n = 68)*

suitable locations for a given role in preference to, or equal to, either the classroom or self-access mode only. In cases where the respondent only marked a single location, the findings show that roles for the computer were more commonly recorded as appropriate for the self-access mode in preference to the classroom; only in raising awareness was this not the case.

The scope of CALL   (Q. 1.2.3)

Figure 5.4 indicates the topics that respondents to the CALL Survey considered to be within the scope of CALL discussion. The response to this question clearly illustrates the breadth of CALL, and a strong response is given to all categories. Of the 84 respondents, 11.9 per cent marked all categories. A further twelve topics were also listed and they are as follows: interactive audio, adaptive testing, text analysis, response evaluation and assessment, feedback systems, CMI and traditional CAI techniques, video digitizing, animation, making movies by computer, simulations and adventures, optical character recognition, and CD-ROM.

These findings support the view that CALL is difficult to circumscribe precisely and that there is clearly overlap with other related fields of endeavour. Moreover, the responses show that the key practitioners exhibit a keen interest in topics, fields, and disciplines

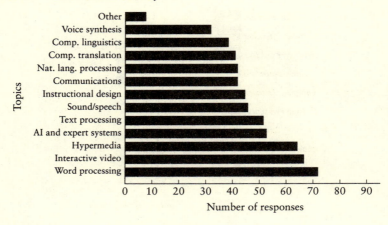

FIGURE 5.4   *Scope of CALL discussion (n = 84)*

across the technological spectrum, and variously related to the study and practice of CALL itself.

Initial orientation and points of departure   (Q. 1.4.6, 1.4.10)

The literature showed a wide range of starting-points for conceptualizing CALL including theories of instruction, theories of learning, curriculum imperatives, experiments with new technology, exercise types, learning problems, the development of a language skill, and the delivery of materials to large numbers of students. Figure 5.5 depicts the CALL Survey findings. In all 12.1 per cent marked only one category and 57.6 per cent marked three or more categories showing a difficulty in specifying a single initial orientation (Q. 1.4.6). Respondents preferred to indicate a small group of factors contributing to the initial orientation.

The two most frequent initial orientations registered by respondents were certain potentials of the computer, and the respondent's language-teaching methodology: 82.8 per cent of respondents marked one or other or both of these categories. There was a broad three-way division between those that orient themselves towards the technology initially, those that orient themselves towards the methodology, and those that attempt to integrate both technology and methodology.

A wide range of other starting-points was described by respond-

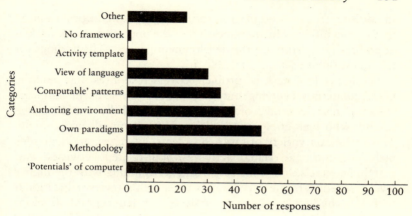

FIGURE 5.5   *Initial orientation (n = 99)*

ents. These were recorded in the 'Other' category in Figure 5.5, and they are:

the needs of my students;
practical instances where the computer can facilitate learning;
paradigms with greatest potential to help learning without aiming to displace teachers;
evolving strategy: pattern based originally, but now environment based;
money considerations;
general cognitive goals and processes;
the language components I want to teach at the time;
views of institutional organization;
the existing curriculum;
motivating students;
basically things that teachers find monotonous/boring but that the computer can do as well or better;
international exchanges of information (using tele-communications);
integration with course or teaching methods;
time;
personal computing ability;
colleagues' requests;
a variety of initial orientations;
instructional design.

In addition to a closed question specifically seeking information on initial orientation, a further question of the open-ended type looked at points of departure for the development process. The findings for this question are set out in Table 5.2.

The lower level task or problem covers responses that describe CALL materials evolving out of practical problems in language teaching and learning, often first recognized by the language teacher who then goes and develops CALL materials accordingly. This includes a variety of tasks, problems, exercises, and activities including grammar-related activities, skill-related activities, and matching exercises. In contrast, workers beginning with the higher level theoretical framework 'conduct research', 'review educational theory', 'conduct preliminary analysis', or 'conceptual development'. Specific examples include examining 'linguistic descriptions of an aspect of language', 'error analysis', 'reading strategies', and techniques of 'speech analysis and synthesis'. This accords more with a top-down approach to CALL materials development using a clear theoretical basis as the starting-point for development.

The other major category arising covers CALL packages that have in some way been derived from a computer application, or a CALL program that already exists. This occurred a number of times in conditions where a CALL author saw an existing application with limitations or constraints of some kind. This led to the author trying to improve the program in some way, adapt it to suit

TABLE 5.2   *Points of departure*

Process of development	No. of responses	Percentage
Lower level task or problem	17	18.6
Higher level theoretical framework	16	17.6
Derived from existing CALL applications	13	14.3
Derived from existing teaching materials	6	6.6
Investigations into hardware and/or software	6	6.6
Syllabus specifications	4	4.4
Matching activity to authoring tool	4	4.4
Other	25	27.5

Note: Sample size of 91. Responses are mutually exclusive.

a different hardware platform, or develop the existing program or concept in some other way that more precisely met the author's needs, students, and resources.

The minor categories in Table 5.2 are CALL materials derived from existing resources and applications, investigations into hardware and/or software, syllabus specifications, and matching an activity to an authoring tool. CALL materials derived from existing applications are distinguished from CALL materials derived from existing teaching and learning materials of a more traditional type, such as a set text or a video. In the former the *concept* is utilized in the new CALL materials; in the latter the material *content* is employed.

For instance, seeing a videodisc application might lead an author to develop a new package using the same technology or instructional design strategy (concept); on the other hand, material from a textbook may be used to provide the basis for a CALL activity (content). One respondent estimated that in the USA, 50 per cent of CALL software accompanies and supports existing language texts. In some instances the CALL materials are so intimately tied to the text that they are 'virtually useless' if you do not have the text. Specific examples of the initial orientations are given in the appropriate categories.

Lower level task or problem
Usually I start with a 'problem', for example, how to teach the interrogative form in class. Then I devise a skeleton program which gradually develops into something with various tools (for the teacher/student) which I had not thought would be there in the first place.
Higher level theoretical framework
I was prompted by Rutherford's work on grammatical consciousness-raising to create a hypertext reading passage which specifically addressed the issues he raises.
Existing CALL applications
Some programs were 'triggered' by papers on EFL or other CALL programs (listings) where aspects of the English language were presented in a way that made them interesting 'computerwise'.
Existing teaching materials
I was approached by the BBC to develop some materials for their German language course. Lengthy discussions on principle ini-

tially led to a short period of intensive programming and further revisions.

Investigations into hardware and software

In CLEF (our major package) we wanted to research the potential of the colour microcomputer. We made it handle fairly traditional tutorial modules, but it did them in ways no other medium could match.

Syllabus specifications

We wanted computer backup for compulsory grammar objectives; began pilot study because we had a very good computer person (ESL, computers, Dip. Ed. and foreign languages in his background) to do scripting and so on; trialled with students; then implemented in course.

Matching activity to hardware and software capabilities

Saw the compatibility of *HyperCard* with an activity (Mazes) that I had used effectively in class.

Hardware and software   (Q. 1.3.5, 1.4.1, 1.4.2, 1.4.3, 1.4.4)

A very high proportion of respondents, 88.5 per cent, owned their own computer. As far as institutional provision was concerned, 28.9 per cent of respondents had a microcomputer or terminal access made available to them at home, while the remainder did not have such a facility. The generic types of computer used for CALL are shown in Figure 5.6.

The hardware that has been used for CALL is shown in Figure 5.7. That IBM PC compatibles and Macintosh machines are becoming the *de facto* standards is supported in the findings from this survey. The approximate ratio of IBM compatible to Macintosh machines stands at approximately 7:3. In spite of these conditions at present, a large number of other machines have been used for CALL materials development.

This hardware was all marked for CALL use at some time. A number of these machines are now obsolete and current student access to them is highly unlikely. Therefore, given that CALL materials have been developed for these machines, the question of upgrades arises. If these programs were not upgraded, their use would cease along with the demise of the computer concerned. Thus, aside from the intrinsic interest that the CALL author may

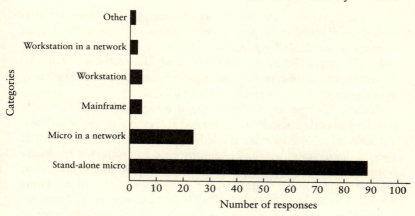

FIGURE 5.6   *Computer used for CALL (n = 100)*

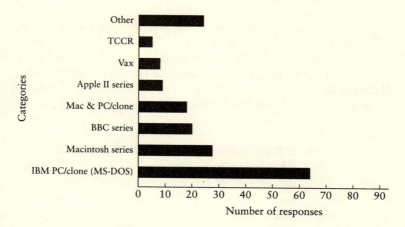

FIGURE 5.7   *Hardware used for CALL (n = 87)*

have in developing the program, the absence of a computer to run the program would prevent widespread use by students.

Sixty-eight different authoring tools were reported in the CALL Survey. Although a vast range of authoring aids is now available, it is noticeable that experienced CALL practitioners still frequently use high-level programming languages such as BASIC, *Pascal*, and

C. *HyperCard* was the most used authoring tool aside from an actual programming language. Other approaches to authoring appear to be favoured by practitioners.

In addition to the twelve authoring tools illustrated in Figure 5.8, a further fifty-six different tools were used giving rise to the exceptionally large 'Other' category in the figure.

In the CALL Survey the assumption was made that CALL practitioners would generally have more involvement in the selection of software than of hardware for CALL materials development. Further, *de facto* standards had been observed emerging for hardware, but not for software. Therefore, in the question on the criteria for the selection of authoring tools, the emphasis was placed on criteria for software selection rather than hardware selection. Given the close association between hardware and software, that the software must always be selected on the basis of the hardware available to run it, a single question on selection criteria on this issue was thought reasonable.

The availability of software is the principal reason governing software choice, as shown in Table 5.3. With regard to availability, respondents commented that the software might be available because it is supplied with the hardware as a package, sometimes free of charge as, for example, with BASIC and *HyperCard*; or it might already be available on the hardware because of a previous pur-

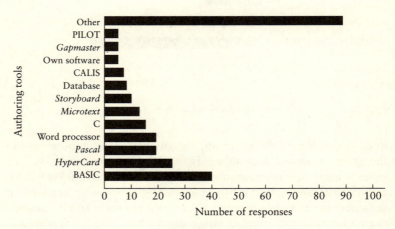

FIGURE 5.8   *Software used for CALL (n = 87)*

TABLE 5.3 *Criteria for software choice*

Reason for choice of software	No. of responses
Availability (on hardware or at institution)	27
Ease of use	18
Flexibility	16
Choice of third party	9
Respondent wrote program	9
Other program capabilities	8
Matches respondent's skills	7
Facilitates specific function	6
Can create materials quickly	5

Note: Sample size of 87.

chase made by the institution. Ease of use and flexibility followed as the next most significant reasons governing software choice.

Once the hardware has been selected, often by the institution or forces external to the CALL author, the fact that certain items of software are often packaged with the hardware is often sufficient reason for that particular software tool to be used for CALL materials development. Two comments from the interviews are pertinent here: one respondent says 'it's been a matter of what's been available where I am' and the software tools, in this case DAL and BASIC, were chosen because 'both times it was what I was stuck with because that's what they had'; another, who has written much CALL material from scratch using a high-level programming language, remarks, 'I would always use something ready-made if it's available'.

'Ease of use' and 'flexibility' were also significant criteria underpinning software selection. Authoring programs were the most popular category chosen on the basis of Ease of Use, and again BASIC was the most frequently marked response with regard to Flexibility. One respondent remarked: 'I would certainly like to see more flexibility, more features which an author can invoke if he or she wants to but doesn't have to' although 'I do experience a certain satisfaction at managing to work within the constraints'. Interestingly, cost was not listed amongst the major criteria for software selection and only two respondents mentioned this factor.

The role of the teacher (as contributor)   (Q. 2.4.3, 2.6.1)

Three specific questions then followed to assist in describing more precisely the preferred role of the teacher in the implementation of CALL. The aim was to establish whether respondents thought the teacher had a role to play in the actual delivery of CALL. This is part of the exploration of how authors conceptualize CALL, and whether they see the language teacher featuring in the implementation. As far as the teacher's presence is concerned, 79.8 per cent believed CALL to be worthwhile under both conditions, that is *with* a teacher and *without* a teacher present; 10.7 per cent thought that CALL was only worthwhile without the teacher present, 5.9 per cent thought CALL valuable only with the teacher present, and the remaining responses were neutral.

To augment the earlier closed questions on the teacher's role, an open-ended question was also provided to allow for longer, unanticipated answers (Q. 2.6.1). Respondents were asked if the introduction of the computer had modified the teacher's role and if so, in what way. The results are given in Table 5.4a and 5.4b. Of the 27 respondents who answered in the negative, 37.0 per cent anticipated a change in the teacher's role, though it had not occurred as yet. The results at this stage are somewhat equivocal. Although the majority felt some change in role had taken place, a significant number of respondents felt no change had occurred, though some role modification may take place in the future.

Amongst the respondents who felt a change in role had occurred, the most frequent comment was that the computer changed what teachers do in the classroom, particularly in terms of the language

TABLE 5.4a   *Modification of the teacher's role*

Has the computer modified teacher's role?	No. of responses	Percentage
Yes	40	49.5
No	27	33.3
A little	7	8.6
Other	7	8.6

Note: Sample size of 81. Responses are mutually exclusive.

learning activities that occur in lessons. Typically, in explaining how their role had been modified, respondents described the computer taking over the more repetitive aspects of language learning thus freeing the teacher, for example:

- Tedious repetition drill and practice can be turned over to the computer, even turned into games and simulations. Freeing the teacher to do something else or to exploit the skills honed by the computerized drills.
- Able to concentrate on face-to-face skills.
- More time for communicative practice in the classroom.

The development process   (Q. 1.4.9, 1.4.10)

The CALL Survey enquired into how authors prepared for a new project by asking whether they first assimilated what had been written on the subject or began with no particular framework consciously in mind. The answers to this question are summarized in Table 5.5.

The table shows that the majority of respondents do assimilate before they begin a new piece of work. Of those, two respondents said that to first assimilate was important so as not to 'reinvent the wheel'. Of those that did not prepare in this way, one stated that he did so 'not to be unduly influenced by what's been done', and another said that he had 'tried . . . but most researchers seem to resist it'.

The question exploring the development process followed by key

TABLE 5.4b   *Directions of modification*

In what way?	No. of responses
Changed classroom learning activities	8
Helped shift focus to learners	7
Changed teacher's role to counsellor/manager/facilitator	5
Improved students' learning	5
Other	8

Note: Sample size of 40.

TABLE 5.5   *Framework for development*

Framework	No. of responses	Percentage
First assimilate	58	62.5
No particular framework	13	14.5
Both of the above	7	7.5
Own framework	6	6.5
Other	8	9.0

Note: Sample size of 92. Responses are mutually exclusive.

practitioners provided insight into exactly how the process occurred, particularly with regard to whether CALL authors broke down the process into discrete elements which were followed in a particular order, or whether the process followed more of a prototyping or an 'incremental step-wise refinement' approach. Results from the CALL Survey indicated that respondents belong to both camps. Approximately 25 per cent identified a set of more or less discrete elements, with about 25 per cent of those clearly numbering the elements and working through them in a predefined order. Some examples in each category are given.

Discrete element processes
- 1. Conceptualization of learning activity. 2. Matching to suitable software format. 3. Software specification. 4. Programming.
- Thorough research; data collections; design on paper; programming; testing—individual and group.
- First of all the topic/subject area—considerable time on the conceptual development—instructional component, evaluation, error analysis, and so on and how they relate—then produce material—trial it—evaluate and refine it.
- Preliminary analysis; macrodefinition of the project; production; debugging; documentation; evaluation; experimentation; evaluation.

Less structured processes
- Always mixed top-down and bottom-up. Often prototype early, alpha-test, redesign and implement; *HyperCard* is good for quick and dirty prototypes.
- One development I have been through several times is (a) program for student use (b) extension to allow teacher/student 'authoring', that is, data determination.

- Original idea; pilot version; trial (classroom, colleagues); constant improvements.
- My solo efforts involve a lot of trial and error because I am not a real programmer and I hate to read documents. I also lack patience with cameras (focusing), so my digitized pictures often require paint work or replacement (but I recently got a colour scanner!). Generally, I start with a fairly clear idea of what I want to accomplish and tinker until I get a reasonable approximation.

The role of the teacher (as author)   (Q. 2.4.4, 2.4.5)

Of the respondents, 73.2 per cent thought teachers should be involved in CALL materials writing, specifically writing support materials to accompany CALL software packages, whereas only 8.5 per cent did not. As far as language teachers learning to program was concerned, the majority of responses, 52.4 per cent, were against language teachers learning to program, and only 4.8 per cent were unequivocally in favour. However, amongst the answers two further significant trends could be identified: in the first, 21.4 per cent contained responses noting that language teachers did 'not necessarily' have to learn a programming language, that is, it should not be compulsory; in the second, with a response frequency of comparable size, 17.8 per cent, respondents recorded that learning a programming language was a matter of 'personal choice'; 3.6 per cent of responses were neutral. Thus, although the majority were against teachers learning a high-level programming language in favour of using easier authoring tools, a substantial number of respondents indicated that although it was not *necessary*, teachers should still be given the option to decide for themselves.

Some longer comments are worth noting on this question. One respondent wrote that language teachers should not learn a high-level programming language 'unless they want to be serious CALL developers', and according to another respondent, 'not unless they want to write a parser'. A number of respondents thought that the present generation of authoring tools precluded the need to learn to program: 'with products like *HyperCard*, *SuperCard*, and *ToolBook* now on the market the need to learn a high level programming language is becoming less and less important', and 'I think it gives some insights into what is computable, but the increasing availability of powerful authoring tools probably changes this'. Finally, 'Most will find an authoring approach meets their needs within the time they have for developing'.

Materials developed   (Q. 1.3.4, 1.4.12, 2.1.1)

The broad range of activity in CALL is evident in Figure 5.9. For this question respondents were asked to indicate the categories of CALL software for which they had at one time or another developed CALL materials. The findings show the numerous ways that practitioners have conceptualized CALL. The high response rate in the reading and writing categories indicates that these skills may be more amenable to implementation on the computer than the other skills, especially speaking.

In addition to the 14 categories given in the questionnaire, a further 21 categories were recorded by respondents. Due to their size the 'Grammar' and 'Vocabulary' categories have been incorporated into Figure 5.9. The remaining 19 categories, falling into the 'Other' category in Figure 5.9 are listed below as the respondents recorded them:

Dictation	Multimedia/hypermedia	Programming utilities
Vocabulary	Exploratory	Tasks
Concordance	Telematics	Testing
Dialogues	Adventure	Voice recognition
Mazes	Problem solving	Grammar
Phonetics	Translation	Multiple-choice
Drill		

Although the research and development directions that have taken place in CALL have been diverse, the absence of an agreed classification system for describing CALL software has further complicated descriptive analysis in this area. The multidimensional nature of CALL software makes it difficult to categorize using traditional methods of describing language learning materials. At the very least a CALL activity can be viewed in terms of the hardware involved (e.g. interactive video), the language focus or skill (e.g. listening), the extent to which the computer exercises control over learning (e.g. tutorial), the approach to learning (e.g. exploratory learning), and a descriptor to label the precise nature of the activity (e.g. gap-filling). Clearly the categories of CALL software noted in the findings are not mutually exclusive. For example, a CALL

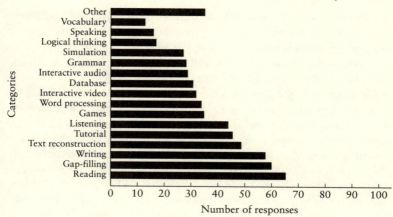

FIGURE 5.9   *Software categories (n = 100)*

program can at once be tutorial and drill, word processing and writing, gap-filling and reading, or exploratory, multimedia and simulation.

In the literature, it is noticeable that some CALL developers rely on commercially developed packages to develop their own materials, while others design new authoring tools from scratch. In the latter, a CALL author may decide to develop their own 'in-house' package for CALL materials development purposes. The CALL Survey examined this question and of the 93 responses a fairly even balance between commercial authoring tools and in-house developed tools was indicated. Examples of 'in-house' development tools are the *Multi-purpose Authoring System*, *FrameTeach*, *Comtext*, *Proforma*, and *Autotutor*. A total of 16.1 per cent of respondents *only* use 'in-house' developed packages, and 9.7 per cent *only* use commercial packages.

Evaluation

The value of CALL   (Q. 1.4.13)

Respondents reported many reasons for believing CALL a valuable teaching/learning resource or technique and the findings are summarized in Table 5.6. It was benefits due to the computer's inherent nature that attracted the most frequent response in the CALL Survey. Of the 40 responses that fell into this category the most common were the computer's ability to provide instant feedback (16), flexibility (8), and large storage capacity (7).

Of interest in the results were the two categories that relate to innovative approaches to language teaching and learning as a result of the introduction of the computer. Methods/activities/tasks unique to the computer included new methodologies such as data-driven learning that would only be feasible with a computer available (see Johns 1990*a*). The views are typified by the following comment when the respondent says that CALL provides, 'New opportunities to provide learning experiences which are impossible without a computer. I am *not* interested in having a program duplicate what can be done by a worksheet, teacher or flashcards.' In the second category, on the diversification of teaching respondents refer to another 'medium', 'teaching/learning mode', or 'aid' that can provide new possibilities, and alternatives in the process of learning a language. Finally, the notion of the computer 'freeing' the teacher for other work also occurred in the answers to this question.

TABLE 5.6   *Reasons for thinking CALL a valuable resource*

Reasons	No. of responses
General characteristics of computer make it suitable	40
Motivating or enjoyable	26
Individualization	21
Autonomous learning, self-access, or self-study use	18
Further practice, or more time on task	14
Methods/activities/tasks unique to computer	13
Frees teacher	12
Links to outside the classroom	8
Diversifies teaching	6
Other	19

Note: Sample size of 100.

Blocks to successful development (Q. 2.6.4)

The major blocks to successful CALL materials are portrayed in Table 5.7. The lack of time for CALL is first. Where a more detailed answer was given, lack of time for materials development was recorded in sixteen instances and lack of time for staff education in three instances. Where funding was mentioned and more detail was provided, respondents maintained that funding was needed for the purchase of hardware and software and for release time for staff to be trained or to develop materials. The lack of time and funding were the most significant blocks, with lack of teacher training, much less frequently recorded, in third position.

The perception of a lack of reward or recognition for CALL work is in a relatively high position and deserves further comment. In relation to this particular hindrance to successful CALL materials development, respondents noted:

- Lack of institutional support—lack of recognition of 'academic' validity, for example, in terms of lack of time and lack

TABLE 5.7   *Blocks to successful development*

Blocks	No. of responses
Lack of time	35
Lack of funding	24
Lack of teacher training	10
Lack of reward/recognition	9
Teaching staff perceptions of CALL	8
Level of expertise required	8
Lack of agreed standards	7
Level of acceptance in wider context	7
Publishing problems	7
Problems organizing team work	6
Professional intransigence	6
Lack of information sharing	5
Lack of suitable software	5
Other	13

Note: Sample size of 100.

of incentives built into the institutions' value judgements and priorities.

- In general, the attitude on the part of many university administrators that programming by humanities faculty members is not to be rewarded as highly as conventional research and publication.
- Time allocated to development; uncertainty about this software development 'helping' in promotion.

Whereas publishing papers, for example, is considered academically 'valid', little or no weight appears to be given to work in CALL.

The eight responses in the category 'Teaching staff perceptions of CALL' reflect the fact that CALL as a technique can still not be said to be part of mainstream language teaching and learning. Many language teachers remain sceptical about CALL as illustrated in this response on the need for: 'Tangible proof that CALL is worth the time and effort'. While CALL remains a specialized interest on the periphery, it is incumbent on practitioners to conduct careful evaluation so that others might be convinced of its value. 'Lack of agreed standards' refers to hardware and software standards. 'Level of acceptance in wider context' refers to levels of acceptance of CALL by those outside the immediate language teaching community itself, for example key personnel responsible for decision-making with regard to technology within the management of an institution.

Publishing problems also deserve careful consideration given the criticism directed towards poor quality unpublished packages in the literature. Typical responses in the survey are:

- Not enough economic benefit in developing high-quality materials for a small, vertical market.
- The difficulty of publishing CALL software satisfactorily, and consequently the fact that materials do not circulate freely; everyone is working alone.

Arguably, all blocks to successful CALL materials development deserve attention at this stage given the newness of CALL, the high cost of equipment, the time required for training and development, and the current state of knowledge about what constitutes an optimal development environment; only then can this new technique be evaluated on a fair and informed basis, and materials development occur with a reasonable chance of success.

Progress in CALL   (Q. 2.6.5)

Respondents were asked to comment on the progress of CALL so far. The responses were divided into general, representative categories and the findings are shown in Table 5.8. Only 19.1 per cent of responses were unequivocally positive and the majority of responses were mixed.

A large proportion of comments described mixed or negative reactions to CALL so far, and a number of recurring points were made in this regard. Fourteen respondents felt CALL progress had been slow, and nine others felt CALL materials development had now reached a standstill or a dead end.

A number of further comments were made which are worthy of presenting given this mixed reaction from a group of people whom one would expect to consider CALL favourably. These comments are paraphrased below:

• Need for more evaluation;
• Too much isolated development, need more cooperation;
• Too much 'reinventing the wheel';
• Teachers need to be more involved;
• Instructional CALL problematic;
• The few well-funded R. & D. CALL projects are not very portable;
• Too dominated by brand names;
• Staff changes causing loss of CALL skills;
• 'Simple solutions are not necessarily the best ones';
• Constant updating of hardware rendering obsolete some skills in earlier software;

TABLE 5.8   *Progress in CALL*

Progress so far (general)	No. of responses	Percentage
Mixed	45	47.9
Poor/negative remark	25	26.6
Good/positive remark	18	19.1
Just beginning	5	5.3
Other	1	1.1

Note: Sample size of 94. Responses are mutually exclusive.

- Belief that CALL can replace expensive teachers;
- Requirement that new language texts are marketed with software.

As with the blocks to successful CALL materials development described in the previous section, at this stage in the development of CALL as a field of study all concerns need to be seriously considered.

Summary

The 104 sets of responses provide a corpus of material on the conceptual frameworks of key practitioners in CALL. As a group they represent a substantial amount of knowledge and expertise in the field. Communicative language teaching followed by task-based learning and, some way behind, formal grammar instruction, were the three most prominent philosophies of language teaching. Interestingly, respondents as a whole were strongly eclectic with 95.2 per cent marking two or more categories, and 35.6 per cent marking four or more categories. In describing how this philosophy affected materials development, answers were diverse. Respondents variously focused on views of teaching and learning, learner needs, the curriculum, aspects of hardware and software, and the role of the computer. Responses also reflected a desire to pin down specific goals in program design in a clear, precise language. The terminology used was that often associated with CLT. The relative importance attached to views of language teaching/learning and their influence on CALL materials development varied considerably: positions that considered such views as all important to positions that located views of language teaching/learning in a much less pivotal position were observed. Another trend in the responses was to answer this question on how an author's philosophy of teaching/learning relates to CALL in terms of the role of the computer. The tutor and tool roles were clearly apparent with the tool role predominating, and more directive roles such as the manager of tasks or the expert system occurring less frequently.

The scope of CALL discussion was remarkably broad with 11.9 per cent of respondents marking all categories. Clearly, CALL draws on the work of many fields and disciplines at this stage in its development. Word processing was the most frequent response, reflecting again the importance of the tool role of the computer, and the need to include rather than exclude word processing within the parameters of CALL discussion. A robust taxonomy for describing CALL materials was not developed for the purposes of the survey: instead descriptive categories common in the literature were used. In addition to the fourteen categories provided, a further twenty-one categories were recorded forming one of the highest 'Other' categories in the survey. As with the literature findings, descriptors were by no means mutually exclusive and respondents varied as to which facet or dimension of the program was the focus. Thus, the same program could be labelled in a number of different ways.

In both the CALL Survey and the literature, initial orientations were diverse. The most frequent initial orientations were certain potentials of the computer and the language learning methodology. The question on the development process revealed a contrast between those whose point of departure originated from a higher level theoretical framework, and those who began with a lower level task or problem. Existing CALL applications and teaching materials also informed the point of departure taken.

As for the teacher's role, a substantial majority felt CALL to be worthwhile *with* or *without* a teacher present. In conceptualizing CALL, therefore, one might expect frameworks that depend upon a teacher's presence, and those that do not. The Ahmad *et al.* and Farrington models described in the literature reinforce this view. Considered as a whole, it seems CALL authors will use commercial tools if they are available and suitable but, if their needs are not met, they will design their own development tools, and perhaps use a high-level programming language to do so. Authoring tools may begin as 'in-house' products for internal use only, but later, as they become more polished, they may be marketed as commercial products for wider distribution. Many authoring tools developed 'in-house', however, do not reach the wider audience. As far as respondents were concerned CALL was valued particularly because of the innate qualities of the computer: qualities such as large storage capacity and speed. Motivation, individualization, autonomy, practice, and the possibility of approaches that only the computer could provide followed. Many blocks to successful CALL materials were identified, the most important being lack of time and lack of funding for development purposes. Finally, progress in CALL was regarded as mixed: many reasons for this assessment of CALL were given, all of which are worthy of further reflection.

Notes

1. The CALL survey relates to conditions at a particular time, the questionnaire having been completed between September 1990 and March 1991. Inevitably, conditions have changed since that time, especially in terms of the hardware and software used for CALL materials development. In fact in the current climate, with almost monthly innovations in hardware and software, any work on CALL is going to be outdated in one way or another, constrained by the inevitable time-lag between writing and publication. Such limitations apply less to the literature review, however and, as stated earlier, it is hoped that the combination of the findings from the literature, and the survey will provide a more balanced and representative sample than the survey alone could possibly provide.

2. The findings of the CALL survey reported in Chapter 5 are restricted to answers to questions that relate to how CALL has been conceptualized, one of the central themes of the book. The CALL survey also covered working methods, factors for success, and teacher education as they each relate to CALL materials development. A general report on the findings of the CALL survey as a whole is given in Levy (1994c), and teacher education is dealt with in detail in Levy (1989, 1990a, forthcoming a). For further information on any aspects relating to the CALL survey please contact the author. (See also Appendix B.)

3. Q. 1.2.2 (philosophies, methods, and approaches). The label 'philosophy' is used here in order to allow for a more general position to be expressed, one that may not be covered by these more narrowly defined terms such as language teaching methods or approaches.

4. Q. 1.4.7 (philosophy used to encompass all). Here 'philosophy' is used as the umbrella term to denote the teaching/learning orientation of the CALL author, because of potential ambiguity in the meaning and connotation of alternative terms such as 'method', 'approach', and 'methodology' (see Savignon 1983: 24; Richards and Rodgers 1986: 15).

6. Emerging themes and patterns of development

Introduction

When CALL is viewed as a whole, as a body of work, the diversity is remarkable. With no agreed agenda for research and development, with a sensitivity to local conditions, and with the flexibility of the computer, materials developers have conceptualized CALL in many ways, and they have drawn their theoretical base and practical orientation from many sources. As a result the points of departure are numerous. Moreover, the ways in which CALL authors conceptualize CALL are often complex and multifaceted. The initial conceptualization may undergo significant transformation as theoretical ambitions are reconciled with practical realities. Hardware and software characteristics, for example, variously shape and form how the initial concept is transformed into a fully implemented CALL program.

Certain characteristics or trends appear and reappear in reviewing the findings of the literature and the CALL Survey. By no means does this discussion claim to identify all the features that emerge when CALL is conceptualized initially or how it is shaped after the development process has begun, but it does aim to shed some light on initial conceptual frameworks and development processes. Describing CALL development work has been made more difficult by the lack of agreed definitions and a clearly resolved metalanguage for discussion. In the CALL Survey it was not anticipated that any one question could resolve satisfactorily how a person conceptualized CALL. Therefore, the problem of conceptualization was explored in a number of ways using the literature and a number of questions in the CALL Survey. After some preliminary observations on the scope of CALL, and the philosophical orientation of authors, the following items are specifically addressed: research-based and practitioner-led CALL; the Richards and Rodgers's model; closeness of 'fit'; the development process; existing conditions and constraints; and hardware and software. New ways of concep-

tualizing CALL as a result of the capabilities of the Internet
follow. Problems in describing CALL materials conclude the
chapter.

The scope of CALL

The scope of CALL is broad, the topic is clearly interdisciplinary,
and as a result its field of view crosses many boundaries that by
convention separate disciplines and other fields of inquiry. The
breadth of CALL was reinforced in the results of the CALL Survey
question seeking to circumscribe CALL where respondents noted a
wide range of topics for inclusion. Word processing was the most
frequent response followed by multimedia (interactive video and
hypermedia), then artificial intelligence and expert systems. The
placing of word processing at the top of the list, and the fact that all
categories listed received a strong response (11.9% of respondents
marked all categories, and no single category was marked by less
than 38% of respondents), deserves further comment.

Word processing is very much part of CALL, at least according
to the CALL Survey results. Views on whether certain topics lie
within or beyond the field of CALL vary considerably, however,
and word processing is one of these topics. For example, for some
CALL commentators such as John Underwood, word processing
lies outside the CALL domain (1984: 65), while for others such as
Jones and Fortescue word processing lies firmly within it (1987). In
a section on 'Alternatives to CALL', Underwood describes word
processing as the 'best language-related' use of computers (1984:
66). Though the word processor is used in relation to language
learning, it is not regarded as part of CALL, presumably because
the word processor does not perform a tutorial function of some
kind: email for language practice is also excluded on the same
grounds (1984: 66). This view, that CALL encompasses tutors but
not tools such as the word processor, is held by a number of CALL
practitioners and researchers. That this assumption is often implicitly rather than explicitly stated, has led, I believe, to considerable
confusion in CALL, especially in such areas as curriculum integration, evaluation, and the role of the teacher. Tutors and tools
function in different ways and present different problems, a subject

that will be explored in much more detail in Chapter 7. Keeping discussion of the computer tool firmly within CALL is further suggested by reactions to the CALL Survey question on favoured roles for the computer: the tool role of the computer was the most frequent response (Q. 1.2.1). Pragmatically though, aside from the collective views of the respondents, it would seem to be important to include tools such as the word processor and email within the aegis of CALL, so that the effects of the tools on tasks conducted by non-native speakers of English may be firmly on the CALL agenda. Thus far, much of the research on the effects of computing tools, such as the effects of writing media on the writing process, has been conducted by those involved in first-language instruction, particularly English composition writing (see Haas 1988; Bridwell *et al.* 1985; Lutz 1987; Hawisher and Moran 1993). Unless we make the rather dubious assumption that the effects of the word processor on writing will be the same for non-native speakers as for native speakers, who, if not CALL researchers, will instigate the appropriate studies and investigate the effects? The same must be said for databases or archives such as the Oral Language Archive, where resources of various kinds are being used to support language learning.

The strong response to the scope of CALL question across disciplines also points to the difficulty for CALL workers of keeping abreast of developments beyond the CALL domain specifically. Typically, each associated field of work is represented by its own researchers, journals, and conferences. In areas such as CALL, it is becoming increasingly difficult to monitor developments from outside the field that may eventually turn out to be extremely important within it. The solutions to this problem are not easy to find, especially given the recent proliferation of publishing options through electronic journals and other mechanisms of dissemination via the Internet, but such work needs to be encouraged to avoid duplication in CALL, and to ensure that CALL is properly integrated with its neighbouring disciplines to the benefit of all the parties concerned. Some fields such as voice synthesis or computational linguistics which were ranked lowest in the CALL Survey might suddenly mature and become sufficiently potent to become critical considerations for the forward movement of CALL.

Teaching philosophy and CALL

In both the literature and the CALL Survey, Communicative Language Teaching (CLT) emerged as the dominant contemporary approach, underpinned by the notion of 'communicative competence'. The introduction of the term into language teaching has led to ambiguity about the meaning of CLT in practice. According to Savignon (1983: 24) this is because communicative competence refers more to a *philosophy* of language than to a method and, as such, a suite of classroom practices has not been clearly articulated. Richards and Rodgers (1986: 66) in their analysis of language teaching method reflect this view, and liken CLT to an *approach* rather than a method, suggesting an orientation rather than a set of prescriptions. A descriptive vocabulary has come to be associated with communicative language teaching and this helps, to a certain extent, in clarifying the orientation of the communicative language teacher: the vocabulary includes such terms as language use, language functions, authentic language, discourse, fluency, interaction, negotiation, social context, appropriateness, coherence and cohesion (Larsen-Freeman 1986: 123).

The evidence from the literature showed that CLT is open to a number of interpretations at the implementation or procedure level (see Breen 1987*b*: 158; Gray 1990: 262). The CALL Survey findings showed similar results. In relating their teaching philosophy to CALL practice (Q. 1.4.7), respondents did not use the term CLT to describe their materials and, instead, showed a preference for using the more specific, descriptive vocabulary often associated with CLT; for example, they advocated the use of 'authentic language', 'language in context', or 'a concern with language use in social settings'. Such statements are more precise and relate more clearly to specific attributes of the CALL materials produced. Here it is also worth noting that in the CALL Survey formal grammar instruction followed after CLT and task-based learning, showing that in spite of the continued dominance of CLT, there is still considerable support for more formal grammar-oriented approaches (see also Jung 1994: 3).

Many teachers do not subscribe to one particular approach or method, but are eclectic. Stern observes that many teachers consider themselves to be eclectic in the sense that they do not follow a distinct language teaching approach, philosophy, or 'named psychological or linguistic theory' (Stern 1983: 29). Rivers goes further, and recommends an eclectic approach because it allows for the best techniques of all methods to be absorbed and used when appropriate; Rivers also believes eclecticism suits the intuitions of many language teachers (Rivers 1981: 54, 55). This view is compatible with the move away from a language teaching method that is well defined and comprehensive, to an emphasis on the use of techniques that accommodate the specific needs and characteristics of the learner. An eclectic approach is also conspicuous in many CALL projects, and is specifically noted in the KITES (Kids Interactive Television Experience by Satellite) Project, for example, where German and American pupils were linked via electronic mail and videoconferencing (Teichmann 1994: 64). It is also worth noting that when recognized teaching approaches, methods or strategies prove insufficiently powerful to embrace the CALL context, practitioners may well describe their approach as eclectic: though their techniques may be amenable to relatively straightforward description, no existing labels are available to adequately describe them.

To conclude, although the goal of many methodologists appears to be to prepare students to communicate in the foreign language, the means by which this goal is reached is highly variable. The notion of communicative competence for language and the communicative approach for language teaching provide an orientation, but not a prescription for classroom practice. Thus, the philosophy or approach is open to individual interpretation and variation. Practitioners differ in the way in which this philosophy or approach translates into teacher and learner roles, materials, classroom activities and techniques (Richards and Rodgers 1986: 69). As a result, instead of the set of optimal prescriptions for language teaching that was used in the 1950s and 1960s, contemporary views are more circumspect and they reflect the complexity of language teaching and learning when a number of interrelated competencies need to be acquired. For CALL, this means that an author with a CLT philosophy of language teaching and learning, the predominant view in the CALL Survey, may in fact develop and use numerous kinds of CALL activities which all fit the general orientation, but which may in themselves vary significantly. Thus, a set of CALL materials labelled 'communicative' has little meaning at the implementation or procedure level, and is of limited assistance in precisely defining the interactions taking place, or the differences between CALL programs.

Points of departure

From the discussion so far it is clear that authors' points of departure for the design of CALL programs vary greatly in position, scale, and in the problems they address. The CALL projects presented in Table 4.1 are recast here in Table 6.1 to show their points of departure recorded as the authors themselves have described them. The conceptualization of these projects appears to originate from widely differing sources.

TABLE 6.1   *Points of departure in CALL with sample programs*

Points of departure	Sample program(s)
Theory of instruction	TICCIT
Theory of language learning	ALLP, Communicating, CAMILLE/ France InterActive
Interactive, self-paced instruction for large numbers of students	PLATO
Learning strategy	Pinpoint
Research tool	CompLex, MicroConcord
Intelligent tutoring	Miniprof, LINGER
Specific language problem	Kanjicard
Exploring new technology	Kanji City, France InterActive (hypermedia)
Language development and practice	Venture-reader (reading), CLEF (grammar), LEXI-CAL (vocabulary), FLUENT (conversation)
Translation	Littré/BonAccord
Vocabulary instruction	CompLex
Natural Language Processing	Spion
International access to authentic materials	Oral Language Archive (dialogues for L2 learners)
International discussion groups	E-Mail Tandem Network, S-L lists
Computer conferencing	Remote Technical Assistant (text), Multimedia Teleschool (video)

There may well be considerable overlap amongst the categories given: for example, a program designed for 'Intelligent tutoring' might well overlap with one that provides for 'Language development and practice'. In addition, the initial inspiration for programs such as *France InterActive*, derives from two sources: a communicative competence model of SLA was combined with the exploration of a new technology, in this case hypermedia. This list is not meant to represent a typology, that is, a complete list of categories that describe the range of programs satisfactorily. Instead it a list that is not exhaustive or mutually exclusive, of the ways in which authors have described their initial positions in the literature concerning their projects.

Of special note are varying attitudes towards the use of new technology as an initial motivation for design and development. In some cases hardware considerations have an important function in initial thinking; in some cases such considerations are secondary. For instance, in *Kanji City* the individual applications 'were developed more as a vehicle for exploring the possibilities of the hypermedia concept rather than as an implementation of a logical sequence of lessons covering a predefined curriculum' (Ashworth and Stelovsky 1989: 36). Technology took a primary place in the work of Ariew (1984: 43) who says in relation to CAI materials development, the 'first decision dealt with the choice of hardware systems'. Other examples point to a subordinate role for technology as in *Kanjicard* where 'pedagogical principles involved in the instruction of ideographic or logographic scripts' required hypermedia technology (Nakajima 1990: 143).

That the technology should take a subordinate role in the design and development process is a point made by a number of writers (Morgenstern 1986; Hubbard 1988c; Mah 1990). Hubbard (1988c: 8) argues that CALL materials development seems 'to be driven primarily by considerations of technique rather than any coherent methodology' implying that methodology should be the initial consideration. Mah (1990: 229) emphasizes the value of intensive research as a basis for design and describes how the results of research on communicative strategies provided clear guidelines for the content of an interactive videodisc. Finally, it is noteworthy that developers working within an instructional design framework also de-emphasize the selection of media.

The findings from the CALL Survey reinforce the diversity found in the literature. Of the many answers to the question of orientation at the outset of projects, the most popular was towards certain 'potentials' of the computer, for example, the matching capability (Q. 1.4.6). Judging by the popularity of this answer, it appears that when developers begin a new project, they place relatively high emphasis on the capabilities they perceive the computer to have. Therefore, the developer's knowledge of what the computer is and what it can do, will play a central role in shaping the developer's conceptualization of CALL. It is essential, therefore, that developers have a good understanding of the capabilities of the computer; Lian (1991: 2) describes how a more restricted view of the computer can inhibit development. The observation by Lian is primarily aimed at hardware, but the same may be said of software. The approach to authoring that the developer adopts can also place strict limitations on what might be done. Given that 40.4 per cent of respondents marked for initial orientation an authoring environment which they consider promising, developers need to be keenly aware of how this initial orientation might be affecting their conceptualization of CALL.

To bring the strands of the discussion on points of departure together, Table 6.2 shows how differently developers derive their CALL applications and describes their points of departure. Table 6.2 summarizes the information on points of departure collected through the literature and in the CALL Survey.

The table illustrates the numerous ways in which authors approach the conceptualization and subsequent development of CALL materials. A number of recurring themes can be observed from the data collected about authors' conceptual frameworks initially. These themes cannot account for all the descriptions of how CALL has been conceptualized. They do, however, represent identifiable trends among the approaches that have been adopted.

Research-based and practitioner-led CALL

Table 6.2 shows that much development in CALL has been led primarily by the interests and goals of practitioners rather than an overriding theoretical model, or to use the terminology of Kemmis *et al.* (1977: 391) that CALL development is 'practitioner-led' rather than 'research-based'. Practitioner-led CALL may begin with a specific language teaching problem that the CALL author believes

TABLE 6.2   *Points of departure: an overview*

Literature, Table 6.1	CALL Survey, Q. 1.4.10
Theory of instruction	Lower level task or problem
Theory of language learning	Higher level theoretical framework
Interactive self-paced	Existing CALL applications
instruction for large	Existing teaching materials
numbers of students	Investigations into hardware
Learning strategy	and software
Research tool	Syllabus specifications
Intelligent tutoring	Matching activity to hardware and
Specific language problem	software capabilities
Exploring new technology	
Language development and	
practice	
Translation	
Vocabulary instruction	
Natural Language Processing	
International access to authentic	
materials	
International discussion groups	
Computer conferencing	

the computer can address, or an exploration into the use of a new technology such as multimedia. Kemmis *et al.* describe teachers as trusting their 'intuitions as teachers rather than research on learning in deciding when and how to use CALL'. Hart (1995: 29) contrasts theory-driven projects with PLATO which was very much practitioner-led. Though PLATO provided all the necessary data-collection mechanisms that could have facilitated experimentation and research, it was not used in this way, and basic research played a minimal part in the development that took place.

Alternatively, research-based CALL tends to proceed from a higher level in a conceptual framework than practitioner-led CALL (see discussion in the section on the Richards and Rodgers model). Development beginning at a higher level often adopts a top-down approach and seeks to apply a theory to structure CALL materials development. Swartz and Russell (1989) use this strategy in their foreign language Instructional Design Environment (IDE) which allows developers to design, structure, and organize material for advanced tutoring systems. Research-based CALL may begin with a theory of instruction or a theory of language learning. The TICCIT Project, for example, began with a theory of instruction, Component Display Theory, and writers such as Doughty (1991: 1) argue that authors must appeal to theories of second-language acquisition to properly determine CALL software development. Authors such as Bailin (1990: 173) and Hubbard (1992: 40) argue that there needs to be a bridge between the two approaches to allow 'top-down' and 'bottom-up' approaches to be employed and to ensure that 'strategies' and 'tactics' that work in one program may be recognized and used as 'building blocks' in others. In the literature on CALL and the CALL-Survey findings practitioner-led CALL predominated, although there were many examples of research-based or theory-driven CALL also.

Project goals can change as a project evolves, and the *Spion* project is such an example (Molla *et al.* 1988; Sanders and Sanders 1995). Initially *Spion* began as a theory-driven project, in this case with the aim of studying models of language understanding by computer (Sanders and Sanders 1995: 119). However, as the project progressed, the application side of the project grew in significance. Those involved in the project began to see it more as an engineering problem than a problem in basic research, partly because the goal had always been to test *Spion* with end-users. As such, the quality of the end-product was important, it had to be usable, and practical concerns such as the screen design, help options, and so on had to be resolved. As a result Sanders and Sanders describe themselves as being concerned with CALL or ICALL *applications*. They make the perceptive observation that the 'challenges of final implementation are sometimes wholly unrelated to the challenge of design', and, as such, we should not be surprised if user-ready versions of research-based laboratory prototype programs are not forthcoming (1995: 127). This view gives further weight to the argument that perhaps the distinction between research-based and practitioner-led CALL, or the formalists and the proceduralists, is an understandable one, because the goals and the problems are quite different.

The Richards and Rodgers model

The Richards and Rodgers model of language teaching method is helpful for interpreting the higher and lower levels of conceptualization illustrated in Table 6.2. In formulating their model, Richards and Rodgers (1986: 15) emphasize the importance of distinguishing between 'a philosophy of language teaching at the level of theory and principles, and a set of derived procedures for teaching a language'. This distinction arose in the earlier section on authors' language teaching philosophies and CALL, where the CLT 'philosophy' manifested itself in many different ways at the procedural level. The Richards and Rodgers model is hierarchical and it is composed of three levels called Approach, Design and Procedure. It is a refinement of a similar three-level scheme constructed by Anthony (1963: 63–7) which Richards and Rodgers stress has considerable value for highlighting 'different degrees of abstraction and specificity' in language teaching (1986: 15). In the Richards and Rodgers model the level of Approach refers to theories about the nature of language and language learning; the level of Design deals with the objectives of the method, a syllabus model, types of learning and teaching activities, and the roles of the learner, the teacher, and the materials; finally, Richards and Rodgers liken the procedure level to the implementation phase (1986: 16), and describe it as the 'practical realization' of the method (1986: 16, 26). All of these levels are represented in Hubbard's methodological framework where the components at the three levels form an integrated network.

The Approach level corresponds to the higher level theoretical frameworks elaborated in the CALL Survey; the Design level corresponds to the lower level task or problem. Also from Table 6.2, theories of language learning, views of language, syllabus models, roles for the teacher and learner—and by extension the computer roles—and learning and teaching activities all fit comfortably within the Richards and Rodgers model of method.

Richards and Rodgers point out that methodological development does not necessarily proceed from Approach through Design to Procedure and that the process can begin at any of these three levels (1986: 29). They also note that a method may be articulated at one, or more levels. For example, Communicative Language Teaching is precisely described at the level of Approach, but is open to a number of different interpretations at the lower levels; Audiolingualism, on the other hand, is clearly articulated at all levels (1986: 83). A higher level framework, that is at the level of Approach, begins with a theory of some kind, possibly a theory of language, of language instruction, or of language learning. Examples in the CALL Survey gave further examples of CALL activity emanating from theories from general education, linguistics, and literary stylistics. The higher level framework is a comprehensive one and generally employs a top-down approach to design which proceeds through all of the levels described in Richards and Rodgers's model. Generally, a higher level framework is used in the design of tutors. The complexity of structuring a conceptual design for a tutor is recognized by Swartz and Russell (1989) who report on the foreign language Instructional Design Environment (1989: 6). The IDE articulates all of the levels described in the Richards and Rodgers model. The IDE is a design tool that 'provides the means of making explicit a particular curriculum design based on a framework of learning principles, instructional goals and real classroom decisions that are relevant to the course at hand' (Swartz and Russell 1989: 6). The complexity of manipulating the wide variety of elements in CALL materials design warrants the use of sophisticated tools such as IDE.

In contrast, the summary of findings in Table 6.2 shows that many authors focus on the level of Design in their conceptualization of CALL. Projects which first relate to a syllabus, specific tasks or activities, and learner needs operate at this level. They tend to begin at the Design level and then proceed to the Procedure level. The lower level approach is generally not as ambitious or as all-embracing as the higher-level approach but, instead, addresses a known condition, for instance a syllabus specification, or particular language learning problem that the developer feels is amenable to solution via the computer. Examples within this framework found in the CALL Survey include CALL programs addressing a teaching/learning difficulty (e.g. the interrogative), those aimed at developing a learning strategy, and programs to generate learning tasks. CALL materials developed under these circumstances tend to be relatively small-scale productions that address particular problems that the author has encountered with a group of students. Often implicit in this conception of CALL is the close association of the teacher with the development and implementation of the program.

In general, although the Richards and Rodgers model is helpful in providing a frame of reference for tutorial CALL, beginning at the Approach or Design levels, it does not appear to be so helpful in describing the tool role of the computer. Not surprisingly, since it was conceived as a model for the description of teaching methods, the Richards and Rodgers model is less convincing when the computer is viewed as a tool rather than as a tutor.

Closeness of 'fit'

The notion of 'fit' (see Wyatt 1988: 86) between an author's philosophy of language teaching and learning, and the capabilities of the technology is a phenomenon noted in both the literature and the CALL Survey. In the literature, for example, Wyatt (1988: 86) states:

One of the most fundamental issues in the field of CALL is the 'fit' between the computer's capabilities and the demands of language pedagogy. Neither is static: both have undergone very significant developments in the last decade, and continued change is to be expected.

This idea has a number of variants. From the CALL Survey, many authors were clearly trying to reconcile their pedagogy or methodology with the capabilities of the technology (see Q. 1.4.6 and Q. 1.3.6). From the literature, Jung (1989: 20), for instance, writes that a 'two-pronged attack' is required in CALL seeking 'bridge-heads' between psycholinguistics and educational technology. Ingraham and Emery (1991: 326) in their project *France InterActive*, say that for the proper development of a CALL environment, a model of language learning needs to be integrated with a computer-aided learning (CAL) methodology. In their case a hypermedia presentation was determined 'from the outset' (1991: 326) and combined with a 'communicative competence' model of SLA. Pennington emphasizes the quality of the 'match' between 'the properties of the medium, the attributes of the users, and the way in which it is implemented in a given context' (1991*b*: 274). Mitterer *et al.* extend the combination further when they argue that four types of knowledge need to be integrated for effective language learning with technology. They propose that theories of instructional design, language teaching and language learning must be combined with a knowledge of how the technology is most effectively applied (1990: 136).

Instances of this orientation towards the conceptualization of CALL also occurred in the CALL Survey; for instance:

- I attempt to bring together the computer application, instructional design theory, and a teaching methodology.
- Saw the compatibility of HyperCard with an activity (mazes) that I had used effectively in class.

The examples given so far place language teaching and learning or methodological considerations on a par with technological considerations. Viewing each of these areas of knowledge equally the CALL author searches for a successful match or, expressed in another way, aims to establish a fit between the pedagogy, methodology or theory of learning, and the author's perception of the capabilities and limitations of the technology. This view contrasts strongly with an approach that proceeds in a linear fashion from a theoretical position, be it based upon a theory of instructional design, a theory of teaching or a theory of learning, through to an application of the technology.

Traditional instructional design methodologies place media selection at a late stage in the design process: Jonassen states, 'it is heretical to . . . begin with assumptions about which medium to use in designing instruction' (Jonassen 1985: 8, 16). Moreover, in the Andrews and Goodson (1980) model of instructional design, for example, 'media selection' is step eight out of a total of nine steps. In contrast, authors such as Laurillard (1987: 75), make the point that whereas in theory, educational technology advocates a systematic series of steps beginning with needs analysis and progressing to describe learning objectives then learning activities before considering the choice of media, in practice this 'idealistic framework' is not used and the choice of media is first. Also in CALL, Meskill argues that is essential to have an appreciation of the media at the very earliest stages of a project (1991: 54). In the CALL Survey, although an equal weighting was given to methodology and technology by some respondents, other orientations included those where methodology or pedagogy was considered the only determinant, to those where the goal was to explore the potential of the technology.

There is a case for viewing technology and pedagogy as equal partners in CALL. Then, for any given circumstance, the closeness of fit between the two can be assessed. If the fit is not good, then the use of technology will probably be rejected; alternatively, if the fit is a good one then the CALL option is probably feasible.

The development process

Development processes range from those that follow a well-defined, staged path from initial concept to final implementation, to those that are much less formally structured. Some developers identify discrete elements as a way of describing the development process, a technique commonly used by instructional designers. Among these, some CALL authors begin by identifying these elements, and then continue by working through them in a linear fashion so they are in effect stages in a clearly defined sequence. For others such as Meskill (1991), though discrete elements are still articulated, the order is not prescribed. In this case, Meskill (1991: 45) says the elements are not hierarchical but circular, and the emphasis is on 'modifying, rethinking, redefining, rewriting until all these highly interdependent considerations fit together and satisfy one another's definitions and requirements'. For others again, notably Hubbard (1992, 1996) a network of elements is presented with no particular order recommended. Hubbard's network of elements might be seen more as a checklist, where the interrelationships presented in the framework may be viewed, and against which the characteristics and structure of a CALL program under construction can be judged.

Breaking down the development process into discrete components and subcomponents has long been the approach of instructional designers. Andrews and Goodson (1980) compared 40 instructional design models, and while there was some disparity between them the major components were the same in each. The generic model consists of three stages or phases: the analysis phase, the development or synthesis phase, and the evaluation phase (see Jonassen 1988: 2). The tasks associated with these three phases are summarized in Bonner (1988: 5) and are listed below:

- needs assessment, task analysis;
- goals, subgoals, objectives;
- measurement;
- types of skill/learning;
- sequencing goals, subgoals, objectives;
- learner characteristics;
- instructional strategies, learning activities;
- media selection;
- formative evaluation.

The question of whether the development process can be segmented in such a way is a point of conjecture, even amongst instructional designers. In this regard Bonner (1988: 5), who questions traditional approaches in instructional design, especially as a result of findings derived from cognitive theory, advances the following question: 'The important question for instructional design is whether and in what way designers may be limiting the design of good instruction by adhering to the systematic process.' In a similar vein, writers such as Shneiderman who have been most influential in the area of interface design, and who reflect profoundly on the development process, argue that we are not able to break the process down into separate, smaller units. Shneiderman says:

- Design is a *process*; it is not a state and cannot be adequately represented statically;
- The design process is *non-hierarchical*; it is neither strictly bottom-up nor strictly top-down;
- The process is *radically transformational*;
- Design intrinsically involves the *discovery of new goals*. (1987: 391)

The question of whether the development process can or should be systematic and broken into discrete elements is most important. The literature and the CALL Survey provide a range of responses to this issue. The literature provides evidence of more systematic, discrete element processes while responses to the CALL Survey represented the whole spectrum, from highly structured, systematic, linear processes to largely unstructured, iterative ones.

In the discussion of 'fit', it appears CALL authors are trying to reconcile their theory, or their philosophy of teaching and learning, with the capabilities of the technology. Whatever the theoretical perspective or pedagogical purpose, a process of accommodation has to occur as the boundaries set by the development environment are gradually understood through the development process. The CALL context is significant, and the strengths and limitations of our technology—notwithstanding obvious constraints such as funding and access to programming expertise—variously constrain what can and cannot be achieved at any particular time. In constructing the CALL program, the author endeavours to establish a suitable 'fit'. Thus, testing, evaluation, and validation of any theoretical base, particularly one derived from a theory of learning, should occur within the context once the prototype program is complete. If the process is radically transformational as Shneiderman suggests, we should not be too surprised if the initial theoretical base is modified in some way, even to the extent that new theories emerge (for further discussion see Levy, forthcoming *b*).

Ultimately many aspects of the development process may be determined by pragmatic considerations such as the scale and complexity of the project, the number of people involved, and the hardware and software tools that are to be utilized. For large-scale projects employing highly sophisticated technology and development teams, controlling the development process through breaking complex tasks down into more manageable components and staging the work that needs to be completed becomes a necessity.

Existing conditions and constraints

It is rare that authors have been able to conceptualize CALL beyond the bounds set by commercially available hardware. Morgenstern's objective, to 'stretch' the capabilities of existing hardware, and the example of the TICCIT project, where the driving force of a particular instructional design theory led to the redesign of the keyboard are the exceptions in CALL research and development, and only seem to occur when the aims of the project are particularly ambitious and the funding substantial. More often, CALL research and development occurs using readily available computer hardware. Much more of an attempt has been made by CALL authors to create their own software, including special-purpose authoring packages that enable others to create language learning materials easily. Even here though, commercially produced packages dominate.

The hardware and software combination is not the only initial condition that helps shape a CALL author's conceptual framework at the outset. Other points of departure may be determined by a prescribed syllabus or textbook or a decision to use existing materials, such as audio tapes, videos or videodiscs, as a point of departure. Where specific characteristics of the development environment are predetermined, the CALL project has to fit in with the parameters set. Such conditions, to a greater or lesser degree, shape the final outcome. In some cases these initial conditions provide a

very helpful springboard for a project, and one respondent remarked that working within constraints was an enjoyable and
motivating challenge: in other instances initial constraints may
seriously curtail what the author is able to achieve.

Existing hardware may impose constraints due to memory,
speed, or connectivity limitations. If a software development tool is
prescribed, it will have its own unique attributes and may cause the
development to proceed along a path determined more by its inherent strengths and weaknesses than the original CALL concept.
Similarly, in beginning with a set syllabus, text, or videodisc, the
essential setting for the activity is a given and will inevitably shape
the author's view of what is possible or amenable to development
under the circumstances. While such initial conditions may be a
positive advantage in providing the initial impetus for CALL development and may lead to better integration into the broader curriculum once the materials have been completed, the fundamental
impact on an author's conceptualization of CALL, especially if
freedom of choice over an item is not possible for some reason, has
to be acknowledged.

Hardware and software

The perceived capabilities and limitations of the hardware and
software used for CALL will affect a developer's conceptualization.
Both the literature and the CALL Survey findings show the pre-
dominance of the microcomputer in CALL, and we have seen how
an interpretation of CALL *only* in terms of standalone microcomputers can be unnecessarily restrictive. The ascendancy of two or
three particular models of microcomputer in CALL further con-
strains an author's view of what might be accomplished in CALL.

The dominance of specific microcomputers was alluded to as
early as 1986 in the *Byte* computer magazine (Smarte and
Reinhardt 1990: 392) which reported: 'It is interesting to note that
despite the Atari's and Amiga's potential, the general use personal
computer industry remained mostly divided between the MS-DOS
and (growing) Macintosh camps'. Given some of the Amiga's characteristics such as a multitasking functionality, an internal device
for video, stereo sound output, and a built-in English text-to-speech
device with controls for rate, pitch volume, inflection, and gender
of voice, the suitability of these features for language teaching and
learning and their absence in other machines, it is surprising that

these computers have not made more of an impact in language education, at least within the microcomputer context (see Commodore Amiga 2000 HD specifications). Whether hardware is chosen according to the needs of language teachers and learners, or due to factors quite removed from such considerations is questionable.

The software that is used for CALL materials development purposes also has an effect in shaping the final product. Usually some compromise has to be reached between the original conceptualization and the final implementation because of intrinsic limitations in the hardware or software, or simply the complexity of programming to create a certain functionality.

The CALL author is likely to have to adapt working methods to suit the conditions imposed by the hardware and software, most directly by the particular strengths and limitations of the software authoring tool. Any authoring system carries a certain conceptualization of CALL that is inherent in its presentational scheme and in the range of options it offers the author, particularly the interaction options that are available. Only the most flexible option, the high-level programming language, is relatively free of such constraints. Anything less than a high-level programming language carries predetermined structures, a condition that can have the effect of filtering the author's initial conceptualization. For example, an authoring system such as *Authorware* imposes its own structure in the development of a program by requiring the author to build branching structures by placing icons on a course flow line (Levy 1994*b*).

In *Authorware* the authoring interface is based upon the metaphor of the flow chart. Traditional flow chart symbols such as the decision icon and the process or step icon have their equivalents in the eleven icons provided by *Authorware* and these icons are used to develop the flow chart. The flow chart metaphor with its loop and conditional constructs is particularly helpful when branching structures are required in a project. Branching structures allow flexible question by question presentation, answer evaluation, and feedback, and *Authorware* is designed in such a way that such structures can all be written with relative ease. It is worth noting, however, that when the computer is used as a tool rather than a tutor, the flow chart metaphor becomes less relevant (see Chapter 7). In such a case the 'navigation through space' metaphor of hypertext might be more appropriate (see McKnight *et al.* 1991). Hypertext provides the ability to link or browse large amounts of information, without necessarily any evaluation of user input taking place as in a tutor. When compared with the design environment provided by *Authorware*, the hypertext arrangement is much less structured. Answer analysis is provided through *Authorware*'s nine different answer options: text, click/touch area, move object, pulldown menu, keypress, pushbutton, conditional, time/tries limit. It is the parameters of these options that determine the nature of the human–computer interactions that are possible. In the Snowy River Project (Levy 1994*b*) it would have been advantageous to ask open-ended questions requiring comment on why characters in the film speak or act as they do. But restrictions in the answer analysis capabilities of the authoring tool prevented this. As a result, multiple-choice and gap-fill type questions were the predominant choice for the Snowy River Project, corresponding to the click/touch area and text answer options. Given the number of possibilities for text entry and the difficulty of dealing with unanticipated text answers, the text answer option was inevitably limited. *Authorware* does not provide error mark-up features allowing text to be marked to indicate the nature of the error, possibly because *Authorware* is a general authoring system not designed specifically for language use—language-specific authoring systems tend to have more sophisticated mechanisms available for marking text (see Pusack 1983). At the present time even the most sophisticated systems employing artificial intelligence techniques lack the necessary power to derive meaning from text when the input is open-ended.

Hardware and software considerations, therefore, are going to have some effect on the nature of any CALL materials produced, often beyond that planned for in the original conceptualization. Nevertheless, careful selection of the hardware and software tools initially, especially with a view to their strengths and weaknesses in relation to a specific application, can significantly reduce detrimental interference through the development process. The strengths and limitations of a single-site, single-user machine are somewhat redefined for a multi-user, multi-site machine, such as the Internet.

Email and the Internet

Email and the Internet are able to provide opportunities for access and interaction with the world beyond the classroom, and as such enable new conceptual frameworks for CALL to be envisaged. These resources can help enlarge and enrich the space within which language learning can occur. The Internet has the potential to provide greater access to, and interactions with, *Materials*, *People*, and *Learning Environments*. These categories are convenient for this discussion, though the categories overlap and interrelate. The possibility of accessing these new resources means that novel types of language teaching and learning activities may be imagined for the first time.

Materials accessible via email or the Internet vastly increase the content options for CALL authors and language teachers. The materials may be downloaded as is, or incorporated in existing or new CALL applications. Archives and databases can include the usual multimedia options such as text, animations, audio, and video, or a subset thereof. Examples such as the OLA illustrate the importance of preparing such archives with great care, given that users distributed worldwide will have vastly different goals and requirements in using the materials. The OLA is, in my view, a particularly good example of how these diverse needs may be catered for.

Email and the Internet have extended access not only to materials, but also to people, fellow students, teachers, and colleagues around the world. Notable in this area are email exchanges of many kinds, particularly collaborative projects which involve students from different countries and cultures. Students participate in authentic and meaningful communication with a real communicative purpose in mind. Since in the typical case email is the only form of communication between students, who are at a distance from one another, great care is taken in the construction of the text. As Eck *et al.* (1994: 45) observe, rather than completing tasks or assignments for a teacher within the traditional education context and within the confines of the class group, with email the audience for the student texts is real and the motivation purposeful. This in turn invites commitment and accountability on the part of students.

From the point of view of conceptualizing CALL, the traditional bounds of the classroom and the class group are broken. Teachers and their students are now able to reach beyond the learning environment as it is defined locally, and thereby native speakers of the target language are able to become active participants in the learning process. This is a significant advance. No longer is it necessary to restrict a conceptualization of CALL to a single class-room, a single class, or a set of materials held locally. Email and the Internet break the barriers set by the human and material resources at a single site, thereby opening up the possibilities for learning immeasurably.

Email and the Internet have also precipitated new learning envi-ronments. For example, MOOs for language learning are steadily increasing in popularity, and a number are now available for differ-ent languages. MOOs are text based, but it is likely that they will move towards multimedia interfaces soon. At the time of writing, there is much interest in Virtual Reality (VR) environments on the Internet. Specially designed VR browsers (e.g. *Hot Java*) and VR languages (e.g. *Java*) enable three-dimensional, multi-user interac-tive simulations to be created and explored on the World Wide Web (WWW).[1] Such environments provide an exciting prospect for international language and cultural interaction in the future.

It is helpful to summarize some of the interaction types available using email or the Internet. Users may interact with:

(i) a site, to look at something and/or to bring it back (e.g. an archive, downloading), or to publish on the Net (uploading);
(ii) a 'form field' (e.g. a language test);
(iii) a teacher or student (e.g. a pen-pal exchange);
(iv) a group (e.g. a discussion group);
(v) a learning environment (e.g. a MOO).

Hefzallah (1990) provides a very useful overview of different kinds of mediated interaction within the context of telecommunications. In the list above, only the second item has not been covered in the preceding discussion. The 'form field' is one of the more advanced features of the Hypertext Mark-up Language (HTML), used for publishing materials on the WWW. This feature enables interactive forms to be created. Thus, users visiting a WWW site, or receiving documents utilizing form fields can enter information and submit the completed form. Generally, three form fields are available: text fields, 'binary' box fields, and drop-down fields. Using these field types, text entry, true/false, multiple-choice, ranking and gap-filling questions can be implemented. This function has great potential for collecting feedback, language testing, and teaching at a distance. Users located anywhere on the Internet may enter information, or answer questions that are then submitted to the primary site. For example, when visiting a home page on the WWW, the visitor may leave comments or answer a survey. Alternatively, form fields may be used as elements in the construction of language tests. The students complete the test remotely, and then submit their papers for feedback and marks which can be forwarded electronically. In distance education, form fields may be used to create interactive worksheets.

Describing CALL materials

CALL writers have attempted to describe categories for the many kinds of CALL software that have been produced, but, so far, no classification system has been convincing as a general vehicle for description. Classification schemes have included those that describe software by activity type, learning style, language difficulty, language skill, the technology utilized (e.g. interactive video), or the learning methodology (e.g. communicative CALL programs). In the CALL Survey, respondents were asked to mark categories within which they had developed software. In addition to those listed in the survey document itself, many more were added by respondents. Reflecting the findings in the literature, the responses in the CALL Survey showed a wide range of software types, including software associated with the four skills, specific technologies, and tutorial and tool roles for the computer. The software categories are not mutually exclusive and an item of software might fall into a number of categories simultaneously depending on what particular characteristic was the focus. This is not surprising perhaps, given the interactive and dynamic nature of CALL materials and the numerous ways they can be used, viewed, and described.

Further work needs to be conducted on developing a descriptive language for CALL materials that reflects their characteristics satisfactorily. Hubbard's call for a metalanguage to better facilitate CALL discussion and evaluation (Hubbard 1992: 42) is nowhere more urgently needed than for the description of CALL materials. An important first step in this direction has been taken by Chapelle (1994*b*) who argues for a three-level mechanism for the description of CALL activities: texts, genres, and contexts. The level of text refers to 'the actual linguistic data' that eventuate as a result of learner interactions; the level of genre summarizes outcomes at the text level to enable 'meaningful generalizations' to be made; and the level of context 'refers to features of the activities, topics, participants, and language that comprise the text and in which the text is embedded' (1994*b*: 42, 43). By formulating the descriptors at the higher levels of genre and context, derived from actual data on linguistic interactions at the text level, Chapelle suggests a mechanism for preventing the ambiguities that arise with higher levels of description, where a single descriptor may be used incorrectly to encompass many kinds of interaction, or where interactions which are fundamentally different are all gathered together under the same descriptive label.

Summary

The scope of CALL is broad and it draws upon many loosely related fields and disciplines. Though computer tools such as the word processor and electronic mail have on occasion been regarded as outside the realm of CALL, on the basis of the CALL Survey results especially, it is argued that such tools should be included. Though CLT was the broad umbrella term under which many authors described their philosophy of language teaching and learning, more precise terms were used when respondents described how this philosophy was applied in their CALL projects. The label CLT does not appear to be particularly helpful for describing the kind of CALL materials they create: a more precise language is required. Many authors were eclectic in their approach. Not surprisingly perhaps, the lack of a sufficiently powerful language for description was also apparent in the diversity of terms used to describe CALL materials. Materials were viewed from many perspectives, and the descriptors used varied correspondingly. As Hubbard suggests, and for which Chapelle has taken an important first step, to enable discussion, comparison, and evaluation to take place a broadly accepted and accessible descriptive language is required.

The review of the CALL projects completed so far illustrates the many points of departure. In bringing the strands together in Table 6.2, a number of key themes can be identified. Research-based and practitioner-led CALL projects are clearly evident. CALL projects do not necessarily have to be conceptualized top-down, but also emerge from lower-level practical concerns that result in a bottom-up approach. Hubbard's call for a bridge between these approaches appears justified. The Richards and Rodgers model helps to account for the different levels of conceptualization of CALL authors. The highest level in the model, that of Approach, corresponds to the higher level theoretical frameworks proposed by some authors. CALL projects that are articulated at the Approach level are normally specified at the lower levels of Design and Procedure as well. Similarly, CALL projects that begin at the level of Design tend to be specified also at the Procedure level, the level beneath. Such projects often begin with a curriculum specification, a task, or particular learning activity. As Richards and Rodgers point out, methodological development, and I would add CALL materials development, may begin at any level. The third theme concerns the fit between technology and language pedagogy. Reflecting on the closeness of fit at an early stage in a project is a critical acknowledgement of the strengths and limitations of the computer, that the qualities of this particular learning environment must be considered at the outset and that because the computer is not capable of doing all we might like it to do, we have to reconcile what we would like to do with what we are able to do. The development process itself may occur in a number of ways. It may be top-down or bottom-up; it may occur in discrete, sequential, well-defined stages, or it may occur through the progressive refinement of a simple prototype. The scale of the project and the number of people involved in its completion will affect the management and organization of the development process. Similarly the intended audience for the materials, be it a local, or a much wider audience, will affect how development proceeds. Existing conditions and constraints play an important role in shaping CALL projects. CALL authors tend to formulate their programs within the bounds of commercially produced hardware and software.

Conceptual frameworks are both enabled and shaped by the technology. The hardware and software constrain what can be done in ways that are not immediately obvious. Nevertheless, the kinds of interactions that are possible are governed by such constraints, and sooner or later the design has to be reconciled with the capabilities of the hardware and software. The Internet opens up the language learning options, particularly in terms of the materials, the people, and the learning environments to which teachers and learners may now gain access. For materials, archives or databases of digitized language learning materials may be accessed and downloaded from sites worldwide. Teachers and learners can communicate in new ways and with greater flexibility, enabling collaborative learning to take place at a distance. New learning environments that exist only in cyberspace can facilitate learning in ways not formerly imagined.

The emergence of the Internet into the wider domain shows the pace with which technology is evolving, and the speed with which a new entity can become mainstream—at least for most universities in the developed world. However, in spite of the excitement that a new technology causes, from the CALL author's and teacher's point of view there are still questions pertaining to teacher and student training and education, authoring, quality control, integration into the curriculum, and so on. While proving beneficial for students, such new mechanisms of communication clearly have ramifications for the teacher in having to provide the extra assistance. This assistance is needed in helping students to understand and use the new resource, and in preparing appropriate tasks so that the resource may be used to best effect. Also, care must be taken to properly evaluate the effects of tools such as email on the curriculum. Though email opens up many possibilities for written interaction via a keyboard, with limited time available for language study, is attention to the other language skills diminishing as a result? In other words, is the curriculum being skewed towards a certain skill, in a way that is inadvisable; or should this renewed focus on computer-assisted writing be welcomed?

In sum, the new technology needs to be used, tested, and evaluated in the field before its value can be determined. The interactions available via email or the Internet in many ways mirror those in the traditional classroom, but with horizons extended worldwide more materials, more people, and more learning environments can be made available to students. Time and distance need not pose the problems of old. In such environments there are enormous possibilities for collaborative teaching and learning, but we need to be conscious of the effects all the same.

When in the CALL Survey respondents were asked to describe how their language teaching/learning philosophy affected the way in which they developed CALL materials, some chose to answer by ascribing a role to the computer. The roles given were primarily the tutor and tool roles. These two broad roles for the computer were also clearly identifiable in the question specifically on roles. In the next chapter these roles for the computer and their implications are explored in more detail.

Notes

1. *Java* is an object-oriented programming language similar in many ways to recent versions of C, the high-level programming language. For object-oriented languages, in essence, the data and the programming are kept separate from one another in self-contained, working modules, which keep themselves in order as the application is constructed. A powerful use of *Java* is in the creation of 'applets'. These are mini-applications which can be delivered to users over the Internet as part of an HTML page. Applets run on the user's machine in a similar way to an ordinary application.

7. A tutor–tool framework

Introduction

The tutor–tool framework is offered here as a mechanism for addressing a number of concerns in CALL, the most far-reaching being the belief that all CALL is of the tutorial type, characterized by one-to-one interactions where the computer evaluates the student input and then presents the new material accordingly. In my view, this assumption has obscured some very important issues, notably in the areas of methodology, learner training, integration and the curriculum, the roles of the teacher and the learner, and evaluation. My thesis is that an understanding of the tutor and tool roles of the computer can help to clarify these issues, whilst at the same time usefully highlighting aspects of CALL that are too often overlooked.

In general terms, such frameworks are helpful for a number of reasons. In suggesting the tutor–tool framework originally, Taylor argued that a simple scheme for classification was required to help practitioners 'intellectually grasp' the diverse range of activities in educational computing (1980: 2). CALL is faced with similar problems. We have seen the diversity of CALL projects in the CALL Survey, and writers such as Chapelle emphasize that CALL is not one activity but many, often differing widely in function, character, and content (1994*b*). A framework is needed to help comprehend the many approaches being taken. Hubbard (1992: 42) with regard to the creation of a methodological framework for CALL, argues that a framework properly constructed has the benefits of providing: a metalanguage for discussion; a useful structure to conceptualize materials for development and research; and an 'integrated set of evaluation criteria for determining the fit of software with the teacher's views, the learner's needs, and the syllabus goals and constraints'. Hubbard's intention is not to suggest a paradigm or model to actively guide development in the field, but to suggest a non-dogmatic and flexible framework, based on existing frameworks, that can be used for discussion of materials development, evaluation, and implementation issues. Such a position is adopted here also, though the framework suggested is quite different from the one suggested by Hubbard. For materials to be developed in a coherent fashion, evaluation must take place. Dunkel's comprehensive article evaluating CAI and CALL shows how complex and insufficient this process has been (Dunkel 1991b). For effective evaluation to occur the major types of CALL have to be delineated. If the framework is a good one it will help practitioners make sense of what is already occurring in CALL, and it may assist developers and language teachers determine how CALL might be conceptualized in the future.

The conceptual framework

The broad conceptual framework proposed for CALL is the one originating from Taylor (1980), that of the tutor, tool, and tutee. The roles of tutor, tool, and tutee have been discussed in the CAI literature, and in relation to expert systems and artificial intelligence (Jonassen 1988; Chan 1989; Lippert 1989: 11). In the domain of artificial intelligence and education, Lippert finds applications of expert systems within each of the tutor, tool, and tutee roles: intelligent tutoring systems fit the tutor role, aids to support decision-making correspond to the tool role, and knowledge engineering places the computer in the role of tutee (1989: 11). This framework has further advantages. The role of the computer is often referred to in the literature and in the CALL Survey for describing CALL conceptualizations and subsequent use. Roles are 'non-dogmatic', and can complement each other, and such a view of CALL appears appropriate at the present time where there are a number of theories and models of second-language acquisition, many not tested in the context of CALL. Furthermore, Taylor's framework can be readily understood in relation to other taxonomies, such as Higgins's magister and pedagogue, Wyatt's instructor, collaborator, and facilitator and Phillips's games, expert systems, and prosthetic models, which can be accommodated within Taylor's classification, though some elaboration and extension will be necessary (see Higgins 1983; Wyatt 1984c; Phillips 1987). In the typology by Taylor, the primary distinction is that between the tutor and tool roles of the computer and this will be the major focus in the discussion that follows. Although these roles have been applied to CALL using different terminology (see Wyatt 1984*c*), the full implications have not as yet been explored.

At the outset it should be noted that the tutor–tool framework is presented as a means of providing an organizational schema in a diverse and complex field. It is not the only framework that could be applied, but it is a valuable one for current CALL activity. Like Hubbard's framework, Taylor's typology applied to CALL is meant to be 'non-dogmatic'. As Taylor suggests, one is not meant to be 'bound' by the framework but to use it when it proves valuable—the extent of its utility in CALL has yet to be tested (1980: 10).

Definition

Before continuing, we need to be clear about what is meant by the computer tutor and the computer tool. The essence of Taylor's original definition of the tutor is that the computer *evaluates* the learner, and then proceeds on this basis (1980: 3–4). Evaluation of the student by the computer is what sets the computer tutor apart from the tool. The tutor evaluates, the tool does not. For the tutor the computer is programmed to make decisions by evaluating the data that has been made available to it. Certain actions follow as a result. If learner input is the basis for the evaluation, the input may be judged right or wrong, or the evaluation of the input and the actions that follow may proceed with more subtlety. The computer tutor may make its judgement known to the student immediately through displaying feedback perhaps, or the result of an assessment may be withheld from the student's view and utilized in other ways, by reordering or restructuring the order of presentation of the content perhaps. In an Intelligent Tutoring System, for instance, a judgement might cause the student model to be refined, or it might lead the system to present the student with some remedial material that would not otherwise have been presented. Through all this, however, the fundamental decision, to program the computer to evaluate, has been made.

Merrill *et al.* (1986: 330) liken the tutor role to Computer-Assisted Instruction (CAI) and say: 'CAI is commonly used to refer to tutor applications, such as drill and practice, tutorials, simulations and games.' Computer tutoring extends much beyond activities such as drill and practice, however, as Last (1989: 32) rightly points out. Tutoring systems developed under the umbrella terms, ICAI and ITS, cater for much more sophisticated interactions. Such techniques have allowed software to be 'more individualized, interactive, and adaptive and therefore introduce instructional strategies beyond CAI's drills, tutorials, games and simulations' (Lippert 1989: 11).

Two assumptions are now made for the tutor role. First, the tutor role is assumed to imply that a teacher is not present. Secondly, the tutor role is held to imply that CALL work is taking place in self-access mode outside the conventional language classroom. With regard to the first point, Kearsley (1987: 93) observes: 'My impression of CAI, both traditional and intelligent, is that designers envision their programs as being temporary substitutes for the teacher'. The first assumption then, is that in the tutor role the intention is for the computer to be a *temporary* substitute for the teacher. However, this assumption is quite different from one which says that the computer in the tutor role *permanently* replaces the teacher. As Dunkel comments, 'researchers and users have come to reject the idea that CAI or CALL might serve as the totality of instruction' (1991*b*: 16), and the assumption of permanent replacement is not made here, even though some might argue that the computer is able to fulfil this role. The second assumption, an extension of the first, assumes that work with the computer as tutor occurs outside the classroom without a teacher present.

The question arises as to whether spelling checkers or grammar checkers are tutors or tools. On the one hand, they might be considered tutors because they judge correctness; on the other hand, they might be considered aids or tools because of their peripheral function in supporting the writing process. Here, I prefer to align them with the tutorial role of the computer, because they are programmed to evaluate correctness. Grammar and spelling checkers are only tutors in a very simple sense though, because, in the main, they make their evaluations or judgements item by item.

In contrast, the tool role for the computer is fundamentally non-directive. Tools are neutral, and how they are used is not predetermined. Since guidance is not available via the computer program, if language learners use tools, they will need to learn how to use them to best effect. The language teacher may well have a pivotal role to play in giving the student direction, or the learners themselves will have the knowledge and expertise to be self-directed, that is, to work autonomously. Although this may also be desirable with the computer as a tutor, for the computer as a tool, it is often essential that the teacher works with the student to help prepare for work at the computer. Computer work may then occur in the classroom, or in a self-access centre or computer laboratory. It is not assumed that when the computer is being used as a tool, the computer work must be completed in the classroom, though this may often occur. The tool tradition makes no assumption about the numbers of students working at a single computer, and so none is made here. These fundamental roles of the computer as tutor and as tool are now examined in more detail.

The tutor: the teacher in the machine

The roots of the tradition that places the computer in the role of tutor lie, to a large extent, in behaviourism and programmed instruction. Skinner's paper, 'The science of learning and the art of teaching', provides the imperative for the use of technology in the classroom. It uses a model of learning as a prescription for change in the classroom. This paper has been particularly influential in its view of education as a 'technology' (1954: 90, 93) and as an advocate of the use of specially designed machines for educational purposes. At a time when computers were in their infancy, especially in education, Skinner argued for the use of 'mechanical and electrical devices' to provide the optimal conditions of learning. These conditions provided for immediate and precise reinforcement of student answers, individual treatment, and progress at the desired rate.

Two beliefs become apparent through Skinner's paper. The first is the separateness of the work of the mechanical device and the work of the teacher. There is no suggestion of the teacher working with the machine and the learner to create an effective learning environment. The second view, related to the first, is the suggestion that the quality of the learning provided by the teacher is somehow inferior to that which the computer can provide. There is a strong sense that the machines are the preferred option for teaching and learning. Skinner says: 'the contingencies (the teacher) provides are far from optimal' (1954: 9), and as a 'reinforcing mechanism, the teacher is out of date' (1954: 94). Though the major tenets of behaviourism have been vanquished for the most part in language teaching and learning, in my view other aspects of the Skinner position persist. Views that suggest CALL activities may not be conducted collaboratively with the teacher, student, and computer working in unison, or that CALL work is only viable in the computer laboratory and not in the classroom can be traced back to the particular conceptualization of CALL advocated by Skinner. This is not to suggest that CALL in the computer laboratory or self-access centre, perhaps without a teacher, is not valuable, but it is imperative to recognize, as did the respondents to the CALL Survey, that this is by no means the sole option.

The publication of Skinner's article is said to have triggered the programmed instruction movement (Gagné 1987: 30). In turn this movement was the direct antecedent to Computer-Assisted Instruction (Schoen and Hunt 1977: 72; Osguthorpe and Zhou 1989: 9). If one considers ICAI as the most recent manifestation of CAI, then the development of this tradition can be traced back for almost forty years.

Early CAI has been closely associated with the role of the computer as instructor and the two predominant computer activities were drill and practice exercises and tutorial programs (Wyatt 1984c: 6). Wyatt summarizes the essence of early CAI as follows:

In the instructional role, the computer program presents material and conducts practice activities as an authority figure. It teaches students in a highly pre-planned fashion, and they have only to follow the directions and work at producing the anticipated language forms and responses. Students are actively involved in the learning process, but their role is that of responder rather than initiator. (1984c: 7)

Early CAI has steadily evolved, especially with regard to the level of sophistication of the computer–human interaction. The modern field of ICAI or ITS uses artificial intelligence techniques in a variety of ways. These include, for example, building a model of what the student knows at any particular time and then providing the appropriate instruction accordingly. Or it might involve the use of natural language processing to provide for the use of natural, or close to natural, language interaction between computer and student (Brierley 1991). Contemporary roles for the computer in the ICAI domain are described by Kearsley, who identifies five major paradigms for research and development: mixed initiative dialogues, coaches, diagnostic tutors, microworlds, and articulate expert systems (1987: 5). The adaptive intelligent tutoring systems of today that model learner performance, then guide the learner through the material accordingly, bear little resemblance to early programmatic CAI systems. Yet, although the computer in the role of tutor has evolved and matured, with computer tutors, the notion of the teacher in the machine rather than the teacher working with the student alongside the machine has remained.

The tool: the teacher/student and the machine

A role for the computer as a tool has been widely discussed in general and in relation to CALL (Weizenbaum 1984: 17; Brierley and Kemble 1991). This role for the computer is a fundamental one, it is the basis for the computer's widespread acceptance and use, and in the sense that the computer is an example of a tool used to augment human capabilities, it has had a long history (Phillips 1987: 282). In contrast to the tutor role of the computer, which is intended to emulate or replace the teacher in some way, the function of the computer as a tool is to enhance or improve the efficiency of the work of the teacher or student.

To illustrate the essence of the computer tool, Winograd and Flores seriously analyse the nature of the word processor (1986: 5–6, 36–7, 143, 164, 175). Their discussion is illuminating and it has important implications for the design of computing tools. The main points of their analysis are repeated here.

The first point concerns the transparency of the tool to the user. When working with a word processor, for example, the user is creating and modifying text that appears on the screen. The focus is not on the intervening mechanisms and devices that allow this to happen, unless there is a 'breakdown' of some kind, as in a computer problem, or a user who is unfamiliar with the keyboard. Rather, the focus is essentially the same as it is with other writing instruments such as the pen and paper. Winograd and Flores argue that it is the 'transparency of interaction that is of the utmost importance in the design of tools, including computer systems, but it is not best achieved by attempting to mimic human faculties' (1986: 164). Thus, a successful word processor lets the user operate on the words and paragraphs without being aware of formulating and giving commands. The user is focusing on the writing 'domain' rather than the computing domain. Winograd and Flores claim that it is only with a poor design that users are forced to deal with complexities that belong to the wrong domain (1986: 165).

The second point underpinning a successful tool lies in the close correspondence between the domain of the tool and the surrounding environment. Witness Winograd and Flores for word processing:

Its domain is the superficial stuff of language-letters and punctuation marks, words, sentences, and paragraphs. A word processor does not 'understand' language, but can be used to manipulate text structures that have meaning to those who create and read them. The impact comes not because the programs are 'smart' but because they let people operate effectively in a systematic domain that is relevant to human work (1986: 175).

To summarize this view, it is what people *do* that is the central concern, and then as a corollary, how computers can help them do it better (see Winograd and Flores 1986: 143). These questions can only be answered in relation to a background and set of concerns. In language teaching and learning, therefore, we must ask what people need to do in this context. There needs to be a close correspondence between the domain of the tool and the domain of the language learner so that the two domains may complement each other.

Winograd and Flores provide a framework for thinking about the design of computer tools for language learning. Designers need to consider what language learners need to do in their work and to specify this activity precisely. Syllabus demands, the objectives of the teachers, and the learners and research on teaching and learning are all potential contributors to the design of language learning tools because what constitutes authentic or inauthentic labour depends upon the contexts and the processes of learning. Thus defined, the objective in the design of the tool must be to enhance authentic labour and reduce inauthentic labour (see Kemmis *et al.* 1977).

Situating other frameworks and taxonomies

In this section a number of other taxonomies will be considered in relation to the tutor, tool, tutee distinction. In some cases the fit between taxonomies is clear, in others it is less compatible. In the latter case, suggestions are made for an improved taxonomy which will reconcile the other systems.

The taxonomies of Higgins and Wyatt fit most comfortably into Taylor's framework. Whereas Taylor's framework originated in the context of general child education in the school, the distinctions proposed by Higgins and Wyatt have been independently proposed by practitioners in the field of CALL, thus showing the broad applicability of the tutor, tool, tutee division.

Rather than speaking of the tutor or teacher role as such, Higgins (1983) contrasts the magister role of the computer with the role of pedagogue. As magister, the computer presents a body of knowledge to the student and 'chooses the order in which things happen, what is to be learned, and what kind of activity will be carried out' (Higgins 1983: 4). Higgins associates the magister role with programmed learning and, in the sense that the computer has the control, it is similar to early CAI programs. In contrast, the pedagogue role is the computer as 'slave', and it becomes 'a task setter, an opponent in a game, an environment, a conversational partner, a stooge or a tool' (Higgins 1983: 4). The pedagogue role is clearly more oriented towards the computer as a tool in Taylor's typology.

Wyatt's categories of role for the computer in CALL, namely instructor, collaborator, and facilitator, map directly onto Taylor's roles of tutor, tutee, and tool, respectively. Wyatt is one of the few writers on CALL to elaborate a collaborative, or tutee, role for the computer in CALL. In this role Wyatt describes the distinguishing characteristic of the students taking the initiative in any interactions with the computer. Wyatt's definition of collaborative is not as restrictive as Taylor's definition of the tutee—the student does not have to learn to program the computer—but the sense of the initiative being taken by the student is maintained. Wyatt writes of students 'trying to discover items of information that the computer alone possesses', and a simulation where 'students are themselves responsible for initiating and directing the activities that occur in the learning environment' (Wyatt 1984c: 8). Wyatt's collaborative role is also similar in many ways to the Conjectural role described by Kemmis *et al.* and discussed a little later in this chapter.

Phillips proposes three models that have the potential to reach paradigmatic status for CALL: the games model, the expert systems model, and the prosthetic model (1987). The latter two models fit comfortably within the tutor and tool categories discussed above.

The expert system model is closest to the tutor role of the computer, and Phillips attributes this model with a 'far more central and directive role for the computer' (Phillips 1987: 281). Phillips also likens this model to the magister role of the computer described by Higgins. Phillips emphasizes the use of AI to develop expert systems that can draw inferences and form judgements, so that the student can be successfully evaluated (1987: 281). Phillips's prosthetic model is so called because it focuses attention on the role of the computer as compensating for human limitations (1987: 282). According to Phillips at least, it is the compensatory features that qualify this model as prosthetic. The examples he gives are all tools and they include the word processor, databases, and spreadsheets. In 1987, Phillips described the games model as the dominant model, and judges its popularity to be the result of a reaction against tutorial CALL (Phillips 1987: 277). Such software has the characteristic features of a game with such elements as competition, either against the computer or between two or more players, a scoring system, and the notion of winning and losing. In attempting to relate Phillips models to the tutor–tool framework, the games model is more problematic and cannot immediately be accommodated so it is now given further consideration.

The games model was derived from close observation of the characteristics of CALL programs on microcomputers available at that time. Programs that fit this model have three characteristics according to Phillips: intrinsic motivation, the element of competition, and a set of rules that govern play. Phillips argues that this model has inherent limitations, especially affecting conceptualization and program design. The discrete nature of games activities and their small scale militate against their effective integration into the broader language learning curriculum. But more limiting, and of greater import perhaps, is the restricted variety of good games ideas. Phillips (1987: 279) gives the example of the business simulation that requires the student to run a food store and itemizes the many instances of programs based upon this idea (e.g. *Fast Food*—British Council). Similarly, the text reconstruction idea has many implementations (see Chapter 2). When a small number of text manipulation programs, small-scale simulations, and various matching activities are considered, the range of genuinely different CALL activities within this genre is clearly limited.

Therefore, Phillip's position is that though the games model played an important role in the early development of microcomputer CALL, it now stands as a model with considerable limitations. Whereas CALL programs will no doubt continue to be constructed around the games model, it does not appear that this model has the capacity to stand as a separate model. This was also the position finally taken by Taylor (1980: 10) who seriously considered extending the tutor, tool, tutee framework by adding a fourth mode, that of *toy,* which could, of course, include games. On reflection, however, Taylor decided that such software could be subsumed within one or more of the modes already described. Table 8.1 shows the roles and models discussed so far in relation to Taylor's original. Prescott's recent taxonomy is included to show that Taylor's roles continue to be reinvented.

The instructional role is again present in the typology developed by Kemmis *et al.* (1977). Kemmis's typology remains valuable, I believe, because it was derived from work on thirty-five projects and studies, all completed within the context of learning with computers. As the instructor, the role of the computer is the presentation of content, task prescription, and student motivation. This view fits comfortably within the tutor model already described. The two other roles for the computer suggested, are the Revelatory role and Conjectural role (Kemmis *et al.* 1977: 25–7). These roles are now considered with examples.

Consider first the revelatory role. The learning that takes place in this case is by exploration and discovery, as in a simulation for

TABLE 7.1   *The role of the computer in CALL*

	Higgins (1983)	Wyatt (1984c)	Phillips (1987)	Prescott (1995)
Tutor	Magister	Instructor	Expert system	Instruction instruments
Tool	Pedagogue	Facilitator	Prosthetic	Production instruments
Tutee		(Collaborator)		
Toy			Games	

example. Kemmis *et al.* speak of the computer 'revealing key ideas to the learner', and describe a view of learning that 'emphasizes closing the gap between the structure of the student's knowledge and the structure of the discipline' (1977: 25). Implicit in this view is the presence of a model of the significant concepts and knowledge structure of the discipline; through interaction with the computer the concepts are gradually revealed, or discovered by the learner. As such, this is a good example of inductive learning, where an understanding of a number of individual instances helps direct the learner to the discovery of a general rule or principle.

An illustration of this principle in practice in the CALL area is the *Loan* program described by Higgins and Johns (1984: 73). In this program students investigate a range of request forms that the computer generates for a particular situation. The students have to decide which is the most appropriate request form for a given situation and, thereby, are 'led to discuss and work out the principles that the program is using to relate language to situation' (1984: 74).

Within this framework Kemmis *et al.* also describe the computer's role in providing a rich learning environment and emphasize its information-handling qualities. Activities which require students to process a range of visual, auditory, and textual information, as in many multimedia applications, could also be situated within this model of learning. The underlying rules or principles may be more or less hidden for the learner, but as long as an underlying knowledge structure is present, the revelatory label would be appropriate. An example in language learning could be where a student is presented with a series of situations where a certain gesture is used. By reflecting on the visual and auditory context of use, the learner could discover the 'rule' or principle underpinning the use of that particular gesture.

The *Conjectural* role is where the computer provides a 'manipulable space/field/ "scratch pad"/language, for creating or articulating models, programs, plans or conceptual structures' (Kemmis *et al.* 1977: 25–7). This paradigm, according to Kemmis *et al.*, fits the learning approach of theorists such as Papert and involves the belief that 'knowledge is created through experience and evolves as a psychological and social process' (Kemmis *et al.* 1977: 26).

The best-known example of this idea is Seymour Papert's work with the LOGO language and the design of a microworld called

Mathland for certain kinds of mathematical thinking (Papert 1980). Papert variously describes a microworld as 'a "place" ... where certain kinds of ... thinking could hatch and grow with particular ease', 'an incubator', and 'a "growing place" for a specific species of powerful ideas or intellectual structures' (Papert 1980: 125).

The concept of the microworld developed by Papert has been considered in the field of language learning. Higgins (1982, 1985) developed a series of prototype programs called *Grammarland* by analogy with Papert's *Mathland* (Higgins 1982: 49). Higgins describes *Grammarland* as an attempt to 'create a miniature universe of discourse and a program which will manipulate things in that universe, answer questions about it, ask questions, or do any of these things at random if the user merely wants a demonstration' (Higgins 1982: 51). The microworld concept is also used in the Athena Language Learning Project (see Kramsch *et al.* 1985: 33), and Rowe (1990: 3) describes a language discovery environment for interactive video which is derived from Papert's microworld. In one of the most highly elaborated systems involving microworlds, Hamburger (1994) describes a second-language tutoring system called FLUENT (Foreign Language Understanding Engendered by Naturalistic Techniques). The latest prototype, FLUENT-2, provides a conversational partner for the user which realistically immerses the beginning student in the new language. The system incorporates the large natural language processing system developed for the ALLP Project which was described in Chapter 2. One graphical presentation of a microworld in FLUENT is called Kitchen World. Here the learner manipulates a human figure with a movable hand which is employed to manipulate objects in the Kitchen environment. Activities require learners to produce words, phrases, and sentences to achieve simple goals, and the system responds appropriately at each stage. The most recent manifestation of the microworld concept are the virtual worlds created in cyberspace, where users, and potentially language learners, can explore their shared environment and interact with each other at a distance as they do it.

Situating the conjectural and revelatory viewpoints in relation to the tutor–tool division is otherwise complicated by their reciprocal nature. The same computer activity can be viewed in two ways, one conjectural and one revelatory, depending on the focus at the time.

By way of illustration, consider concordancing as an example. Johns has written extensively on using this approach in language learning, and has described a methodology for the use of concordancers in the classroom (Johns 1986; 1988; 1990*a*; 1990*b*). Johns focuses on the *revelatory* nature of the activity when he says: 'By concentrating and making it easy to compare the contexts within which a particular item occurs, it organizes data in a way that encourages and facilitates inference and generalization' (1986: 159). On the other hand, concordancing work can equally facilitate hypothesis testing, or *conjectural* learning as evidenced by Johns when he says: 'Without questions given in advance, it leads the learner to generate his or her own questions, and to test them out against the evidence' (1986: 160).

The essential difference between the two kinds of learning becomes apparent when considering the source of the initiative in human–computer interactions (see Figure 7.1). In revelatory learning, the focus is on the computer supplying the appropriate data that reveal the pattern or the underlying rule. In conjectural learning it is the student that takes the initiative and interrogates the computer, testing an hypothesis that the student has already formulated. The latter role is more defensible in the case of concordancing because the computer is simply locating instances of a word in a text and presenting it to the user. There is no tangible knowledge structure built into the program that governs the selection of the items presented to the user—a word is located in a text or group of texts and it is simply grouped and presented. If there is a recognizable pattern, it is often more by good fortune than by design. If, on the other hand, instances were selected according to some guiding

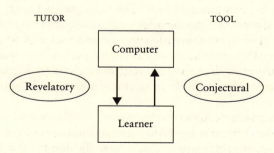

FIGURE 7.1   *The reciprocal nature of revelatory and conjectural learning*

principle built into the computer program, then the concordancing work would more properly fit into revelatory learning.

This discussion of concordancing gives an insight into how revelatory and conjectural learning might be situated in relation to the tutor–tool framework. Revelatory learning, in the sense that the control for what is presented resides in the computer program, is more akin to a tutor. Just as a teacher might present examples of an idea or concept for the purposes of illustration, to reveal the idea to the student, the computer can selectively present material to lead the student to an understanding of the idea. However, rather than deductive learning where the rule precedes the examples, the approach is inductive, with examples preceding the rule. Still the locus of control is with the teacher or tutor.

On the other hand, conjectural learning demands that the student take the initiative. The student, either independently or in collaboration with the teacher, decides on the hypothesis to be tested. In this case the computer acts as a tool: it simply locates and presents the information that the student uses to either substantiate or disprove the hypothesis. Under these circumstances the locus of control is with the student.

To conclude, therefore, it appears that the two kinds of learning articulated by Kemmis *et al.* do broadly fit into the tutor/tool categories, but it has been necessary to expand the categories beyond their original descriptions. The tutor category needs to include both deductive and inductive approaches to encompass learning that occurs as a direct result from exposure to the rule, or more subtly, through exposure to a sequence of events that lead the student to an appreciation of the rule.

The notion of conjectural learning also extends the traditional notion of the computer as tool. The example of Papert's work is helpful in illustrating the expanded definition of the computer tool. The concept of the microworld shows that a tool may be devised in such a way that new ideas and concepts can be manipulated and tested. Further evidence in this respect is given by Lippert (1989: 11) who gives the example of decision-making aids matching the tool role.

This discussion leads to the view that revelatory and conjectural roles for the computer are rather special instances of the tutor and tool. The similarities are visible when the locus of control, the source of initiative, and the requirement for external intervention

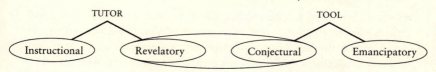

FIGURE 7.2   *Tutor and tool roles with learning paradigms*

(e.g. the teacher) are considered; the differences are apparent in the design techniques required, revelatory and conjectural learning often necessitating a very different approach to that dictated by traditional methods, especially for the initial conceptualization and later implementation. The interrelationship of the roles for the computer developed by Kemmis *et al.* and the tutor/tool roles are illustrated in Figure 7.2.

The strength of the tutor, tool, tutee typology as a general guide is that it can provide a viable, general framework for a discussion of many outstanding issues in CALL. These roles for the computer are well established in the broader context as well as in the area of language learning. CALL practitioners have independently advanced these roles for the computer in language learning, and a wide range of materials have been produced within their boundaries. The use of the computer as a tool, with the specific example of the word processor, has proved to be one of the most fruitful uses of the computer in CALL. Next, the implications of the tutor–tool framework is discussed in relation to methodology, the teacher, the learner, integration, and evaluation.

Implications

Overview

The tutor–tool framework has implications for program design, methodology, teacher and learner expectations, the teacher's role and the relationship of work completed at the computer with work completed away from it. The discussion argues that many models of CALL, whilst purporting to be general models for CALL, are in actuality models derived from a conceptualization of CALL as tutor, overlooking, for example, the role the teacher might play in the implementation phase. Though the notion of tutor may be nowhere included in the model, the pervasive effect of early CAI approaches to the use of the computer in CALL often has led to the omission of the teacher in present-day frameworks. As a result, when considering CALL, it is necessary to distinguish between the tutor and tool roles for discussion to be meaningful. The tutor and tool approaches will now be dealt with in turn, and this will be followed by a SWOT (Strengths, Weaknesses, Opportunities, and Threats) analysis applied to them.

Methodology and the learning environment

Long defines methodology as 'the instructional strategies and learning processes employed by both teachers and learners in performing tasks which they engage in separately, in groups or as a whole class' (1990: 34). With the computer tool the methodology—the instructional strategies, the learning processes, and the tasks—resides outside the domain of the computer, and the various aspects that combine to form a methodology have to be devised by the language teacher or the student, or both together. In the role of tutor, the methodology used in CALL is predominantly expressed through the design of the computer program, as in TICCIT for example, where the instructional strategy is built into the program, or in projects like *France InterActive* where a specific CALL methodology is built into the program (Ingraham and Emery 1991). Wyatt appears to be speaking of a computer tutor when he perceptively observes that the computer 'is a medium that reveals the methodological assumptions of its authors with unusual clarity' (Wyatt 1984*a*: 10). On the other hand, for the computer as tool, the environment external to the computer is considered to be the critical factor in determining the success or failure of a program (see C. Jones 1986: 171; G. Jones 1986: 179).

Computer tools may be used to facilitate new learning environments. At the same time, computer tools in themselves are neutral. They are designed to perform certain functions which may or may not lend themselves in some way to language learning. If these tools do have the potential to contribute in some respect to language teaching and learning, then the critical issue is how exactly these tools should be used to support the process.

The use of concordancing programs is one example of computer tools that have potential for language teaching and learning. At its most basic, all a concordancer does is search through a text, or a collection of texts, picking out all the instances of a keyword or phrase, then presenting the results in context on the screen. The concordancer utilizes the machine's ability to search quickly and reliably, and as such it makes full use of the innate qualities of the computer, its storage capacity, its speed and its accuracy. Whether this particular function of the computer is of any value in language teaching and learning is beside the point as far as the designer is concerned. The goal in the design of such a tool will be in choosing the best algorithm to facilitate high-speed searches. Then the CALL fraternity might consider how best to make use of this tool. Tribble and Jones (1990) provide many ideas on how the concordancer might be used. For Johns the tool precipitated a new methodology, a concordance-based methodology, later named data-driven learning (Johns 1986: 158; Johns 1990*a*: 2).

Another good example of the computer tool in language learning is email. Again once the tool has been recognized as having potential in language teaching and learning, the question of how it might best be used to support language learning is the all-important question to be resolved. Again it requires methodologists with experience in language teaching and learning and the technology to suggest an approach. Warschauer (1995) addresses this question for email in his book 'Email for English Teaching'. He introduces the ways in which teachers can use email and the Internet in collaborative work locally and at a distance. He considers how these tools might be utilized for accessing ESL materials and resources, and for cross-cultural communication. Importantly, he concludes with a section on how the various components might be integrated into an educational program.

In describing a set of principles for the design of CALL software, Hubbard argues that, 'First, in the earliest stages of the design process, individual software developers and development teams should describe the language teaching approach to be targeted' (1988*b*: 251). In a later article, Hubbard (1992: 39) goes on to articulate his methodological framework which links together CALL materials development, evaluation, and implementation. Hubbard makes the assumption that the issues that require consideration in creating CALL materials are the same as those which must be taken into account in describing a language teaching method (1992: 63).[1] In making this assumption, Hubbard orientates his framework more towards the teacher than the tool. The methodological framework appears to work well when the computer is cast in the role of tutor and where all of the levels and their components need to be considered. When the computer acts as a tool, however, a number of the components appear to have little or no relevance. The network of elements that make up Hubbard's methodological framework, is based upon Richards and Rodgers's analysis of method discussed at length in Chapter 6. To recap, this model is hierarchical, and conceptualizes language teaching method at the three levels of Approach, Design, and Procedure. With this in mind, each level will now be discussed.

At the level of Approach, the components here described tend to be external to the program itself. With a tool, for example, linguistic assumptions do not have to be made 'as explicit as possible' in the program as maintained by Hubbard (1992: 47). Although this correctly applies to a tutor, for a tool such thinking tends to occur outside the domain of the program. Rather than the initial conceptualization involving the means of delivery, that is, the computer delivery system as for a tutor, for a tool the initial conceptualization has already been formulated and the objective is to design or match the attributes of the tool to the existing framework. In the first instance, the machine is explicitly tied to the initial conceptualization, as indicated by Hubbard's inclusion of the computer delivery system at the level of Approach; in the case of the tool, if it is to be utilized at all, it must be compatible with a framework that has already been articulated.

At the level of Design, with the computer as tool, again only a small number of the components of Hubbard's framework appear to have relevance. Of these elements, language difficulty, in the sense of accommodating the language proficiency levels of users, program difficulty, the overall operational complexity of the program, and hardware and programming language considerations deserve careful consideration by the designer of a tool for language learners. On the other hand, the other components do not have direct relevance. In a concordancing program, for example, the tasks would be set by the teacher or would be devised by the learner apart from the computer, making program focus, learning style, and classroom management factors externally determined. Similarly the learner focus, the language skill area on which the software concentrates, is externally determined since the software is quite passive in its role as a tool, and the content, for a concordancer at least, is the database of texts or corpora and this would normally be chosen by the teacher—the functioning of the program as a tool is not in any way dependent on the material it is required to process.

It is at the level of Procedure that Hubbard's framework is most problematic. Having this level in the methodological framework means that the program is devised in such a way as to include 'the tactics and strategies used by teachers when the method is being used' (Richards and Rodgers 1986: 28). Whilst this is applicable if the role of the computer as tutor is assumed, it cannot be wholly accepted if the computer operates as a tool. With regard to elements prescribed at the Procedure level, the fundamentally neutral role of the computer as tool would not require input judging and feedback to be included as Hubbard maintains. However, the nature of the presentational scheme, for example the use of colour, graphics and sound, the screen layout, and the help and control options would still need to be addressed as Hubbard suggests.

For the computer as a tool, looking at the appropriateness of the components at the three levels shows that many elements are not relevant and, in fact, the separation in terms of levels is not appropriate. For a tool, generic, and on the whole non-language, specific design elements are the major concern, though factors such as the language level of the instructions used during the program's operation and general levels of operational complexity do have a bearing on the design of a tool for language learners. But, for the most part, rather than appealing to a specialized framework for CALL program design derived from a model of a language teaching method, in the case of a tool it would appear more appropriate to analyse the tasks the students need to complete, then look carefully at the design of the tool. For the tutor, there needs to be a methodology built into the CALL program governing instructional variables such as the presentational scheme and the modes of human–computer interaction; for the tool, the methodology resides outside the computer which holds an entirely neutral position as far as methodology is concerned.

The teacher

The teacher may have a minimal role, or be excluded altogether, if the CALL materials have been conceived as a self-contained, tutorial package; alternatively, the teacher may play a pivotal role in the actual delivery of the materials, which is often the case with a tool. In the tutorial tradition, there is a separateness between CALL and non-CALL work. In contrast, for the computer as a tool, generally many more demands are made on the teacher. Such demands can include task setting and learner training, which tend to be more extensive with the tool compared with the tutor. A good example is the use of concordancing techniques in language learning, where considerable attention has to be given to the construction of the tasks and the concordances that will best support them (see Tribble and Jones 1990). With a view to using the computer as a tool, Jordan (1988: 142) marks three areas that should be considered in a 'teacher-based' approach for designers of CALL programs: 'taking advantage of the teacher's presence; facilitating use by teacher and students-authoring facilities; using the computer for visual presentations'. The teacher may be involved in assisting students as they work at the computer or designing broader tasks that in some way involve the computer for their successful completion. Only with an awareness of these two distinct roles of the computer will the teacher be able to respond accordingly.

The tool role is likely to place greater demands on the teacher in preparing for the computer's use, and the notion of using the computer to 'free' the teacher, a notion often associated with computer tutors, is not likely to be the case with computer tools. This view is further supported by the examples earlier on the use of the concordancer. For the effective use of email, Warschauer (1995) suggests the language teacher needs to:

- choose the appropriate software;
- learn how to use the email system confidently;
- train students;
- organize access to computers;
- prepare handouts, including basic easy to read instructions;
- organize assistance for students in the early stages of use;
- prepare suitable task-based learning projects;
- monitor progress, and provide guidance on an ongoing basis.

Though extra assistance may be available in some instances, usually all of these tasks will fall to the language teacher. For computing tools, such as the concordancer or email, considerable effort has to be put into creating suitable language learning tasks, and in creating a suitable working environment within which the tools can be used effectively.

The learner

One of the oft-stated benefits that the computer brings to language learning is greater learner autonomy, and recent CALL collections emphasize learner centredness and learner-driven CALL (Jung and Vanderplank 1994: p. viii). Gremmo and Riley (1995), in giving a historical overview of autonomy, self-direction, and self-access in language teaching and learning, note recent and increasing discussion of issues related to learner autonomy. They provide a useful background, and track the evolution of these issues by reviewing philosophical developments in education, wider access to education, reactions against behaviourism, and new options provided by educational technology. Though educational technology has contributed to the spread of autonomy and self-access, Gremmo and Riley remark that the cost is often a 'retrograde and unreflecting pedagogy' (1995: 153). In fact, they are rather critical of the contribution of such fields as CALL, and they argue that they are far from essential for the understanding and practice of self-directed learning. They also stress that learner training for autonomous learning in this context is absolutely essential (1995: 160).

Learner training for successful learner autonomy and self-access use will be necessary in all circumstances. However the training required will differ for computer tutors and computer tools. If the computer tutor has been well designed, it will have a tutorial, context-sensitive help, and a management system that will both guide the learner and be responsive to the particular needs and level of the learner. For the computer tutor, feedback mechanisms must be error free, and feedback must be provided at the appropriate times. If the computer tutor satisfies such criteria, then it can provide real autonomous learning opportunities for the student. However, in the role of tutor, the computer, the teacher, and the student have to 'trust' the computer to do its job properly. Control is delegated to the computer to manage the learning, and in consequence, students will rely on its judgements. If the computer cannot be relied upon, it should probably not be allowed this relationship with the learner.

For the computer tool, less is required of the computer program in terms of teaching or managing the student, because the computer's role is neutral and it does not evaluate the learner as such. On the other hand, the computer is not managing the interactions either; the learner has the responsibility here and will have to determine whether the use of the tool is appropriate and how best to make use of it. Really knowing how to use a computer tool is not a trivial issue, and learning training will be needed, either through the auspices of the teacher in conventional classes or through some other kind of provision. For collaborative email projects, Eck *et al.* stress the considerable demands placed on learners who, as well as needing technical know-how, have to conduct extensive planning and long-term coordination (1994: 46). For a tool, a tutorial might be well able to help the student learn the mechanical operation of the program, but it is not designed, nor should it be expected, to be able to provide guidance on when the program should be used, and whether it is suitable for the task at hand: only the student can do that.

Integration and the curriculum

That proper integration of CALL is critical for its ultimate success has been noted by many authors including Rüschoff (1984), Farrington (1986: 199), Benwell (1986: 2), Garrett (1991: 42), Robinson (1990: 160), and Warschauer (1995: 49, 52, 62). Garrett also claims that 'integration of CALL and classroom activities can be mutually supportive and result in more efficient learning' (Garrett 1988: 194). Robinson (1991: 160) reports the findings of two studies by Robinson *et al.* (1985) and Verano (1987) and concludes: 'These findings highlight the importance of integrating individual CALL work with the total program of language instruction, including the classroom, rather than configuring it as an independent, supplementary activity.' According to Farrington (1986) and Garrett (1991), if CALL is ever to be accepted by the language teaching community as a whole, CALL work must become a fully integrated component of the language teaching and learning environment. Therefore, the question of how materials integration is to be accomplished when tutor and tool roles for the computer are proposed, is one of some moment.

Before discussing how integration relates to the tutor and the tool roles of the computer, it is helpful to introduce two special terms, 'logical' and 'physical', borrowed from the field of structured analysis. In the area of computer systems development, structured analysis refers to the systematic study of some business area or application, usually leading to the specification of a new system. In structured analysis logical and physical are usually used to describe two kinds of system model. The point of note for this discussion is that the logical model is implementation-*independent* whereas the physical model is implementation-*dependent* (DeMarco 1979: 230). This terminology is useful in CALL because integration is a twofold problem. It involves the 'logical' problem of deciding what aspects of language work should be handled by the computer and what should be in the hands of the teacher or student. Also it involves the 'physical' problem, concerning implementation-dependent factors, which closely involves the role of the teacher, locating the computers appropriately, in the classroom or self-access centre for example, plus the concomitant access issues. Whilst liberties are being taken with the use of the term 'physical', as strictly defined within structured analysis, the issue of the training of students in the requisite computing skills might also be considered an aspect of the physical problem, because if an experienced teacher is not present or available, some tutorial substitute needs to be offered. That the logical and physical sides can have an independent existence, is shown in circumstances where the logical problems have been resolved satisfactorily, but the physical problems have not, thus preventing full and effective integration of CALL work into the broader curriculum.

In the tutorial tradition, the logical problem reduces to deciding what work should be completed at the computer and what work should be completed away from it. There is a separateness between CALL and non-CALL work, derived as discussed previously from Skinner. This separateness extends from the logical to the physical dimension and would usually result in the computers in one space, a laboratory or self-access centre, and a classroom without computers, but with a teacher, in another. CALL work is completed in a special computer area, ostensibly under the control of the computer, while non-CALL work, work that requires the special qualities of the human teacher, is conducted in the classroom, ultimately under the control of the teacher. Both computer and teacher may relinquish control of their respective spaces, either by design or on principle, but the ultimate control still lies with each of them. An example of this kind of scenario is given by Benwell (1986), who, in an imaginative and flexible way, describes a 'German morning' that lasts for four hours. Basically, the class is divided in two with one half working orally with two teachers and the other half doing practical 'remedial and reinforcing work' using computers in a computer laboratory. The groups are then switched. This arrangement is flexible and allows for smaller sized groups when working with the teachers. The notion of 'freeing' the teacher is also employed by Benwell, in this case to facilitate 'intensive oral work' (1986: 4).

In the tradition of the computer as tool, logical and physical integration pose different problems. Logically, there need be no division of labour as such, because of the mutually supportive, complementary nature of human and tool. With the computer tool, the goal is full integration, both logically and physically. Unlike the tutor, there need be no division of labour as such. Instead with the tool, the student and the computer, and possibly the teacher, engage in a collaborative effort to accomplish a learning task. If the computer tool can assist, it will be used; if it is inappropriate it will not. Chris Jones (1986) describes a wide range of examples in which CALL work can be integrated into classroom work in the way just described. Although the computer is not always being used as a tool specifically, all the activities 'involve the learners in work away from as well as at the keyboard, and all depend on co-ordination and advance planning by the teacher' (C. Jones 1986: 177). As such the computer is not the central focus; instead it functions as a support for the teacher and learner.

From the physical perspective, for students to be able to use the computer as a language learning tool whenever they need it, computers have to be readily available in the classroom as well as the self-access centre, or computer laboratory. At present, it is often the case that computers are located in a space quite separate from the classroom. This arrangement makes it difficult to use the computer regularly as a tool, especially if learners require training or tasks need to be formulated, perhaps with the help of the teacher. However, as computers become more compact, the use of special-purpose computer tools in the classroom, at the moment only represented by spelling checkers and word translation machines, might become far more common. For example, small hand-held machines, those that can recognize hand-writing such as the computers described under the name of Newton technology, are likely to appear in the classroom in the future (see Weiman and Moran 1992: 129).

Finally, in this discussion of integration and the use of the computer as a tool, the problem of students using the computer in the self-access centre needs to be recognized. Whereas in the classroom students have the teacher on hand to orchestrate the learning tasks to which the computer as tool contributes, in the self-access centre such support is often not available. Tools, unlike tutors, do not provide a framework for the tasks to be completed and so the onus is on the teacher or the student to prepare the way for the use of the computer in this circumstance.

Evaluation

Evaluation studies to date have shown a tendency to view all CALL materials as tutorial in nature. Treating all CALL activity as one kind of instructional activity has led to considerable confusion in evaluating its effectiveness (see Dunkel 1991*b*). The tutor–tool distinction is a crucial one for evaluation purposes. In my view the evaluation of a computer tool is a twofold problem. First the tool needs to be evaluated in relation to other computer tools of a similar type. Be it a word processor, database, concordancer, email, or videoconferencing system, the system (or program) has first to be able to accomplish its purpose effectively. Questions such as ease of use, the quality of the user interface, screen design and organization, and so on are all issues that would arise at this initial stage. Sensitivity to user characteristics and needs should of course be paramount, especially given that such programs if adopted will be used by non-native speakers. This stage might be referred to as an assessment of the qualities of a system in relation to other systems of the same generic type. Then, the computer tool needs to be considered in relation to how it might be used in language teaching or learning. What methodology is appropriate for this particular tool? The second stage would aim to evaluate the tool in its context of use, in this case for language learning. Such an approach distinguishes between the tool itself, and the learning environment into

204 The tutor–tool framework

which it is incorporated. A perfectly good tool may be used incorrectly, or it may simply be inappropriate for the task. In an evaluation study, therefore, negative results may refer to problems with the computer program or system, but they may just as easily refer to inappropriate use of the tool, or poorly defined or unsuitable learning tasks.

The computer tool must be evaluated on the basis of its effectiveness in supporting the task for which it was designed: the learning task itself is beyond the domain of the computer. The computer does not set the task. Instead the learner comes to the computer with a task that the use of the computer can help the learner complete through enhancing the process or product in some way. The tutor, on the other hand, needs to be evaluated according to its effectiveness in helping students learn directly, not indirectly as with the tool. The function of a tool is not to teach, though in the use of a tool one may inadvertently learn, and once proficient with the use of a tool, one may accomplish tasks more efficiently and effectively. The difference in perspective is an important one.

This point emerges from an investigation of the positive and negative potentials of word processing (Pennington 1991b). In reviewing a wide range of research studies, Pennington notes the mixed results of effectiveness evaluations for the word processor. This is not surprising given that the criteria used for many of the evaluations at this time assumed that the computer was a tutor and not a tool. Pennington says, 'the degree of success of any application of word processing in an ESL setting will ultimately be determined by the nature of the users and the circumstances of use, rather than directly by the attributes of the medium' (1991b: 267). This statement captures the essence of the issue. The 'attributes of the medium' for word processing are neutral. They can be evaluated, but for the word processor this means evaluating how well the tool helps the user accomplish the task, not how well the computer can teach. The kind of evaluation studies required, therefore, need to be of the kind conducted by Haas (1988), for example, which focus on how the writing medium shapes the writing process. Finally, Pennington emphasizes the crucial role of the teacher in determining the success or failure of word processing with ESL student writers. The qualities of the tool, its neutrality in teaching/ learning terms, and the need for the appropriate guidance to be given by the teacher are emphasized.

Strengths, weaknesses, opportunities, and threats

Tutor: strengths and weaknesses

The strengths of the tutor role for the computer lie in its flexibility to provide language instruction when a teacher is not available. This flexibility can allow students to learn at a 'time, place, and pace' that suits them. Even when a teacher is available and students are attending a regular language course, the computer tutor can provide valuable supplementary work, especially extra language practice.

Ideally, the student can choose to work at any time of day, given access to a computer. That may involve study somewhere on the campus of an institution, in a self-access centre, computer laboratory, library or elsewhere, or through the use of a computer at home, or at a distance. Learner characteristics can be accommodated by the mechanisms in the computer program itself and through allowing the student control over pace, content, and learning styles.

The degree of success of the computer in this role depends upon a number of issues: ease of access to computers, the degree to which computer management and control of human–computer interaction is effective, the aspects of the language that can be covered in this way, the validity of direct teaching of language, and broad teacher acceptance.

In the tutorial role, where the student is generally working alone without the teacher, the computer has reliably to give the student the right kind of guidance and advice every time the program is used; there is no second wave of feedback that can come with a teacher's presence to act as backup (see Rüschoff 1984: 28). The computer program must be completely reliable. If for some reason the student is provided with incorrect or incomplete feedback in answer to a question and the deficiency is not made known to the student, then serious problems can result. The success, therefore, of the computer in the tutorial role hinges on how reliably the program manages the student's learning and on how timely, accurate, and appropriate is the feedback, help, and advice given. This point is supported by Kenning and Kenning (1990: 34) who argue that 'the shortcomings only loom large if the computer–learner dialogue constitutes the sole, or main, component of a learning experience, as in the case of a tutorial package used on a self-access basis'.

One of the goals of the Ng and Olivier study (1987) was to see what aspects of language learning the computer could best address. Supported by results from the questionnaire, Ng and Olivier's results showed that the computer could best handle reading, followed by writing, listening, and speaking in that order. At the moment the computer cannot deal satisfactorily with the teaching and learning of the spoken skill, so unless this skill does not form part of the learner's goal in language study some other form of learning environment is required. The use of the computer as independent tutor, therefore, at present must always be accompanied with a caveat: that it can only deal effectively with certain language skills. In the tutorial tradition, there has also been an emphasis on the computer dealing with the more 'onerous' aspects of language learning such as drill-and-practice. With the restricted number of language skills and the more routine and predictable parts of foreign language teaching being the chief areas of language addressed, the role of the computer as tutor is one that is strictly limited. Again, the tutorial role of the computer is heavily dependent on the level of sophistication of the programs that operate under this banner. That is not to say, however, that the areas of language learning that tutorial programs do address are not of considerable value.

Tutor: opportunities and threats

The urge to build a machine capable of exhibiting human intelligence is proving to be extraordinarily compelling and long-lasting. Current trends indicate that this quest for the intelligent machine will continue for many years to come. For language learners, intelligent tutors that cover aspects of language in a suitably reliable way have the potential to liberate students from the circumstances within which they are currently obliged to learn a language. The experiments that are currently taking place in ICAI and ITS have the potential to provide greater flexibility for students, especially in time and place of study and could open up language learning to those who are currently restricted through geographical isolation and work or home responsibilities. More specifically, improved models of learning have the potential to provide improved CALL environments within which language learning can occur. Increased sophistication of systems promises richer, more efficient, and hence more enjoyable language learning experiences. Whilst the applications of current tutors are limited for language learning, there is no reason not to believe that their functionality will not steadily improve in the future.

In the case of the computer as tutor, the teacher's fear of being displaced by the computer arises. While it is unlikely, given the complexities for the computer of handling natural language and speech understanding, in years to come it is likely that computers will be able to 'free' language teachers from an increasing amount of work that has traditionally been regarded as the teacher's domain of responsibility. Here the central issue concerns delegation of control to the computer. The teacher's and the computer's roles need to be carefully circumscribed within the tutor framework and the tasks ultimately assigned to the computer will need to be carefully examined, especially as computers become more accomplished as intelligent tutors. The delegation of responsibility to the computer to manage learning in this way must be made wisely: just because a computer *can* complete a task does not mean that it *should* (Weizenbaum 1983). At the moment the tasks that are allocated to the computer in CALL or ICALL directly reflect the computer's present capabilities and limitations. So far we have not had to face the dilemma presented by Weizenbaum. On the other hand, as computers increase in sophistication, this issue may not be resolved so simply, without a more assertive stance being taken by the language teaching profession. This mirrors some of the ethical and other considerations being faced in the professions, in medicine, for example, where there exists a real choice and the positions on both sides need to be weighed carefully.

Finally, the potential threat of isolation and mere vicarious experience of language must be considered. Virtual reality, for example, can isolate the individual from the real world with helmets, goggles, and gloves. Such experiences, whilst having the potential to simulate real communicative situations, nevertheless remain illusory. Again Weizenbaum (1983: 111) shows in his discussion of science and the compulsive programmer that people can become locked into worlds created by machines and become isolated as a result. Obviously, to become confident and proficient language users, the goal of the majority of language learners is to be able to interact with people face to face in the same physical space using language to accomplish real world tasks. Quite when the rehearsal, utilizing simulated tasks and simulated environments, should end and the live performance, using tasks and environments that relate to the learner's world after instruction is complete, should begin is a critical issue, and one that will remain in the future.

Tool: strengths and weaknesses

The use of the computer as a tool was its original function and this role continues to be a major one, both within the language teaching field and outside it. The most common instrumental uses of the computer are the word processor, the database, and the spreadsheet. In language teaching, tools have included email, conferencing programs, monolingual, bilingual, and multilingual dictionaries, thesauruses, concordancers, and more recently archives accessible via the Internet such as the OLA. Two extensive surveys have demonstrated the value of the computer as tool. Johnson (1985: III-5) concluded from her survey that 'the use of a computer as a tool to accomplish functional tasks has far greater potential for second language learning than traditional or even communicative CALL.' In an extensive survey of CBI projects, Kearsley *et al.* (1983: 93) observed that the predominant role of the computer in the projects reviewed, was as a tool for the student, indicating a move away from the original philosophy of CAI where computers were employed to 'deliver instruction'.

The fundamental qualities of a tool largely determine the strengths and weaknesses of the computer in this role. The tool is designed to assist the human, so that tasks may be accomplished more efficiently and more effectively with the aid of the tool than without it. The human is in direct control of the tool. The tool itself is quite neutral in terms of how it is used, and it can equally be used for the wrong purpose, or in the wrong way, as for the right one. In comparison with the tutor, the tool is non-directive whilst the tutor is directive, the latter offering some form of guidance or determining structure within which interaction can take place. The tool does not have a methodology attached to it as does the tutor, and so, as with any tool, the student needs to learn how to use it effectively. The strengths of the tool, therefore, lie in its versatility and capacity to augment human capacities; the weaknesses derive from its neutrality and the fact that it offers the user no guidance on its use in context, that is, beyond the mechanics of its actual operation. For example, having done the tutorial one may be familiar with all the functions of a word processor, but still not be able to write.

The word processor is a good example of a tool used in CALL and it remains the most popular. It offers no feedback, or comment on what the student writes: it is merely a convenient tool that allows text manipulation, editing, and revision to be accomplished more easily. Whether the word processor improves writing or makes it more effective is debatable on the basis of research so far conducted (Pennington 1991*b*), but it undoubtedly allows words, sentences, and paragraphs to be changed or moved more easily than the preceding technology, pen and paper. The act of writing involves the creation of words, sentences, and paragraphs and frequently revision. It is for this basic manipulative function that the tool is designed. Whether it improves writing or not is really beside the point, since the tool was not designed primarily for this purpose, although writing improvement may well be a corollary given the ease with which text can be manipulated.

Tool: opportunities and threats

There are many opportunities for the use of the computer as a tool in CALL. As well as the more well-known applications such as the word processor or email, new learning environments such as MOOs are becoming available on the Internet. They are best exploited by first considering what learning tasks are desirable for a particular group of students, and then searching for possible computer applications that could assist with them. The computer applications would likely make use of the main characteristics of the computer, its ability to store large quantities of visual, audio, and textual information (e.g. multimedia) and its ability to search, locate, and retrieve quickly (e.g. concordancing). Applications that use the computer as a convenient scratch pad for the initial conception and development of ideas (e.g. a word processor), or for the manipulation and or/testing of ideas (e.g. microworlds) are other possibilities. More specific language learning applications are likely to derive from a clearer understanding of the cognitive processes that are involved. It is only when these processes are reasonably clear that specialized tool will be designed to help activate or in some other way support them.

In a language learning environment, given the neutrality of computer tools, it is essential that students are able to seek and find advice on when and how to use the tools most effectively. With no guidelines built in, students will need assistance from teachers, and teachers from CALL researchers, to obtain the appropriate guidelines. For example, Haas has shown that word processors have affected planning for both learner writers and experienced writers (Haas 1988). Both groups plan less with the word processor when compared to pen and paper. This knowledge might lead teachers and through them learners, to complete the initial planning stages of a piece of writing on paper, only using the word processor for later stages in the writing process. If such advice is not forthcoming, there is the threat that tools will be used inappropriately and fragmentation will result. The question of integrating CALL work and non-CALL work is similarly defined. When a teacher is present with students working on CALL in the classroom, guidance and advice is available when required. In the self-access centre, however, careful preparation will need to occur so that students have the requisite learning strategies to use computer tools confidently and appropriately in their work.

Summary

Ascribing roles to the computer has been a frequent means of describing patterns of computer use in teaching and learning. Acronyms for computer roles such as CML, CBE, or CALL indicate the degree of centrality of the computer in presenting materials, and the extent to which control is conferred to the machine. In computer–learner interactions, the computer can be highly directive, entirely non-directive, or operate in either way at different times. To capture the quality of this distinction, the tutor, tool, tutee description of the roles of the computer, drawn from educational computing and proposed by Taylor in 1980, is most helpful. With the computer as tutor, the computer's role is central; with the computer as tool, the computer's role is supplementary to the teacher and the student. The tutor–tool distinction can easily be substantiated in CALL: both roles for the computer are well-established and have a long history. The tutor–tool framework fits with other frameworks by CALL authors such as Higgins (1983), Wyatt (1984c), Phillips (1987), and Prescott (1995). Many of the roles for the computer presented by CALL authors had in fact originated earlier in general educational computing circles. The tutor role is derived from Skinner's work which implies a separateness of the work of the computer, and the work of the teacher in language learning, the latter being 'freed' for more humanistic work. On the other hand, the tool role for the computer, which is its fundamental role and one illustrated in CALL by the popularity of the word processor, leads to a more pivotal role for the language teacher or learner, and a less directive role for the computer.

The implications of these roles were discussed in terms of the learning environment, the methodology, the role of the teacher and learner, integration and the curriculum, and evaluation. A specific CALL methodology is required for the computer as tutor but not for the computer as tool, because in the latter case the computer's function is neutral and therefore subsumed in the general methodology being used. Hubbard's framework for CALL materials development which assumes that all CALL is tutorial in nature, is not generally applicable to the computer as a tool. Similarly, the Richards and Rodgers model of Approach, Design, and Procedure which was conceived as a means of describing a teaching method and which is used by Hubbard as a basis for his methodological framework for CALL, only has limited application for the computer tool.

The teacher's role will vary according to whether the computer is acting as a tutor or as a tool. With a tutor, the computer can be relied upon to manage the interactions, and, ideally at least, the program will adapt to the student's needs, level, and ability, then present material accordingly. With a tool, it will often fall to the teacher to ensure that the student knows how to make best use of the tool, and so a learner training component will often be required. Further work may be involved in setting tasks, or helping students to set them, ensuring the tool is appropriate to the task, and helping students appreciate any effects of the tool on the task. All in all, with the tool, the teacher's role is likely to be more demanding. Likewise, the learner will need to know what to do, and understand when to use the tool and how to make use of it. Unlike the tutor, the tool is not guiding the student in any way, but providing a support service so to speak, to assist in the accomplishment of the task. To do this effectively the task will need to be clearly defined and the tool will need to be appropriate for its completion.

The question of the integration of CALL is one where the computer as tutor may be more easily managed than the computer as tool. With the computer as tutor the materials are designed to be self-contained and to be used in a stand-alone way without the teacher present. Therefore, if all the computers reside in a self-access centre, computer laboratory, or library and a teacher is not available, in theory the CALL materials can still be used effectively. Alternatively, with the computer being used as a tool, the role of the computer is non-directive and the user needs to know what he or she is doing. Successful integration of CALL then becomes more problematic because the computer, the student, and the teacher need to be in an environment where all can function effectively. For the tool role to be viable, computers have to be readily accessible in the classroom as well as the self-access centre, and teachers and learners need to have the confidence and expertise to get the best out of them. Careful integration of CALL work needs to take place if it is not to become fragmented.

The evaluation of a tool is different from a tutor, and different criteria must apply. Treating all CALL as one kind of instructional activity has led to considerable confusion in evaluating its effectiveness (see Dunkel 1991*b*); recognizing the two principal roles of the computer as tutor and tool would help resolve some of these difficulties. With the computer as tutor the focus should be on measuring learning outcomes in an appropriate way. With the computer as tool the focus should be on evaluating the tool in relation to the task. A perfectly good tool may be unsuitable for the task, and the best tool will contribute little to a task that is ill defined or inappropriate. First, the tool and the task have to be evaluated independently; then the tool can be evaluated in relation to the task. Thus, for the evaluation of CALL tools to be accomplished successfully, teachers and learners must be very clear about the tasks—only then can the tool be evaluated effectively.

An analysis of the strengths, weaknesses, opportunities, and threats concludes the chapter. Strengths and weaknesses refer to the current situation; opportunities and threats refer to the future. The strengths of the computer tutor lie in its potential to supplement, or to some extent replace, the human teacher by providing learning opportunities that are more convenient for the learner, or that accommodate individual learner characteristics and needs with more precision. With the tutor, the learner relies on the guidance and feedback the computer provides so it should be accurate, appropriate, and timely. As the technology develops, the computer tutor may be able to deal with more aspects of language learning, involving speech recognition and synthesis perhaps, and much more sophisticated mechanisms for 'understanding'. Its limitations need to be understood, however. Ultimately, whatever the computer may or may not be able to do, it may not be necessarily wise to delegate responsibility to the computer to do it. Though computer-mediated forms of communication are likely to increase, for many learners skills in handling face to face interactions in the same physical space will remain the priority, and this facet of language use with all its attendant unpredictability will need to be conserved in the teaching and learning of languages, so that learners are able to acquire the skills that are needed.

The decision to delegate responsibility to a computer to evaluate the language learner directly should not be taken lightly. We need to avoid the temptation to allow the computer a more powerful role than is justified by its capabilities. Even with the simplest programs that evaluate, such as spelling checkers, incorrect advice can be given because the data the computer has to form its judgement may not include information that is needed to make a suitably informed decision. Moving beyond the word to judging the correctness of phrases or sentences is even more complex. Real world knowledge may be needed to evaluate appropriately. After a comprehensive evaluation study of grammar checkers, Bolt is most critical of their usefulness (1993). If, on the other hand, a grammar checker is not used to evaluate but to identify or to highlight then the problem is qualitatively different (see Garton and Levy 1993/4; Levy and Garton 1994). Provided that the students know in advance that the computer is *identifying* possible problem areas and not making immediate corrections, then the role of the computer is clear. Such approaches also fully utilize the students' intelligence. Provided the students are clear about the role of the computer, and any limitations a computer tutor is known to have, then they will not be drawn into ascribing to the computer an infallibility that is not warranted, and they will use their own judgements to filter the feedback they receive. It should be emphasized, however, that students expect a computer tutor to give the right advice on all occasions—the students' default setting so to speak is that a computer tutor knows what it is doing.

The tool function of the computer was its original purpose. It remains central in all domains of use including language teaching and learning where word processing and electronic mail are two prominent examples. Computer tools offer support for humans in the completion of tasks. The tools can enable these tasks to be undertaken, or in a variety of ways they may enhance the process or the product. To be successful, teachers and learners need to be clear about the tasks that require completion, they need to understand the tools that provide the support, and they need to know how best to make effective use of these tools. This requires training, both in the mechanics of the operation of the tool and in understanding the effects of the tool on the task. Opportunities are boundless at this point in the development of CALL, although clearly some tools will prove more useful than others. Threats to the use of computer tools in CALL derive from a misunderstanding of this role of the computer which may lead to shortfalls in providing the necessary infrastructure to support teachers and learners.

Although work on tools has been conducted and promoted within the CALL community (see e.g. Brierley and Kemble 1991), the computer tools of the 1980s arose in the commercial rather than the educational world; the focus in CALL was on tutors. This has been particularly true in the theoretical frameworks that have been proposed to guide CALL materials development. In contrast, procedures emanating from the field of human–computer interface design and task analysis appear to be more appropriate to guide materials development when the computer is envisioned as a tool (see Merrill 1978; 1980b; Shneiderman 1987). It is noteworthy that Kohn (1994: 32), in suggesting reasons for some of the deficiencies in current CALL, says that there has been too much emphasis on special-purpose rather than general purpose technology. Generic computer tools deserve much more attention in CALL, and further work needs to be conducted on theoretical frameworks, principles, and guidelines that embrace this role of the computer.

Notes

1. In a recent publication, Hubbard (1996) acknowledges the bounds of his methodological framework. He restricts his field of view to CALL 'courseware' which he likens to the 'tutor' use of CALL (p. 15). Hubbard's work was published after the manuscript for this book was completed. The present critique, therefore, should be read with Hubbard's acknowledgement firmly in mind.

8.   On the nature of CALL

Theory and application

This reflection on the nature of CALL begins by considering the oft-stated maxim that developments in CALL should not be technology-led (e.g. Murison-Bowie 1993). Quite rightly, such statements are motivated by a widely held concern that practitioners should not be blindly led by the latest technological innovation, but should have a carefully conceived set of principles to act as a guide. However, once the decision has been made to introduce technology, at a fundamental level it must be acknowledged that we are technology-led, at least in the sense that on the whole the technology is presented to us first, before we conceive of it, or consider what we might do with it. For example, the hardware we use in education, typically popular microcomputers of the IBM PC or Apple Mac style, or the communications systems and protocols that enable us to communicate with each other around the globe, have been conceived by engineers who are not primarily concerned with education, let alone language learning. In the initial stages of the development of a new technology, it would be most unusual for an educationalist or language teacher to have any input (although there have been notable exceptions as in the development of the BBC microcomputer, or the development of the customized keyboard in the TICCIT project). The more elemental concerns, especially of hardware design, have only been approached in large-scale, well-funded projects and then in the broader educational context, rather than CALL particularly. In the history of CALL, involvement in such fundamental questions of design has been rare. Market forces then further shape the choice of hardware and software that we and our students ultimately have available to us. Again, as CALL practitioners, typically we have little to do with this process. Market forces have determined the relative position of the Amiga series of computers in education, for instance, irrespective of the view of educationalists on the merits of this machine. On the whole, we receive our technology commercially packaged, and then we consider how best to make use of it: in this sense, we are most certainly technology-led.

We might argue, perhaps, that at this level the technology is somehow neutral in terms of the CALL applications we create—a kind of generic computing machine that is unfettered by any kind of constraint—and that the particular microcomputer we use is ultimately immaterial. However, as we have seen, the hardware and software we employ inevitably shape our CALL conceptualizations, and for any machine, we are immediately faced with its strengths and limitations, and the way in which the hardware and software combine to structure the working environment and the range of interactions that can be created with it. Further, the regular introduction of new models of computer has a very potent effect, often precipitating the view that when a computer is two- or three-years old, it has to be replaced, and that the educational institution is somehow inferior if it does not have the very latest technology. On the whole CALL practitioners have little to do with this process, and like it or not are obliged to move on to new hardware and software, even if the existing environment is perfectly adequate for the task at hand and a substantial number of CALL materials have been developed for it. Of course, some readers may be wishing they had this problem, when dated equipment really does need to be upgraded to facilitate the kind of work teachers and learners would like to accomplish. Clearly there has to be a balance: for some a four- or five-year plan works very well. There also has to be a process whereby CALL users can be included in the negotiations that take place. Appreciating the nature of the wider environment at a time where technological innovation is a formidable driving force for accelerating change in our society is an essential first step in understanding the nature of CALL, and it is only against this background that CALL can be understood.

Theory and application in CALL

In observing how CALL has been conceptualized throughout this book, it is clear that some developers prefer to begin with a clearly articulated theory. For example Liou says 'Well-grounded theoretical motivation for technological innovations should always lead CALL courseware development' (1994: 47). For those who begin with a theory to guide and motivate their work, not surprisingly the field of second-language acquisition has been suggested most frequently as the favoured source. For example, Doughty describes how the Negotiated Interaction Model and the Cognitive Processing Model derived from SLA theory motivate her work in interactive videodisc software research and development (Doughty 1991). Other theoretical sources that have been suggested emanate from Instructional Design, or the study of systems (see Chapter 3). This discussion does not attempt to compare such theories or to argue in favour of a particular position, but it does reflect on what a theory of CALL might look like, on some of the potential difficulties in formulating such a theory, and on some of the features it might be expected to have.

A useful way to begin is to look at the key arguments presented by Carroll (1991) who, in the context of Human–Computer Interaction (HCI) research, helped lead a three-day discussion on the role of psychological theory in the design of HCI. The result was a profound examination of the issues, and I believe the arguments are helpful for CALL.

Theory is only valuable in as much as it encompasses the context of the application. Consider the analogy of bridge-building, for example (Carroll 1991: 2). The Romans built very effective bridges centuries before the dynamics of such structures were analysed and understood. Presumably, in early times development proceeded through a process of trial and error, and a recognition of the principles associated with best practice (see Moonen and Stanchev 1993). The theories available at the time where not powerful enough to be able to inform the designers and the builders of the bridges. However, with the advent of a more complete scientific understanding of the properties of materials and the laws which govern how they deform under stress, the practice of bridge-building could be 'codified', that is the rules of thumb and the general principles derived from experience could be made explicit. Theories have now been devised that are directly applicable to the context of bridge-building. Such theories now enable bridge-building not only to be codified, but optimized so that bridges can be constructed in such a way that they perform their function with the most efficient use of materials and at minimum cost. The analogy of the bridge points to the essential ingredient for understanding the relationship between theory and application: that theory must be sensitive to the context of the application if it is to be any use to the practitioner. In Roman times theory had not advanced to the point where it could be applied to the context of bridge-building. Only with modern theory, however, drawn from basic science, could bridge-building truly become an application (Carroll 1991: 2).

What then are the implications of this discussion for CALL? First, for theory to be useful, it must be applicable to the context of CALL. On the whole the theories that have been applied to the CALL context have originated outside of it. If the theory has emerged in a non-CALL context, without concern for the unique characteristics of CALL, then its value in that context must be carefully considered. For any in doubt about the unique qualities of CALL, one need look no further than the nature of human–computer interactions mediated by a screen, keyboard, or mouse, or the immature technology that only partially supports speech synthesis and recognition. Further limitations appear through the processes of CALL materials development, in the software programs required to author new materials, even if high-level programming languages are employed. Propositions that derive from assumptions that equate human–computer interactions with human–human interactions, or presume the direct equivalence of learning with a machine to learning with a teacher are in danger of insensitivity to the context of CALL. To date it must be said that very few theoretical perspectives have grown out of such an understanding.

Secondly, a theory of CALL must address significant aspects of the target domain, some of which may be unique attributes of that domain, and may therefore, 'resist effective analysis by the standard methods, concepts and theories of the basic science' (Carroll 1991: 2). Of course, the techniques of the parent discipline have evolved to meet *its* needs, not necessarily the needs of the application. A good example in CALL is the use of traditional evaluation methods to evaluate the effectiveness of CALL tools (see Dunkel 1991*b*). Pennington (1995; forthcoming) draws attention to the limitations of pre-testing and post-testing research techniques, for instance, to evaluate the effects of the word processor. Instead, she argues for longitudinal research designs that are capable of capturing the long-term changes that writers undergo as they adjust their working methods to match the properties of the medium. In this regard, Pennington points out that research findings on the value of the word processor have become more positive of late. Before 1989 research results were rather mixed, perhaps even leaning towards the negative; between 1989 and 1993 research findings became more positive; since 1993 research findings have been very favourable towards the word processor. She suggests that such changes reflect in part more accurate and appropriate measurement techniques that capture more profound long-term effects occurring in the learner writer. This example is a clear indication that some types of CALL—and I would argue the tool types particularly—are distinct, and researchers may require novel research techniques to resolve and observe the effects. Again research techniques from outside the field need to be applied to CALL with a degree of caution.

Thirdly, the theory must be process appropriate, that is, it must be able to accommodate the processes of the application. Liou, for example, whilst acknowledging the primary importance of theory in courseware development is immediately faced with the 'how-to' aspects (1994: 47). Arguably, much current theory applied to CALL is not process appropriate. It is not presented in a way that can be utilized by practitioners in the process of CALL materials development, and so it is limited in its value at the procedural level, the 'how to' aspects. Current theory may provide an initial orientation, or a philosophical position—a little like the Communicative Language Teaching philosophy provides an orientation for language teachers—but it is not able to provide direction on the finer, lower-level detail required by CALL authors when constructing new programs. For theory to be of real value to the CALL author it must be specific and applicable to the CALL context. The value of specific theories developed for CALL environments would be in their sensitivity to the CALL context, and in their capacity to meet specificity and applicability requirements.

In ICALL some researchers are developing a theory of learning from within so to speak, taking account of any contextual constraints imposed by the computer right from the start. For example Harrington (1994) in the *CompLex* project has designed the project in such a way that the learning environment can be examined and refined as it is created. Harrington describes *CompLex* as a 'a research tool facilitating the systematic study of L2 lexico-semantic development and organization' (1994: 484). Thus, by tracking the learner as the program is used, the researcher can make adjustments and modifications, and fine-tune the program as it is developed. This tying together of theory and application, where the two are developed hand in hand right from the start, enables theory to inform the development of the application and vice versa, and it also seems a valuable way to ensure by default that the context of CALL is accommodated fully.

As an alternative to beginning with a theory, some writers on CALL have articulated CALL frameworks as a set of principles. For example, Oxford (1993) presents a 'desiderata' for Intelligent CALL by formulating nine key elements that are essential, if current thinking on language teaching and learning is to be heeded.

1. Communicative competence must be the cornerstone of ICALL.
2. ICALL must provide appropriate language assistance tailored to meet student needs.
3. ICALL must offer rich, authentic language input.
4. The ICALL student model must be based in part on a variety of learning styles.
5. ICALL material is most easily learned through associations, which are facilitated by interesting and relevant themes and meaningful language tasks.
6. ICALL must involve interactions of many kinds, and these interactions need not be just student–tutor interactions.
7. ICALL must provide useful, appropriate error correction suited to the student's changing needs.
8. ICALL must involve all relevant language skills and must use each skill to support all other skills.
9. ICALL must teach students to become increasingly self-directed and self-confident language learners through explicit training in the use of learning strategies.

Few would dispute the general wisdom of this set of prescriptions in the present climate of communicative CALL: the question, however, concerns their value to the ICALL practitioner in building ICALL software. Here I would argue that such prescriptions are of limited value. The statements certainly provide a clear orientation, but they do not meet the specificity and applicability requirements described earlier.

Whatever, the over-arching theoretical rationale for a CALL project, screens still need to be designed, optimal menu designs need to be selected, colours need to be chosen, and so on. Theories developed in HCI, which almost by definition are context appropriate, can provide a basis for the decisions that have to be made in this area. As the design of systems that support collaborative learning and the work of a group become more common, theory may also be drawn from emerging fields such as Computer-Supported Cooperative Work (CSCW).[1] Theories derived from CSCW will be more directly applicable to group interactions where learners are involved with each other collaboratively at a distance.

In the Introduction, I posed the problem of where a theory of CALL should come from. In answer, I would most closely agree with Mitterer *et al.* who say, 'we identify four types of knowledge which must be integrated in order to produce effective language learning environments: a theory of instructional design, a theory of language teaching, a theory of language learning, and knowledge of the applicability of technology' (1990: 136). A theory of language learning would almost certainly derive from the field of second-language acquisition. Knowledge of the applicability of technology relates to the notion of fit described earlier. I would also add human–computer interaction as a valuable source. So rather than a specific theory of CALL so to speak, an integrated theoretical framework which combines theoretical perspectives drawn from a number of related disciplines may provide a solution (see also Levy, forthcoming *b*).

As stated at the beginning of this section on theory and CALL, although some CALL authors argue for a theoretical position as a point of departure, many others clearly do not. My own view is that theory development is important in CALL. The reasons for valuing theory are expressed very well in the HCI discussion, where all participants acknowledged the value of insights from psychology in order to '*understand* how we do what we do in design, so that we can do it deliberately and repeatedly in diverse and novel situations' (Carroll 1991: 1). Participants were agreed about the need to 'codify' their understandings of design practice. In other words, practical knowledge gained from experience needs to be put in a form where it can be shared and communicated. Codification makes practical knowledge tangible so that it can be used and refined by practitioners and, most importantly, taught to others.

Technological innovation: counter-effects

Aside from the interplay between theory and application, there seems to me to be a further element that is central to an understanding of the nature of CALL. This element hinges on an appreciation of the effects of technological innovation on the ways in which people work, on the processes of reading and writing for instance, and on traditional domains of discussion in language teaching and learning, for example the curriculum, methodology, and the roles of the teacher and learner. Technology precipitates change, often in ways that can be difficult to predict in advance. When, for example, a curriculum specification that does not contain a fully integrated view of technology is used as a point of departure in CALL, the way in which technology is employed can be seriously constrained. It is false to assume that the curriculum specification is the only variable. In my view, if the curriculum is inflexible, and technological options are simply forced to fit within its boundaries, then the way in which the technology is used is likely to be mundane and unimaginative. The possibility that the introduction of technology can fundamentally alter the curriculum, or another of the traditional areas of discussion in language teaching, is too easily overlooked. In practice the introduction of a new technology, from a simple word processor to an Internet connection, will immediately affect the range of learning opportunities available and the ways in which learning tasks may be formulated and carried out. In a perceptive note, Phillips detects that there is a dialogue, so to speak, between the technology and its context of use when he says: 'The ELT profession needs to accommodate the new technology within its theories of language teaching methodology. This will almost certainly require some rethinking of methodology' (1985*b*: 114). The influence runs in two directions as the technology and the methodology exert a mutual effect upon one another. A key element in understanding the nature of CALL, then, is to attempt to understand some of its effects.

In discussing the effects, it is helpful to make a notional distinction between direct effects and indirect effects. Direct effects are more immediate, they concern what users do as they work at the computer. Examples include the effects of word processor and email use on writing, the effects of hypertext on reading strategies, or the effects of videoconferencing when used to facilitate face to face communication at a distance. The direct effects can be observed by recording the data entered or transmitted, or by observing what is occurring at the computer as students work on a task. On the other hand, indirect effects occur away from the immediate domain of the computer. They concern effects of technology on broader issues such as the curriculum, the role of the teacher, and so on. These effects are longer range, less immediately obvious, and are held to influence the environment within which CALL is conceptualized and used. To provide a few more illustrations of what I mean, some examples are discussed in a little more detail.

The way in which our students read and write is much affected by the technology they employ to assist them in these activities. New phenomena emerge as students adjust to using new computing tools and become familiar with them. For example, the word processor has had far-reaching direct effects on both the process and the product of writing (see Pennington 1993). Haas provides a well-constructed introduction to the direct effects in her paper, *How the Writing Medium Shapes the Writing Process: Effects of Word Processing on Planning* (Haas 1988). Compared with pen and paper, with the word processor Haas concludes that there is less planning overall, and specifically there is less conceptual planning and more sequential planning. The effects were the same for experienced and student writers. Also, intriguingly, writers respond very differently when allowed to use both the word processor and pen and paper as they wished. Some chose not to use pen and paper at all, while another wrote out the whole text by hand first, before typing it all into the computer. Though some writers chose not to use pen and paper, all chose to use the word processor at some stage. Haas has also written a companion piece on reading problems of writers using the word processor (Haas 1987).

The ways in which students write also changes when email is the tool that is employed. Written communication mediated via a computer in this way is reminiscent of spoken dialogue, a phenomenon first recognized by Daiute (1985), and later independently confirmed by Dam *et al.* (1990: 333) among others. Warschauer (1995) provides a concise review of the literature, and broadly divides his discussion into the effects of email in a single classroom and the effects of email for intercultural exchange. In the first category, Warschauer reports on the work of Wang (1993) who, like Haas for the word processor, compared email with the pen and paper equivalent. In writing dialogue journals using email, ESL students wrote more, asked more questions, and used different language functions more frequently compared with pen and paper. Another observation widely noted is the greater equality of participation among students when email is used (Warschauer 1995: 44). In the second category, email for cross-cultural exchanges, Warschauer reports on the work of Tella (1991; 1992*a*; 1992*b*). Using an ethnographic research design, Tella used observation, interviews, analysis of text messages, and meticulous tracking of the content and timing of the exchanges to assist in an analysis of the effects. Compared with traditional classroom exchanges, Tella noted a move towards a more learner-centred, individualized learning environment, more practice in open-ended situations, more editing and revision of composition through collaborative work, and general qualitative improvements in writing throughout. Effects were also noted in reading: reading became more public and collaborative, and new reading styles developed to accommodate different kinds of text. The way in which we read also changes when technology mediates the interaction between human and computer. For instance, McAleese (1993*b*) examines the effects when we read hypertext documents.

For textual and visual computer conferencing new phenomena are being observed also. Kalaja and Leppänen note the variation in the linguistic and textual strategies of participants, and suggest that, in the absence of prior experience, participants appear to adopt conventions from other written and spoken genres with which they are familiar (1994: 90). With videoconferencing, Hiraga and Fujii observe that students are less relaxed with this technology (1994: 77). They argue for more case studies and experiments in this area to test different teaching techniques and strategies. Such issues are in fact being addressed already, but in fields like HCI, not in CALL, and not with second-language learners and their learning environments in mind (see Dix *et al.* 1993: 470). Whatever the technology, teachers and researchers are observing new phenomena in their language classrooms, and efforts must continue to understand the effects, particularly to aid in the successful integration of technology-related activities with the more traditional ones.

Exactly how researchers might investigate these effects still requires further exploration. In the last section on theory and application we saw how, in evaluating the effects of the word processor, existing traditional research designs might need to be refined in order to capture the changes brought about by the introduction of a new technology. For the evaluation of multimedia Andrews and Isaacs (1995: 12) go as far as to say that experimental approaches are totally inappropriate for evaluation. Clearly new approaches do need to be considered and they are being trialled by writers on CALL. For example, Eck *et al.* (1994: 50) describe a procedure for analysing message flow and intermessage reference for email interactions. In a more descriptive vein, Hiraga and Fujii (1994) have developed their own unique system for evaluating the effects of videoconferencing. In another article, Esch (1995) reports on the work of Rutter (1984) who tested three forms of interaction for their effects: face to face; via a two-way video system in the same room separated by a screen; and over a telephone. Psychological distance significantly affects the language content, style, and outcome of the interaction. Others, such as Martha Crosby and her colleagues at the University of Hawaii, are exploring a multiplicity of techniques designed to capture the effects of new media so that specific elements can be related to learner variables such as visual ability (1994; 1995).

Some of the indirect effects subtly changing the environment in which language learning takes place, concern the curriculum, methodology, and teacher and learner roles. In the CALL survey a number of CALL practitioners noted how their methodology was eclectic, reflecting a view held by many in the wider teaching community. Similarly, an eclectic approach is described by Teichmann (1994) when using email and videoconferencing. Entirely new methodologies are being developed that blend satisfactorily the broad-based approach and orientation that is preferred with the technological opportunities and limitations. The indirect effects on the teacher and learner are significant. Again Teichmann describes the meticulous 'minute by minute' preparation and planning required for a videoconference where email is used by teachers, scholars, and students to prepare the way. Students themselves decide upon the time-plan and the themes to be discussed. In considering the changing roles of the teacher and the student, Davis and Ye-Ling (1994/5) give an illuminating description of some of the organizational and curricula challenges in a long distance collaboration between the USA and Taiwan via the Internet. Differences in campus calendars mean that course descriptions, texts, and assignments have to be exchanged well in advance. Class schedules are quite different, and one class was twice as big as the other. And different technologies are employed at either end so that each collaborator has to adapt to different means of composition and transmission. All in all, such projects highlight the enormous amount of preparation that is required. Of course such changes also substantially affect the curriculum. In this regard Davis and Ye-Ling specifically note the effect on course design, and the need for careful integration of email work with the wider class curriculum. It is particularly important that curriculum specifications include a position statement on technology, and that this is sufficiently flexible to accommodate the new options that technology can provide. A prescriptive, inflexible curriculum, or set text for that matter, can severely curtail some of the most valuable CALL opportunities and reduce CALL to a mundane page-turning exercise. The computer presents the content prescribed in the curriculum, but adds little else to the learning process.

In this brief review, it is quite clear that the introduction of the different kinds of CALL is inducing a corresponding effect, both direct and indirect. These effects need to be investigated and understood within the CALL context, and I feel that a part of the CALL agenda should include this work. Who if not CALL practitioners are going to explore these issues as they relate to language teaching and learning? Clarifying the nature and extent of the effects can help CALL authors and teachers prepare in advance for their CALL classes. Understanding the effects of the word processor on writing for instance can help teachers determine when best to advise their students to make use of the tool, and when students might be better advised to use more traditional methods. In a broader sense, we need to be aware that the introduction of technology can significantly skew the curriculum—if it is allowed to—perhaps promoting reading and writing to the detriment of speaking and listening. On the other hand, if this new emphasis is the result of careful reflection, and it is considered justified and advantageous, then the curriculum should be flexible enough to be able to embrace the changes.

In looking at CALL as a whole, pioneering efforts in such areas as curriculum development, methodology, and evaluation can easily be overlooked because of the way in which projects are written up, often with a title that reflects only their technological orientation, and the type of journal that is used to disseminate the information. By that I mean that papers reflecting on these mainstream issues may be published in specialized CALL journals which, through no fault of their own, may mean that information may not reach the wider audience. Vital issues of methodology, evaluation, and so on are often there, but lie hidden behind a curtain of technology. Conventional methods of evaluation and so on as described in the mainstream literature are, for the most part, inadequate and cannot cope with the demands that stem from an environment where technology is a fully integrated component. CALL workers are not only trying to develop CALL programs using the new technology, they are also addressing traditional questions in language teaching and learning, with few 'tools' to help them, from the established forums for such discussion. As a result, I believe that CALL practitioners need to make inroads into more broad-based forums of discussion including publication in the relevant journals, presentations at conferences, and so on. Highly innovative work is being done, and CALL practitioners—researchers, authors, and teachers—need to write about their experiences not only from the perspective of technology, but most importantly from these other perspectives as well. CALL practitioners are in a position to make significant contributions to contemporary thinking about methodology, evaluation, and the curriculum. In articulating their needs with confidence in the broader context, they can assist in strengthening the links between theory and application that will have benefits to the wider language teaching community much beyond CALL itself. This in turn will help integrate CALL into mainstream thinking on language teaching and learning with benefits for all concerned.

Final remarks

The study of CALL as a body of work has been complicated because it has had to contend with the rate of technological change, and from the uneven introduction of technology into language teaching and learning. While some language teachers and learners have access to the most recent hardware and software, others use technology that is dated. Yet I do not think this is an insurmountable obstacle to broad-based discussion of CALL. Such issues as integration, methodology, materials description and development, and roles for the computer and the teacher remain issues for all, as they have over a prolonged period of time. Some of the most imaginative programs have been written with inexpensive machinery, and mundane CALL programs have been produced for the most advanced equipment. We can learn from each other's experiences and we should continue to share them.

If I were to think of a metaphor of CALL at the moment, I would describe a set of parallel lines like the chronologies in history books that highlight the exploits of key figures over a period of time. CALL projects have many starting-points, some theoretical and some practical, and many end-points also. Projects appear to be addressing a whole variety of questions or problems in language teaching and learning, from simply providing learning opportunities at a time and place convenient to the student, to providing learning environments that are unique to the computer and which could not be constructed in any other way. When projects are written up and published, though they describe their own derivation they rarely mention other projects of a similar type or appear to build upon them in any way—hence the metaphor using parallel lines rather than ones that intersect. The domain of the project is self-contained within the bounds of the project itself.

In 1987, Phillips pointed to the absence of a 'prevailing model' in CALL, or a clear paradigm to direct development (1987: 275). A research agenda, a path for development, or even the problems to which CALL provides the solution have not been agreed and, without this, CALL is somewhat fragmented, and moving in many different directions at the same time. Such CALL characteristics appear to be set in a pre-paradigm stage (see Kuhn 1970: 163, 178). Early attempts are being made to present theories, models, or sets of principles as potential paradigms and to assert their authority, but on the whole, it is not yet clear which direction or source will be most fruitful. Matthews's observation rings true. For ICALL Matthews (1994: 533) says that the development of ICALL has 'often tended to proceed in an ad-hoc fashion'. He calls for a more 'principled framework' in ICALL, and sets as the point of departure for the field the question: 'Which grammar framework might best form the basis of the syntactic component of an ICALL system?' (1994: 533). We can expect more calls for a collective response in CALL, as we search for the optimum path to take. However, in the past too early an allegiance to a paradigm has been a trap. We have seen that it can lock us into a view of CALL that is unnecessarily constraining, and limits its enormous potential. In the absence of a paradigm, like Jones, I prefer to talk of roles rather than models of paradigms. Jones says: 'When something new comes along, it can simply be added to a continually evolving body of knowledge and experience. When roles are seen as "models" they compete. As roles, they are complementary' (1988: 12). It is in this spirit that a tutor–tool framework outlining the roles of the computer has been offered.

The path from the initial conceptualization of CALL materials to final implementation and regular use with language learners is not an easy one. To enhance the early stages of a project, there are benefits in absorbing the research and development findings of other fields of endeavour, variously related to the field of CALL. The history of language teaching methodology warns against using theory and research from other disciplines indiscriminately but, with suitable critical appraisal of their applicability, assessing and sometimes using such findings can be most advantageous for CALL. Increased specialization in many disciplines that use new technology does not make cross-fertilization easy. Specialized journals, distributed electronically and through the print media, and subject-specific conferences work against information exchange, but if CALL is to build upon what has gone before, it has to acknowledge and review findings in other related fields.

For CALL authors, an agreed metalanguage for discussion, for materials development, and for evaluation is essential. As Hubbard suggests, we need to be able to identify desirable elements in CALL programs and use them as building blocks in new programs. In other words, we need more than a general feeling that something works: we need to know exactly what it is that makes a CALL program successful so that we can share the knowledge with others and use the successful elements again. Here again the tutor–tool distinction is important. For tutors these elements may be coded into the program on the computer; for tools the key elements may lie outside the immediate domain of the computer and reside in the careful construction of learning tasks.

Models or frameworks are needed to guide CALL materials development, and the models or frameworks need to be sensitive to the specific needs of practitioners. The tutor and tool roles, reflecting two of the most established roles of the computer, provide a useful perspective but they are only a beginning. As yet there is no agreed framework for development, although the Richards and Rodgers model and Hubbard's framework derived from it go a considerable way towards providing a framework against which CALL tutors may be developed and evaluated. For tool applications, the emerging discipline of HCI should prove most useful, particularly in shedding light on how systems influence and are influenced by the groups and social contexts in which they are placed. Though work on tools is under way in CALL, the notion of the computer as tutor, especially in methodological discussions of CALL and in evaluation studies, still predominates. More research is required to refine tool models and frameworks further.

With regard to CALL materials, there is much to be gained by placing CALL materials in the wider and more general language learning materials context. For example, this perspective helps to account for the popularity of tools such as the word processor in CALL. In the broader context, the current interest in task-based and procedural syllabuses and the move towards developing process-oriented materials which are a means to an end rather than an end in themselves helps to explain the value of using the computer as a tool, a role that gained the highest rating in the survey. In fact the need for process-oriented materials as well as content-oriented materials accords well with the twin roles of the computer as tutor and as tool.

The number of hardware and software tools for CALL materials development remains problematic. So far, CALL authors have been largely subject to commercial imperatives and have played a minor role in the selection of hardware and software, particularly hardware. As a result, large quantities of CALL materials are lost when machines become obsolete. The computer, instead of being a means to an end, as a vehicle for the creation of CALL materials, has too often become an end in itself, in the sense that CALL materials cease to exist when computers are replaced. This proliferation in development tools means that CALL materials exchange is difficult at best; and that common ground for research and development, and the metalanguage alluded to above, is entirely lost. The solution is the articulation of standards for CALL development tools and development processes, and this is occurring with some of the larger CALL consortiums such as the TELL Consortium. Approached in the right way, standards can be helpful, although there is a fine line between standards that guide and provide a mechanism for helpful dialogue and the exchange of materials, and standards that curtail imagination and innovative uses of the technology. This course of action is difficult, especially against a background of commercial enterprises vigorously promoting their own hardware and software products, but it is useful in providing a counterbalance, so that CALL practitioners do feel they can exert an influence where it is justified.

Most CALL materials are locally produced and unpublished. Publication of CALL materials is difficult because, unlike a book which is self-contained, CALL materials require a computer to function and this immediately restricts the potential market. The small market and the diversity and expense of equipment reduce the viability of publication. The advantages, however, are many and include the provision of cross-checks through the participation of editors and possibly programmers, and the prerequisite that proper testing and evaluation has been conducted, and that the documentation is comprehensive and complete. Every effort should be made to publish CALL materials. This helps to ensure that CALL materials are complete with full documentation and that they are properly tested. Only then will CALL be given a reasonable chance for fair evaluation of its value in the wider language teaching community.

In conclusion, however, it is to the language teacher, to the potential CALL user and CALL author, that we should return. The survey showed that teacher-related factors were the most important in determining the success of CALL materials development. From the literature, Farrington (1989: 70) and Sussex (1991: 21) assert that language teachers must be involved in CALL if it is to flourish in the future. It is language teachers who exert ultimate control over what materials are chosen and subsequently used by students in the classroom. Even if the CALL materials are designed to be stand-alone, as with a computer tutor perhaps, in the long term students are only likely to make use of the materials if encouraged to do so by their teacher. Moreover, given that few would argue that a computer can look after all of a language learner's needs, the teacher is going to continue to be involved in some way or another. On the other hand, if the computer is used as a tool, the teacher is intimately involved in setting tasks and in guiding students in the optimal use of the computer in their work. Thus, if CALL is marginalized it will largely be the result of the collective views of language teachers, and by that I mean teachers who are not presently using CALL.

Those recommending CALL to language teachers, while proclaiming the benefits of the new technological options, often overlook the implications for language teachers, especially when the computer is cast in the role of tool rather than tutor. Computer tools, worthy as they are, do require time, effort, and commitment on the part of language teachers. Generally speaking, if language teachers can gain access to CALL materials at reasonable cost in terms of time and effort then I believe they will use them. Ultimately, it is a question of cost versus gain. We can lower the cost by making the technology more accessible, programs more user-friendly, using frameworks that have been devised to guide and assist language teachers and CALL authors. For CALL materials development to be successful and to make significant in-roads into mainstream language teaching practice, substantial support must be given to the language teacher, who must be acknowledged as a key contributing factor. Only then will the future success of CALL be assured.

Notes

1. Dix *et al.* characterize the essential difference between HCI and CSCW by suggesting that the principal axis in HCI is psychology–computing whereas the principal axis in CSCW is sociology–computing (1993: 424).

Appendix A: The CALL Survey

Computer Assisted Language Learning (CALL) Materials Development
Survey: part 1

1   CALL materials development: individual factors

The first part of the survey seeks to establish your educational background, your language teaching philosophy and the extent of your experience in CALL. The questions that follow then relate directly to determining your approach to the development of CALL materials.

Throughout the survey the general term 'CALL materials' is used to include materials produced using various authoring tools *and* software produced using high level programming languages such as Pascal or BASIC.

1.1   Personal language teaching/learning experience

1.1.1   Which languages do you speak? (Indicate degree of fluency.)

_____

1.1.2   In what subject(s) was/were your first degree/second degree/later degrees?

_____

1.1.3   Would you consider yourself to have principally a scientific or a humanities background?

_____

1.1.4   In what kind of educational institution have you been predominantly employed? Indicate the approximate number of student users of CALL programs.

_____

1.1.5   How many years have you taught languages? _____

1.1.6   Which language do you usually teach? _____

1.2   Theoretical basis

1.2.1   Choose the term(s) that best refer(s) to your notion of the role of the computer in language learning. You may select more than one. If relevant indicate by the appropriate box 'S' for Self-Access use, 'C' for classroom use or 'SC' for both.

- ☐ (a) A tool (e.g. word processing)
- ☐ (b) An expert system
- ☐ (c) A surrogate teacher
- ☐ (d) A useful provider of mechanical language practice
- ☐ (e) A manager of tasks
- ☐ (f) A complement to classroom instruction
- ☐ (g) A means of raising awareness (e.g. visual representation of sounds)
- ☐ (h) A database of textual and visual materials
- ☐ (i) An aid to communication (e.g. electronic mail)
- ☐ (j) Other (please specify)

1.2.2   Below is a list of language teaching philosophies, methods and approaches. Please tick the box(es) that best describe your own. You may select more than one.

- ☐ (a) Audiolingual
- ☐ (b) Cognitive code learning
- ☐ (c) Communicative language teaching
- ☐ (d) Community language learning
- ☐ (e) Direct method
- ☐ (f) Formal grammar instruction
- ☐ (g) Functional/notional approaches
- ☐ (h) Grammar translation
- ☐ (i) Oral approach
- ☐ (j) Situational language teaching
- ☐ (k) Structuro-global audio visual
- ☐ (l) Suggestopedia
- ☐ (m) Task-based learning
- ☐ (n) The natural approach
- ☐ (o) The silent way
- ☐ (p) Total physical response
- ☐ (q) Other (please specify)

1.2.3   Below is a list of items that might be considered to be within the scope of CALL discussion. Please tick the box(es) that you would include. You may select more than one.

- ☐ (a) Artificial intelligence and expert systems
- ☐ (b) Communications technologies

☐ (c) Computational linguistics
☐ (d) Computer translation
☐ (e) Hypermedia
☐ (f) Instructional design
☐ (g) Interactive video
☐ (h) Multi-lingual word processing
☐ (i) Natural language processing
☐ (j) Sound/speech production and understanding
☐ (k) Text indexing and retrieval (including concordancing)
☐ (l) Voice synthesis
☐ (m) Word processing
☐ (n) Other (please specify)

1.3   CALL experience

1.3.1 Please indicate the extent of your experience in CALL. Tick the box below that best describes your own experience.

☐ (a) I have taken at least one CALL course as a learner.
☐ (b) I have looked into CALL (read about it, or attended an introductory course, seminar or conference, etc.).
☐ (c) I have examined and evaluated at least one commercial software package.
☐ (d) I have developed my own materials using a CALL authoring package.
☐ (e) I have participated in the design and/or development of at least one CALL software package.
☐ (f) I regularly design, develop and write CALL software programs.

1.3.2 How many years have you been:

(a) observing the development or implementation of CALL?

_____

(b) directly participating in the implementation (or delivery) of CALL? _____

(c) developing CALL materials? _____

1.3.3 As far as you can remember, when and under what circumstances did you begin to be interested in computer assisted language learning?

_____
_____
_____
_____

1.3.4   Tick the categories of CALL software for which you have at one time or another developed your own materials.

☐   (a)   Speaking
☐   (b)   Listening
☐   (c)   Reading
☐   (d)   Writing
☐   (e)   Database
☐   (f)   Games
☐   (g)   Gap-filling
☐   (h)   Simulation
☐   (i)   Text reconstruction
☐   (j)   Tutorial
☐   (k)   Word processing
☐   (l)   Logical thinking
☐   (m)   Interactive audio
☐   (n)   Interactive video
☐   (o)   Other (please specify)

1.3.5   In question 1.3.4, in the space above next to the software categories, indicate the software and hardware you used (e.g. C on a VAX or Hypercard on the Mac).

1.3.6   In what aspects of CALL are you chiefly interested?

_____

_____

1.4   Development methods and approaches

1.4.1A   If you personally own a computer, please state the computer type and style.

_____

1.4.1B   If you regularly use a computer at work, please state the computer type and style.

_____

1.4.1C   Does your institution provide you with a computer that you can use at home? _____

1.4.2   When developing CALL materials, what kind of computer do you use most? Please tick the appropriate box(es). You may select more than one.

☐   (a)   Standalone microcomputer
☐   (b)   Microcomputer in a network

☐ (c) Mainframe computer
☐ (d) Workstation
☐ (e) Workstation in a network
☐ (f) Other multi-user systems and terminals

1.4.3 When developing CALL materials, what kind of software do you normally use? Please tick the appropriate box(es). You may select more than one.

☐ (a) An authoring system (e.g. Course of Action)
name:
☐ (b) An authoring program (e.g. Storyboard)
name:
☐ (c) An authoring language (e.g. PILOT)
name:
☐ (d) An authoring environment (e.g. Hypercard)
name:
☐ (e) A high level programming language (e.g. Pascal)
name:
☐ (f) Other (please specify)
name:

1.4.4 Why did you choose the software named in 1.4.3 for CALL materials development?

_____
_____
_____
_____

1.4.5 How did you learn to use the software named in 1.4.3 for CALL materials development? You:

☐ (a) were self-taught
☐ (b) were taught by colleagues
☐ (c) attended a formal course (please specify)

1.4.6 When developing new CALL materials, which of the following considerations do you initially orientate yourself towards? Please tick the appropriate box(es). You may select more than one.

☐ (a) Your view of language (e.g. Chomsky)
☐ (b) Your language learning methodology (e.g. The Silent Way)
☐ (c) Patterns in the language that seem 'computable' (e.g. verb endings)
☐ (d) Your own paradigms for CALL development and use

☐ (e) Certain 'potentials' of the computer (e.g. the matching capability)
☐ (f) A CALL activity template (e.g. Crossword Magic)
☐ (g) An authoring environment that you consider promising (e.g. Hypercard)
☐ (h) No particular framework
☐ (i) Other considerations (please specify)

1.4.7 How does your philosophy of language teaching/learning affect the way in which you develop CALL materials?

_____

_____

_____

_____

1.4.8 Do you normally develop CALL materials on your own or with others? If you generally work with others, could you describe your role and the roles of the other members of the team.

_____

_____

_____

_____

1.4.9 Before beginning a piece of CALL research work, do you first assimilate what has already been written on the subject, or do you prefer to work with no particular framework consciously in mind?

_____

_____

1.4.10 Have you a distinct recollection of the process of development of some CALL materials that you have developed? If so, please describe their genesis.

_____

_____

_____

_____

1.4.11 In your opinion what are the key skills language teachers need to become competent developers of CALL materials?

_____

_____

_____

1.4.12 Describe the CALL materials you have produced. (Please attach further pages of notes or documentation if necessary.)

_____

_____

_____

_____

1.4.13 What are your main reasons for thinking CALL a valuable teaching/learning resource or technique?

_____

_____

_____

_____

Computer Assisted Language Learning (CALL) Materials Development

Survey: part 2

2   CALL materials development: external factors

The second part of the survey attempts to measure external factors, drawn from the literature and discussion with key practitioners, that appear to influence the successful development of CALL materials. In estimating success, you should base your response on your own criteria for a successful project.

In sections 2.1 to 2.5 the questions are grouped into a graded general response followed by a more specific response. For the specific responses you are asked to rank items from each list of alternatives in order of importance to you. Each box should be marked 1, 2, 3 etc. with *1 representing the most important factor*. If any factors are not relevant in your situation leave the box blank. If you have difficulty in ranking items simply tick the appropriate box(es) instead.

If you wish to qualify or explain your response, please feel free to add notes in the margin or attach an additional page of your own to the questionnaire.

2.1   General developmental factors

2.1.1 To what extent are the CALL materials developed at your institution based on commercial software packages, or on in-house developed packages?

Commercial: _____% In-house: _____%

2.1.2 How many staff in your institution are regularly involved in CALL materials development? In what capacities?

_____

2.1.3 Place numbers in each of the boxes to rank the factors that you consider to be the most critical to the successful development of CALL materials.

☐ (a)   The cost of computer hardware
☐ (b)   The cost of CALL software
☐ (c)   The time allocated to staff education
☐ (d)   Well-packaged CALL materials
☐ (e)   Powerful software authoring tools
☐ (f)   Versatile, general purpose computing languages

☐ (g) A clear paradigm to guide developers
☐ (h) Other (please specify)

2.2 Hardware

2.2.1 How important do you believe is the availability of suitable hardware to the successful development of CALL materials?

Important   Not Important
   1   2   3   4   5   6   7   8   9   10

2.2.2 Place numbers in each of the boxes to rank the factors which you consider most significantly contribute to the successful development of CALL materials.

☐ (a) A particular infrastructure of computers in the institution (please specify)
☐ (b) Availability of networked systems
☐ (c) Availability of microcomputers
☐ (d) Availability of special purpose CALL hardware (please specify)
☐ (e) Hardware with sufficient memory and speed
☐ (f) Accessibility of hardware to students
☐ (g) Access to computer-based communications
☐ (h) Other (please specify)

2.3 Software

2.3.1 How important do you believe is the availability of suitable authoring tools to the successful development of CALL materials?

Important   Not Important
   1   2   3   4   5   6   7   8   9   10

2.3.2 Place numbers in each of the boxes to rank the factors which you consider most significantly contribute to the successful development of CALL materials.

☐ (a) High quality authoring systems (e.g. Course of Action)
☐ (b) High quality authoring packages (e.g. Storyboard)
☐ (c) High quality authoring languages (e.g. PILOT)
☐ (d) Networking capability of programs
☐ (e) Portability of programs
☐ (f) User-friendly software development packages
☐ (g) Clear, readable documentation
☐ (h) Other (please specify)

2.3.3 Place numbers in each of the boxes to rank the factors which you consider most significantly contribute to a successful CALL software package. The package should:

- ☐ (a) be easy to use for teacher and student
- ☐ (b) have an authoring capability
- ☐ (c) have high quality instructional design
- ☐ (d) have a networking capability
- ☐ (e) run on readily available computer hardware
- ☐ (f) be available in different versions for different computers
- ☐ (g) contain relevant pre-packaged material content
- ☐ (h) contain clear, readable documentation with teaching ideas
- ☐ (i) be of high technical quality
- ☐ (j) other (please specify)

2.4 The teacher's role

2.4.1 How important do you believe is the role of the teacher/instructor in the development of CALL materials?

Important _____ Not Important
      1   2   3   4   5   6   7   8   9   10

2.4.2 Place numbers in each of the boxes to rank the teacher-determined factors which you consider most significantly contribute to the successful development of CALL materials. The teacher's:

- ☐ (a) general level of confidence/competence with computers
- ☐ (b) ability to make use of commercially-produced products
- ☐ (c) confidence in using commercial authoring tools to produce CALL materials
- ☐ (d) ability to use a high-level programming language
- ☐ (e) ability to understand what is 'computable'
- ☐ (f) considered opinion on the validity of CALL
- ☐ (g) other (please specify)

2.4.3 Is CALL worthwhile WITH the teacher present, or WITHOUT the teacher present, or both?

_____

2.4.4 Should language teachers write support materials to accompany software packages?

_____

2.4.5 Should languages teachers learn a high level programming language?

_____

2.5   Management

2.5.1   How important do you believe are the attitudes and expectations of the administration or management of the institution to the successful development of CALL materials?

Important   Not Important

1	2	3	4	5	6	7	8	9	10

2.5.2   Place numbers in each of the boxes to rank the factors which you consider most significantly contribute to the successful development of CALL materials. Administrative attitudes and conventions which contribute include:

☐   (a)   level of provision of computing facilities
☐   (b)   level of commitment to the efficacy of CALL
☐   (c)   level of institutional interest in CALL
☐   (d)   level of professional advancement for staff who engage in CALL
☐   (e)   level of interest of key personnel
☐   (f)   realistic expectations held by administrators or funding authorities
☐   (g)   predictability of support from the administration
☐   (h)   internal institutional and interpersonal politics
☐   (i)   time allocation for staff to author CALL materials
☐   (j)   other (please specify)

2.6   Current practice

2.6.1   Do you think the introduction of computers has modified the teacher's role in language teaching and learning? If so, in what way?

_____
_____
_____
_____
_____

2.6.2   What staff education, training or development courses, workshops or activities have been available in CALL to language teachers at your institution during the last year? Indicate whether these activities were internal or external to your institution.

_____
_____
_____
_____

2.6.3 In what way does your institution support your CALL activities at the moment? What else could be done to encourage and support the development of CALL materials?

_____
_____
_____
_____
_____

2.6.4 What do you consider to be the most significant block to successful CALL materials development at the present time?

_____
_____
_____
_____
_____

2.6.5 How would you summarise CALL progress so far?

_____
_____
_____
_____
_____

2.7   The future

2.7.1 In your view, where lies the most potential for CALL materials development in the future?

_____
_____
_____
_____
_____

2.8   Follow up

THIS SECTION WILL BE REMOVED BEFORE DATA ENTRY BEGINS.

2.8.1 Contact Name: _____

2.8.2 Are you prepared to supply further information on request which could be published to verify the observations from this study?

_____

2.8.3 Would you like to suggest the name(s) of a colleague(s) working in the field to whom a questionnaire might be sent?

If so, please give Contact Name: _____
Address: _____
_____
_____

Contact Name: _____
Address: _____
_____
_____

* Demonstration copies of CALL materials, and articles or other documentation not readily available in the literature that relate to projects in which you have been involved, would greatly help to support the observations. I would appreciate the inclusion of such material with your responses.

Thank you for your help and for your valuable time.

Appendix B: The design of the CALL Survey

There were fifty-two questions in the final version of the questionnaire (see Appendix A). For some of the more complex areas, both a closed question and an open-ended question were included, as in trying to establish initial orientation on a CALL project, for example (Q. 1.4.6). This combination acts as a cross-check, it guards against the registering of an item simply because it is supplied as a possible answer, and it gives an opportunity to provide more detail. The majority of the closed questions contained a set of possible item answers where each item had to be checked or ranked according to its significance for the question concerned. The questionnaire was divided into two parts and eleven sections as follows:

Part 1

CALL materials development: individual factors

   1.1 Personal language teaching/learning experience
   1.2 Theoretical basis
   1.3 CALL experience
   1.4 Development methods and approaches

Part 2

CALL materials development: external factors

   2.1 General developmental factors
   2.2 Hardware
   2.3 Software
   2.4 Teacher education
   2.5 Management
   2.6 Current practice
   2.7 The future

The first part of the survey sought to establish an individual respondent's educational background, language teaching philosophy, and CALL experience. The second part of the questionnaire focused more on external factors, such as the development environment and the level of institutional support available, rather than the individually determined factors canvassed in the first part. In Part 2 the aim was to establish the most important factors that influenced the *successful* development of CALL materials. Since the order of importance of items was of interest in Part 2,

TABLE B.1   *The indicators and the survey questions*

Topic with indicators	Question number
Details of respondents	
Language teaching and CALL experience	1.1, 1.3.1, 1.3.2
Conceptualization	
Language teaching/learning philosophy	1.2.2, 1.4.7
Role of the computer	1.2.1
Scope of CALL	1.2.3
Initial orientation and points of departure	1.4.6, 1.4.10
Hardware and software	1.3.5, 1.4.1, 1.4.2, 1.4.3, 1.4.4
Role of the teacher (as contributor)	2.4.3, 2.6.1
The development process	1.4.9, 1.4.10
Role of the teacher (as author)	2.4.4, 2.4.5
Materials developed	1.3.4, 1.4.12, 2.1.1
Evaluation	1.4.13, 2.6.4, 2.6.5

respondents were asked to rank items, whereas in Part 1 respondents were simply asked to select one or more items.

The layout of the questionnaire did not reflect the form of the component indicators exactly. As the objectives of the study were translated into questions in a survey format, they were necessarily modified by the following considerations: the need to group the closed and open-ended questions together; the occasional need to ask more than one question on the same topic; and the need to organize the content and layout of the questionnaire so that it was meaningful and logical as a document in its own right. Nevertheless, there is rightfully a close correspondence between the research objectives and the questionnaire, as shown in Table B.1.

This book focuses on how CALL has been conceptualized. As a result, the contents of Table B.1 only include matters relating to conceptualization. Other sections in the CALL survey that relate to issues such as working methods, teacher education, and factors for success have been omitted. A full discussion of teacher education and CALL is given in Levy (forthcoming *a*).

Appendix C: Miscellaneous charts

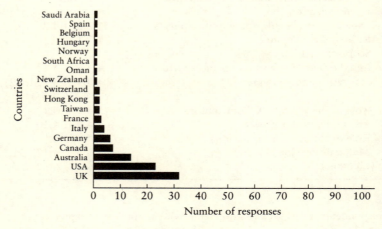

FIGURE C.1   *Country of respondents (n = 104)*

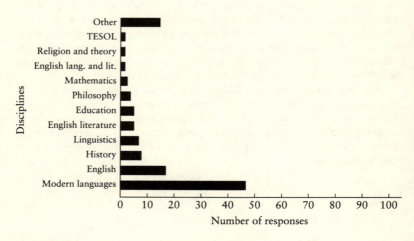

FIGURE C.2   *First degree taken by respondents (n = 104)*

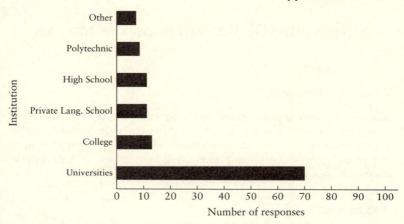

FIGURE C.3 *Institutional affiliation of respondents (n = 102)*

Appendix D: Resources on the Internet

Caveat for Web sites

Since the Internet is growing and changing every day, it is impossible to guarantee that the addresses provided in this section are correct on publication. Machines may break down, be disconnected for some reason, or moved and given a new name. Nevertheless, every effort has been made to choose the more stable and reliable sites.

The Internet

Understanding the Internet
http://www.screen.com/start

Internet Assistant On-line Companion
http://www.vmedia.com/hpia.html

Dummy's guide
ftp://ftp.eenet.ee/pub/guides/bdg/bdg_3.html

The Internet Bookshop
http://www.bookshop.co.uk

Netscape home page
http://home.netscape.com

Hardware and software: general

Intel
http://www.intel.com/

Apple Computers Inc. (Netscape & Apple etc.)
http://www.apple.com/

IBM
http://www.ibm.com/

Sun (includes Hot Java browser and Java language)
http://www.sun.com/

Microsoft
http://www.microsoft.com/

Adobe
http://www.adobe.com

Multimedia

Macromedia
http://www.macromedia.com

Australian Multimedia Magazine
http://www.mm.com.au/amm

Virtual Reality

Virtual Worlds
http://www.virtualworld.com

The VRML Forum (at Wired magazine's web site)
http://vrml.wired.com/

VRML
http://www.w3.org/hypertext/wwwMarkUp/VRML

Web Page Construction

HTML Tutorial: introduction
http://www.cwru.edu/help/introHTML/intro.html

HTML
http://www.w3.org/hypertext/www/MarkUp/MarkUp.html

At Netscape
http://home.netscape.com/home/how-to-create-web-services.html

University of Melbourne
http://www.unimelb.edu.au:8001/courses/

Web Construction (Internet Australia: 68)
http://byerley.cs.waikato.ac.nz/~tonym/html-intro/

Java programming

Java: programming for the Internet
http://java.dnx.com/

Java tools
http://www.construct.net/tools/java

Writing Java programs
http://java.sun.com/tutorial/java/index.html

Applied lingustics, languages and language teaching

Language and Technology Centre of the National Languages and Literacy
Institute of Australia, University of Queensland
http://www.cltr.uq.oz.au:8000/

TESL-EJ: North America
http://www.well.com/www/sokolik/tesl-ej.html

TESL-EJ: Asia
http://www.kyoto-su.ac.jp/information/tesl-ej/

EUROCALL
http://www.cti.hull.ac.uk/eurocall.htm

TELL Consortium
http://www.cti.hull.ac.uk/tell.htm

EFL ODL Project (Ruth Vilmi)
http://www.hut.fi/~rvilmi/email-project.html

Foreign language resources on the Web (UC Campus, Berkeley University)
http://www.itp.berkeley.edu/~thorne/HumanResources.html

Aston University Languages Department
http://sol.aston.ac.uk/home.html

The Language Centre (Sussex University)
http://www.sussex.ac.uk/langc/intro

The Language Centre (Warwick University)
http://www.warwick.ac.uk/WWW/faculties/arts/Lang_C/

The Language Centre (Oxford University)
http://info.ox.ac.uk:80/departments/langcentre/

The World Language Page (Liverpool John Moores University)
http://www.livjm.ac.uk/language/

CALICO
http://www.calico.org

CALICO Courseware development SIG
http://cc.usu.edu/~scott/csig.html

ATELL
http://www.arts.unimelb.edu.au/~ATELL/

On-CALL
http://www.cltr.uq.oz.au:8000/oncall

Foreign language teaching forum
http://www.cortland.edu/www_root/flteach/flteach.html

COBUILD
http://titania.cobuild.collins.co.uk

Collection of language Lists (Oxford University Language Centre)
http://info.ox.ac.uk/departments/langcentre/langlists.html

Wida software
http://www.wida.co.uk/wida/

Concordance program messages
http://ling.rochester.edu/linguist/7-768.html#2

The CALL Cookbook
http://www.owlnet.rice.edu/~ling417/

H-Net Humanities Online
http://h-net.msu.edu

CELIA at Latrobe University
http://www.latrobe.edu.au/www/education/celia/celia.html

SL-Lists: International EFL/ESL email student discussion lists
http://www.latrobe.edu.au/www/education/sl/sl.html

Survey of the State of the Art in Human Language Technology
http://www.cse.ogi.edu/CSLU/HLTsurvey/

A selection of Lists

To subscribe to a LISTSERV list send an email message to the subscription address using the keyword Subscribe, the name of the list and your name. Generally, the following patterns of entry are used for subscription, termination and posting messages:

Subscription address:	LISTSERV@hostname
Subscription message:	Subscribe *list* yourname
Termination message:	Signoff *list*
Posting address:	*list*@hostname

Name: **H-NET**—Humanities on-line
Description: seventy scholarly lists for humanists and social scientists with over 30,000 subscribers in sixty-one countries. Each list is edited by a team of scholars and has a board of editors; most of the lists are co-sponsored by a professional society.

Subscription address: LISTSERV@msu.edu
SUBSCRIBE H-MMedia Firstname Surname, Affiliation

Name: **TESL-L**
Description: resource for anyone interested in the education of non-native English-speakers. Eighty-three countries. TESL-L also has an on-line database of TESL/TEFL materials and eight special interest groups, one of which is computer-assisted language learning.

Subscription address: LISTSERV@cunyvm.cuny.edu
SUB TESL-L Firstname Surname

Name: **TESLCA-L**—CALL
Subscription address:

1. Subscribe to TESL-L
2. Send an email message to the TESL-L LISTSERV with the message: SUB TESLCA-L Firstname Lastname

Name: **Linguist**—for discussion of language and linguistics
Subscription address: LISTSERV@tamvm1.tamu.edu

Name: **SLART-L**—second-language acquisition, research, and teaching
Subscription address: LISTSERV@cunyvm.cuny.edu

Name: **FLTEACH**—foreign language teaching for high school and college teachers
Subscription address: LISTSERV@ubvm.cc.buffalo.edu

Name: **Applix**—various aspects of Applied Linguistics
Subscription address: LISTSERV@cltr.uq.oz.au

Name: **MULTI-L**—language and education in multilingual settings
Subscription address: LISTSERV@vm.lbiu.ac.il

Name: **LTEST-L**—language testing
Subscription address: ltest-l@psuvm.psu.edu

Name: **LLTI**—language learning technology international/discussion of CALL
Subscription address: LISTSERV@dartcms.1dartmouth.edu

MUDs and MOOs

To join a MUD or a MOO you need to send a command called Telnet. Telnet is a program that turns your machine into a telnet client so that you can access data and programs on a remote computer, a telnet server, somewhere. Once logged in, you can use the applications on that machine as if it were your own. The basic form of the command in UNIX is ⟨telnet hostname⟩ where 'hostname' is the name of the computer you want to reach. Before sending this command all you usually have to do is log in to your own local system.

Writing Centre
telnet://daedalus.com:7777/

SchMOOze University, a special MOO established for ESL/EFL teachers and students
telnet://arthur.rutgers.edu 8888

French language MOO
telnet://logos.daedalus.com 8888

German language MUDs
telnet://mud.uni-muenster.de:4711
telnet://infosgo.rus.uni-stuttgart.de:3333

'Little Italy', Italian Language MOO
telnet://ipo.tesi.dsi.unimi.it 4444

MundoHispano Spanish language MOO
telnet://io.syr.edu 8888

References

Ahmad, K., Corbett, G., Rodgers, M., and Sussex, R. (1985), *Computers, Language Learning and Language Teaching* (Cambridge: Cambridge University Press).

Alderman, D. L. (1978), *Evaluation of the TICCIT Computer-Assisted Instructional System in the Community College: Final Report* (Princeton: Educational Testing Service).

Allinson, L., and Hammond, N. (1993), 'A Learning Support Environment: The Hitch-Hiker's Guide', in McAleese (1993*a*).

Allwright, R. (1981), 'What Do We Want Teaching Materials For?' *English Language Teaching Journal*, 36/1: 5–18.

Anderson, J. R. (1985), *Cognitive Psychology and its Implications* (New York: W. H. Freeman and Company).

Andrews, D. H., and Goodson, L. A. (1980), 'A Comparative Analysis of Models of Instructional Design', *Journal of Instructional Development*, 3/4: 2–15.

Andrews, D., and Isaacs, G. (1995), 'The Effectiveness of Multimedia as an Instructional Tool within Higher Education' (Brisbane: Tertiary Education Institute, University of Queensland).

Anivan, S. (1990) (ed.), *Language Teaching Methodology for the Nineties*, Anthology Series 24 (Singapore: SEAMEO Regional Language Centre).

Anthony, E. M. (1963), 'Approach, Method and Technique', *English Language Teaching*, 17: 63–7.

Ariew, R. (1984), 'Computer-Assisted Foreign Language Materials: Advantages and Limitations', *CALICO Journal*, 2/1: 43–7.

——(1988), 'Integrating Video and CALL in the Curriculum: The Role of the ACTFL Guidelines', in Smith (1988).

——and Frommer, J. (1987), 'Interaction in the Computer Age', in Rivers (1987).

Ashcraft, M. H. (1993), *Human Memory and Cognition* (New York: Harper Collins).

Asher, J. (1977), *Learning Another Language Through Actions: The Complete Teacher's Guidebook* (Los Gatos, Calif.: Sky Oak Productions).

Ashworth, D., and Stelovsky, J. (1989), 'Kanji City: An Exploration of Hypermedia Applications for CALL', *CALICO Journal*, 6/4: 27–50.

Ashworth, M. (1985), *Beyond Methodology* (Cambridge: Cambridge University Press).

Atkinson, C. J., and Checkland, P. B. (1988), 'Extending the Metaphor System', *Human Relations*, 41/10: 709–25.

Augarton, S. (1984), *Bit by Bit: An Illustrated History of Computers* (New York: Ticknor and Fields).

Austin, R., and Mendlick, F. (1993), 'E-Mail in Modern Language Development', *ReCALL*, 9: 19–23.

Ausubel, D. P. (1960), 'The Use of Advance Organizers in the Learning and Retention of Meaningful Verbal Material', *Journal of Educational Psychology*, 51/5: 267–72.

Bailin, A. (1988), 'Artificial Intelligence and Computer-Assisted Language Instruction: A Perspective', *CALICO Journal*, 5/3: 25–50.

——(1990), 'CALI, Artificial Intelligence, and the Representation of Social Roles', in Craven *et al.* (1990).

——Chappelle, C., Levin, L., Mulford, G., Neuwirth, C., Sanders, A., Sanders, R., and Underwood, J. (1989), 'A Bibliography of Intelligent Computer-Assisted Language Instruction', *Computers and the Humanities*, 23: 85–90.

——and Levin, L. (1989), 'Introduction: Intelligent Computer-Assisted Language Instruction', *Computers and the Humanities*, 23/1: 3–11.

——and Thomson, P. (1988), 'The Use of Natural Language Processing in Computer-Assisted Language Instruction', *Computers and the Humanities*, 22/2: 99–110.

Barker, P., and Yeates, H. (1985), *Introducing Computer-Assisted Learning* (Englewood Cliffs, NJ: Prentice Hall International).

Barson, J., Frommer, J., and Schwartz, M. (1993), 'Foreign Language Learning Using E-Mail in a Task-Oriented Perspective: Interuniversity Experiments in Communication and Collaboration', *Journal of Science Education and Technology*, 2/4: 565–84.

Bartlett, F. C. (1932), *Remembering: A Study in Experimental and Social Psychology* (London: Cambridge University Press).

Batley, E. M., and Freudenstein, R. (1991) (eds.), *CALL for the Nineties: Computer Technology in Language Learning*, ii (Marburg: FIPLV/Eurocentres).

Batson, T. W. (1988), 'The ENFI Project: A Networked Classroom Approach to Writing Instruction', *Academic Computing*, Feb./Mar.: 32–3; 55–6.

Beardon, C., Lumsden, D., and Holmes, G. (1991), *Natural Language and Computational Linguistics: An Introduction* (New York: Horwood).

Beattie, K., McNaught, C., and Wills, S. (1994) (eds.), *Interactive Multimedia in University Education: Designing for Change in Teaching and Learning: Proceedings of the IFIP TC3/WG3.2 Working Conference on the Design, Implementation and Evaluation of Interactive Multimedia in University Settings*, 6–8 July (Melbourne, Victoria, Australia).

Bedell, D. (1994), 'Review of Bitnet/Internet Lists for Language Learning', University of Bridgeport ELI ⟨bedell@cse.bridgeport.edu⟩.

Bedford, A. (1991), 'Methodology for CALL: Beyond Language Teaching Paradigms', in Brierley and Kemble (1991).

Beeching, K. (1982), 'Authentic Material 1', *British Journal of Language Teaching*, 20/1: 17–20.

Benwell, G. A. (1986), 'Integrating the Computer into a Language Course', in Cameron *et al.* (1986).

Berdel, R. L., Locatis, C., Weisberg, M., and Carr, V. (1990), 'Evaluation of Authoring Systems for Hypermedia-Based Instruction', *Journal of Interactive Instruction Development*, spring: 11–15.

Beretta, A. (1991), 'Theory Construction in SLA: Complementarity and Opposition', *Studies in Second Language Acquisition*, 13/4: 493–511.

Best, J. (1989), *Cognitive Psychology* (St Paul: West Publishing Company).

Bickes, G., and Scott, A. (1989), 'On the Computer as a Medium for Language Teaching', *CALICO Journal*, 6/3: 21–34.

Blake, R. (1995), 'Remote Technical Assistant (RTA): Distance Learning for Teaching Foreign Languages', paper presented at the Exeter CALL Conference, 10–12 Sept., Exeter, UK.

Bloch, J., and Bates, J. (1990), 'Developing Interactive Fiction for the Language Classroom: The Contribution of Artificial Intelligence', in Craven *et al.* (1990).

Block, D. (1990), 'Seeking New Bases for SLA Research: Looking to Cognitive Science', *System*, 18/2: 167–76.

——(1991), 'Some Thoughts on DIY Materials Design', *English Language Teaching Journal*, 45/3: 211–17.

Bogdan, R. C., and Biklen, S. K. (1982), *Qualitative Research for Education: An Introduction to Theory and Methods* (Boston: Allyn and Bacon).

Bolitho, R. (1990), 'An Eternal Triangle? Roles for Teacher, Learners and Teaching Materials in a Communicative Approach', in Anivan (1990).

Bolt, P. (1993), 'Grammar Checking Program for Learners of English as a Foreign Language', in Yazdani (1993).

Bonner, J. (1988), 'Implications of Cognitive Theory for Instructional Design: Revisited', *Educational Communication and Technology Journal*, 36/1: 3–14.

Bott, M. F. (1970), 'Computational Linguistics', in Lyons (1970).

Brammerts, H. (1995), *International E-Mail Tandem Network*, http://www.slf.ruhr-uni-bochum.de Update: 5.1.96.

Breen, M. P. (1987a), 'Contemporary Paradigms in Syllabus Design: Part I', *Language Teaching*, 20/1: 81–92.

——(1987b), 'Contemporary Paradigms in Syllabus Design: Part II', *Language Teaching*, 20/2: 157–74.

——(1987c), 'Learner Contributions to Task Design', in Candlin and Murphy (1987).

Breen, M. P., and Candlin, C. N. (1987), 'Which Materials?: A Consumer's and Designer's Guide', in Sheldon (1987).

——— ———and Waters, A. (1979), 'Communicative Materials Design: Some Basic Principles', *RELC Journal*, 10/2: 1–13.

Brett, P. (1994), 'Using Text Reconstruction Software', *ELT Journal*, 48/4: 329–36.

Bridwell, L., Sirc, G., and Brooke, R. (1985), 'Revising and Computing: Case Studies of Student Writers', in Freedman, S.W. (ed.), *The Acquisition of Written Language* (Norwood: Ablex).

Brierley, B. (1991), 'Natural Language Processing', in Brierley and Kemble (1991).

———and Kemble, I. (1991) (eds.), *Computers as a Tool in Language Teaching* (New York: Horwood).

Brocket, A. A., Clark, I. A., and Taylor, O. B. (1992), 'Development of a Human-Computer Interface', *ReCALL*, 7 Nov.: 17–27.

Brücher, K. H. (1993), 'On the Performance anel Efficiency of Authoring Programs in CALL', *CALICO Journal*, 11/2: 5–20.

Brumfit, C., Phillips, M., and Skehan, P. (1985) (eds.), *Computers and English Language Teaching: ELT Documents 122* (Oxford: Pergamon).

Burton, D. M. (1981*a*), 'Automated Concordances and Word Indexes: The Early Sixties and the Early Centres', *Computers and the Humanities*, 15/2: 83–100.

———(1981*b*), 'Automated Concordances and Word Indexes: The Fifties', *Computers and the Humanities*, 15/1: 1–14.

———(1981*c*), 'Automated Concordances and Word Indexes: The Process, The Programs and the Products', *Computers and the Humanities*, 15/3: 139–54.

———(1982), 'Automated Concordances and Word Indexes: Machine Decisions and Editorial Revisions', *Computers and the Humanities*, 16: 195–218.

Bush, M. D., and Crotty, J. (1989), 'Interactive Videodisc in Language Teaching', in Smith (1989).

———Slaton, A., Slayden, M., and Verano, M. (1991) (eds.), *Interactive Videodisc: The 'Why' and the 'How'*: CALICO Monograph Series, ii (Brigham Young University, UT).

Bush, V. (1945), 'As We May Think', *Atlantic Monthly*, 176/1: 101–8.

Butler, J. (1990), 'Concordancing, Teaching and Error Analysis: Some Applications and a Case Study', *System*, 18/3: 343–9.

Cameron, K. C. (1989) (ed.), *Computer-Assisted Language Learning: Program Structure and Principles* (Oxford: Intellect Books).

———Dodd, W. S., and Rahtz, S. P. Q. (1986) (eds.), *Computers and Modern Language Studies* (Chichester: Horwood).

Candlin, C. N., and Breen, M. P. (1979), 'Evaluating and Designing

Language Teaching Materials', *Lancaster Practical Papers in English Language Education*, 2: 172–216.

——and McNamara, T. F. (1989) (eds.), *Language, Learning and Community: Festschrift in Honour of Terry Quinn* (National Centre for English Language Teaching and Research, Macquarie University, Sydney).

——and Murphy, D. F. (1987) (eds.), *Language Learning Tasks*, Lancaster Practical Papers in English Language Education, 7 (Englewood Cliffs, NJ: Prentice Hall International).

Canter, M., Neumann, E., and Fenton, J. (1987), 'Controlling CD-I: Languages and Authoring Systems', in Lambert and Sallis (1987).

Card, S. K. (1993), 'Forward', in Dix *et al.* (1993).

Carroll, J. M. (1991) (ed.), *Designing Interaction: Psychology at the Human–Computer Interface* (Cambridge: Cambridge University Press).

Catt, C. (1991), 'CALL Authoring Programs and Vocabulary Development Exercises', *Computer-Assisted Language Learning*, 4/3: 131–40.

Cerri, S. A. (1989), 'ALICE: Acquisition of Linguistic Items in the Context of Examples', *Instructional Science*, 18/1: 63–92.

Chan, C. (1989), 'Computer Use in the Classroom-II: An Assessment of Using the Computer as a Tool and as Tutee', *Computer Education*, 13/3: 271–7.

Chanier, T. (1994), 'Special Issue Introduction', *Special Issue of the Journal of Artificial Intelligence in Education*, 5/4: 417–28.

Chapelle, C. (1989*a*), 'CALL Research in the 1980s: Setting the Stage for the 1990s', *CALL Digest*, 5/7: 7–9.

——(1989*b*), 'Using Intelligent Computer-Assisted Language Learning', *Computers and the Humanities*, 23/1: 59–70.

——(1990), 'The Discourse of Computer-Assisted Language Learning: Toward a Context for Descriptive Research', *TESOL Quarterly*, 24/2.

——(1994*a*), 'Theoretical Bases for Human–Computer Interaction Research in CALL', in *Proceedings of the CALICO 1994 annual symposium* (Duke University, North Carolina).

——(1994*b*), 'CALL Activities: Are They all the Same?' *System*, 22/1: 33–45.

——and Jamieson, J. (1984), 'Language Lessons on the PLATO IV System', in Wyatt (1984*a*).

Chun, D. M. (1994), 'Using Computer Networking to Facilitate the Acquisition of Interactive Competence', *System*, 22/1: 17–31.

Clark, J. (1988), 'Toward a Research and Development Strategy for CALL', *CALICO Journal*, 5/3: 5–24.

Clark, R. (1985), 'Confounding in Educational Computing Research', *Journal of Educational Computing Research*, 1/2: 137–48.

Clarke, D. F. (1989*a*), 'Design Considerations in Writing CALL Software with Particular Reference to Extended Materials', in Cameron (1989).

——(1989*b*), 'Materials Adaptation: Why Leave it all to the Teacher?' *English Language Teaching Journal*, 43/2: 133–41.

——(1989*c*), 'Communicative Theory and its Influence on Materials Production', *Language Teaching*, 22: 73–86.

Conklin, J. (1987), 'Hypertext: An Introduction and Survey', *Computer*, 20/9: 17–41.

Cook, V. J. (1985), 'Bridging the Gap between Computers and Language Teaching', *ELT Documents*, 122: 13–24.

——(1992), 'Second Language Acquisition and CALL', *ReCALL*, 6: 20–1.

——and Fass, D. (1986), 'Natural Language Processing by Computer and Language Teaching', *System*, 14/2: 163–70.

Cooke, P., and Williams, I. (1993), 'Design Issues in Large Hypertext Systems for Technical Documentation', in McAleese (1993*a*).

Craven, M.-L. (1988), 'Evaluating CUES: Some Problems and Issues in Experimental CALL Research', *CALICO Journal*, 5/3: 51–64.

——(1993), 'Shared Journal Writing in a Social Science Class: ESL Students' Experiences', in Liddell (1993).

——(1995*a*), 'Computer Mediated Communication: Some Thoughts about Extending the Classroom', *Computing News* (York: York University).

——(1995*b*), 'Providing Scaffolding Strategies for ESL Students on a Conferencing System', paper presented at the EUROCALL Conference, 6–9 Sept., Valencia, Spain.

——Sinyor, R., and Paramskas, D. (1990) (eds.), *CALL: Papers and Reports* (La Jolla: Athelstan).

Crookall, D., Coleman, D. W., and Oxford, R. L. (1992), 'Computer-Mediated Language Learning Environments', *CALL*, 5/1–2: 93–120.

Crosby, M., Stelovsky, J., and Ashworth, D. (1994), 'Hypermedia as a Facilitator for Retention: A Case Study using Kanji City', *CALL*, 7/1: 3–13.

—— —— ——(1995), 'Evaluation of Multimedia Interfaces in Transcription: A Case Study', paper presented at the Exeter CALL Conference, 10–12 Sept., Exeter, UK.

CU-SeeMe Development Team (1996), *CU-SeeMe: Desktop Videoconferencing from Cornell University*, http://cu-seeme.cornell.edu/ Update: 24.12.95.

Cumming, G., Sussex, R., and Cropp, S. (1994), 'The Teacher–Learner–Computer Triangle in CALL Frameworks for Interaction and Advice', *CALL*, 7/2: 107–23.

Curran, C. (1976), *Counseling-Learning in Second Languages* (Apple River, Ill.: Apple River Press).

Daiute, C. (1985), *Writing and Computers* (Reading, Mass.: Addison-Wesley).

Dalgish, G. (1985), 'Some Computer-Assisted ESL Research and Courseware Development', *Computers and Composition*, 2: 45–62.

Dam, L., Legenhausen, L., and Wolff, D. (1990), 'Text Production in the Foreign Language Classroom and the Word Processor', *System*, 18/3: 325–34.

Das, B. K. (1988) (ed.), *Materials for Language Learning and Teaching*, Anthology Series 22 (Singapore: SEAMEO Regional Language Centre).

Davies, G. (1985), *Talking Basic* (Eastbourne: Cassell Computing).

——(1986), 'Authoring CALL Courseware: A Practical Approach', in Leech and Candlin (1986).

——(1987), 'CALL: Past, Present and Future', *Modern Languages*, 68: 68–77.

——(1989), 'CALL and NCCALL in the United Kingdom: Past, Present and Future', in Smith (1989).

——(1993), 'CALL in the new Europe: The Spirit of Cooperation', in Liddell (1993).

——(1996), 'Total Text Reconstruction Programs: A Brief History', unpublished article. Personal communication.

——and Higgins, J. (1982), *Computers, Language and Language Learning* (London: CILT).

————(1985), *Computers in Language Learning: A Teacher's Guide* (London: CILT).

Davis, B. H., and Ye-Ling, C. (1994/5), 'Long-Distance Collaboration with On-Line Conferencing', *TESOL Journal*, 4/2: 28–31.

Dede, C. (1980), 'Educational Technology: The Next Ten Years', *Instructional Innovator*, 25/3: 17–23.

——(1986), 'A Review and Synthesis of Recent Research in Intelligent Computer-Assisted Instruction', *International Journal of Man-Machine Studies*, 24: 329–53.

——(1987), 'Enpowering Environments, Hypermedia and Microworlds', *The Computing Teacher*, 15/3: 20–4.

——(1988), 'The Role of Hypertext in Transforming Information into Knowledge', in Ryan, W. C. (ed.), *Proceedings: National Educational Computing Conference* (Dallas, Tex.: Eugene).

Demaizière, F. (1991), 'From Linguistics to Courseware Design', *CALL*, 4/2: 67–79.

DeMarco, T. (1979), *Structured Analysis and System Specification* (Englewood Cliffs, NJ: Yourdon Press).

Digital Equipment Corporation (1983), *Introduction to Computer-Based Education* (Bedford, Mass.: Digital Equipment Corporation).

Dix, A., Finlay, J., Abowd, G., and Beale, R. (1993) (eds.), *Human–Computer Interaction* (Hemel Hempstead: Prentice Hall).

Dixon, R. (1981), 'PLATO Reaches International Students with English Lessons', *Studies in Language Learning*, 3: 98–112.

Doughty, C. (1988), 'Relating Second-Language Acquisition Theory to CALL Research and Application', in Smith (1988).

——(1991), 'Theoretical Motivations for IVD Software Research and Development', in Bush *et al.* (1991).

Dubin, F., and Olshtain, E. (1986), *Course Design* (Cambridge: Cambridge University Press).

Dunkel, P. (1987*a*), 'Computer-Assisted Instruction (CAI) and Computer-Assisted Language Learning (CALL): Past Dilemmas and Future Prospects for Audible CALL', *The Modern Language Journal*, 71: 250–60.

——(1987*b*), 'The Effectiveness Literature on CAI/CALL and Computing: Implications of the Research for Limited English Proficient Learners', *TESOL Quarterly*, 21: 367–72.

——(1991*a*) (ed.), *Computer-Assisted Language Learning and Testing* (New York: Newbury House).

——(1991*b*), 'The Effectiveness Research on Computer-Assisted Instruction and Computer-Assisted Language Learning', in Dunkel (1991*a*).

Eck, A., Legenhausen, L., and Wolff, D. (1994), 'Assessing Telecommunications Projects: Project Types and their Educational Potential', in Jung and Vanderplank (1994).

Ellis, R. (1985), *Understanding Second Language Acquisition* (Oxford: Oxford University Press).

——(1994), *The Study of Second Language Acquisition* (Oxford: Oxford University Press).

Eltis, K., and Low, B. (1985), *A Review of the Teaching Process in the Adult Migrant Education Program*, Report to the committee of review of the Adult Migrant Education Program (Department of Immigration and Ethnic Affairs, Canberra).

England, E. (1989), 'Instructional Design: Its Relevance for CALL', *CALICO Journal*, 6/3: 35–42.

Esch, E. M. (1995), 'Exploring the Concept of Distance for Language Learning', *ReCALL*, 7/1: 5–11.

Esling, J. H. (1990), 'Researching the Effects of Networking', in Dunkel (1990*a*).

Essinger, J., and Hicks, R. (1991), *Making Computers More Human: Designing for Human-Computer Interaction* (Oxford: Elsevier Advanced Technology).

Faiola, T. (1989), 'Improving Courseware Development Efficiency: The

Effects of Authoring Systems on Team Roles and Communication', *Educational Technology*, 29/8: 16–19.

Farghaly, A. (1989), 'A Model for Intelligent Computer-Assisted Language Instruction (MICALI)', *Computers and the Humanities*, 23/3: 235–50.

Farrington, B. (1986), ' "Triangular Mode" Working: The *Littré* Project in the Field', in Higgins (1986*a*).

——(1987), *Littré* (Scottish Computer-Based French Learning Project, University of Aberdeen, Aberdeen).

——(1989), 'AI: "Grandeur" or "Servitude?" ', in Cameron (1989).

——(1995), 'Authoring Materials for *BonAccord*', paper presented at the EUROCALL Conference, 6–9 Sept., Valencia, Spain.

Fesl, G. (1994), 'European Foreign Language Learning in the Multimedia Teleschool', in Jung and Vanderplank (1994).

Flagg, B. N. (1990), *Formative Evaluation for Educational Technologies* (Hillsdale, NJ: Lawrence Erlbaum).

Fox, J. (1986*a*), Review of Leech and Candlin (1986), *System*, 14/2: 234–5.

——(1986*b*) (ed.), *Special Issue: Computer-Assisted Language Learning* (UAE Papers in Linguistics, University of East Anglia, Norwich).

——(1993), 'EC Research in Language Learning and IT—Some Experiences with LINGUA', *Journal of Computer Assisted Learning*, 9: 100–6.

——Matthews, A., Matthews, C., and Rope, A. (1990), *Educational Technology and Modern Language Learning*, prepared for the Learning Technology Unit by the University of East Anglia and the Bell Educational Trust, the Training Agency, Norwich.

French, J. R. (1991), 'Machine Translation', in Brierley and Kemble (1991).

Fritze, P. (1994), 'A Visual Mapping Approach to the Evaluation of Multimedia Learning Materials', in Beattie *et al.* (1994).

Frommer, J. (1989), 'Listening, Looking and Learning with *MacLang*', *CALICO Journal*, 6/4: 51–71.

Gagné, R. M. (1987), *Instrucional Technology: Foundations* (Hillsdale, NJ: Lawrence Erlbaum).

——Briggs, L. J., and Wager, W. W. (1988), *Principles of Instructional Design*, 3rd edn. (New York: Holt, Rinehart, and Winston).

——and Dick, W. (1983), 'Instructional Psychology', *Annual Review of Psychology*, 34: 261–95.

Gaines, B. R. (1985), 'From Ergonomics to the Fifth Generation: 30 Years of Human–Computer Interaction Studies', in Shackel, B. (ed.), *Human–Computer Interaction—Interact '84 Proceedings of the IFIP Conference* (Amsterdam: North-Holland).

Gale, L. (1983), 'Montevidisco: An Anecdotal History of an Interactive Videodisc', *CALICO Journal*, 1/1: 42–6.

Gale, L. (1989), 'Macario, Montevidisco, and Interactive Digame: Developing Interactive Video for Language Instruction', in Smith (1989).

Garfinkel, S. L. (1988), 'A Second Wind for Athena', *Technology Review*, Nov.–Dec.

Garrett, N. (1988), 'A Psycholinguistic Perspective on Grammar and CALL', in Smith (1988).

——(1991), 'CARLA comes to CALL', *Computer-Assisted Language Learning*, 4/1: 41–5.

—— and Hart, R. (1989), 'Language, the Teacher, the Student and the Computer: New Roles Defined', *Foreign Language Annals*, 22/5: 499–501.

Garton, J. (1992), 'Learning how to Manage Text with Interactive Multimedia', *ON-CALL*, 7/1: 17–22.

—— and Levy, M. (1993/4), 'A CALL Model for a Writing Advisor', *CAELL Journal*, 4/4: 15–20.

Gayeski, D. M. (1993), *Multimedia for Learning: Development, Application, Evaluation* (Englewood Cliffs, NJ: Educational Technology Publications).

Geens, D. (1981), 'Computer-Driven Remedial Teaching of Foreign Languages', in Bailey R. W. (ed.), *Computing in the Humanities* (Ann Arbor: The University of Michigan).

Gibbs, S., Tsichritzis, D., Fitas, A., Konstantas, D., and Yeorgaroundakis, Y. (1987), 'Muse: A Multimedia Filing System', *IEEE Software*, 4/2: 4–15.

Gimeno-Sanz, A. (1993) (ed.), *English for Specific Purposes (ESP) Studies* (Valencia: Universidad Politécnica de Valencia).

Ginsberg, M. (1988), 'Multivalued Logics: A Uniform Approach to Reasoning in Artificial Intelligence', *Computational Intelligence*, 4: 265–316.

Goodwin, A. A., Hamrick, J., and Stewart, T. C. (1993), 'Instructional Delivery via Electronic Mail', *TESOL Journal*, 3/1: 24–7.

Gordon, S. (1994), *Systematic Training Program Design: Maximizing Effectiveness and Minimizing Liability* (Englewood Cliffs, NJ: Prentice Hall).

Gray, K. (1990), 'Syllabus Design for the General Class: What Happens to Theory when you Apply it', *English Language Teaching Journal*, 44/4: 261–9.

Greene, J. (1986), *Language Understanding: A Cognitive Approach* (Milton Keynes: Open University Press).

Gremmo, M.-J., and Riley, P. (1995), 'Autonomy, Self-Dirction and Self Access in Language Teaching and Learning', *System*, 23/2: 151–64.

Grishman, R. (1986), *Computational Linguistics: An Introduction* (Cambridge: Cambridge University Press).

Griswold, R. E. (1990), *An Overview of Version 8 of the Icon Programming Language* (Department of Computer Science, The University of Arizona, Arizona).

Haas, C. (1987), *'Seeing it on the Screen Isn't Really Seeing It': Reading Problems of Writers using Word Processing* (Pittsburgh: Carnegie Mellon University).

——(1988), *How the Writing Medium Shapes the Writing Process: Effects of Word Processing on Planning* (Pittsburgh: Carnegie Mellon University).

Hagan, S. (1995), 'User Preferences in Open and Distance Language Learning: What are the Options for Multimedia', *ReCALL*, 7/1: 20–5.

Hamburger, H. (1994), 'Foreign Language Immersion: Science, Practice, and System', *Journal of Artificial Intelligence in Education*, 5/4: 429–54.

Hardisty, D., and Windeatt, S. (1989), *CALL* (Oxford: Oxford University Press).

Harmon, P. (1987), 'Intelligent Job Aids: How AI will change Training in the Next Five Years', in Kearsley (1987).

——and King, D. (1985), *Expert Systems* (London: John Wiley and Sons).

Harrington, M. (1994), '*CompLex*: A Tool for the Development of L2 Vocabulary Knowledge', *Journal of Artificial Intelligence in Education*, 5/4: 481–500.

Hart, R. S. (1981) (ed.), 'The PLATO system and Language Study', special issue of *Studies in Language Learning*, 3/1.

——(1995), 'The Illinois PLATO Foreign Languages Project', *CALICO Journal*, 12/4: 15–37.

Haukum, R., and Malone, E. (1987), 'A Survey of Level III Videodisc Delivery Systems', in Lambert and Sallis (1987).

Havelock, R. C. (1973a), *Planning for Innovation through Dissemination and Utilization of Knowledge* (Ann Arbor: The University of Michigan).

——(1973b), 'What do we Know from Research about the Process of Research Utilization' (Ann Arbor: The University of Michigan). Prepared for the conference: Making Population/Family Planning Useful, East-West Communication Institute, East-West Centre, University of Hawaii, Honolulu, Hawaii, 3–7 Dec. 1973.

——and Havelock, M. C. (1973), *Training for Change Agents: A Guide to the Design of Training Programs in Education and Other Fields* (Ann Arbor: The University of Michigan).

Hawisher, G. E., and LeBlanc, P. (1992) (eds.), *Re-Imagining Computers and Composition: Teaching and Research in the Virtual Age* (Portsmouth, NH: Heinemann).

——and Moran, C. (1993), 'Electronic Mail and the Writing Instructor', *College English*, 55/6: 627–43.

Hefzallah, I. M. (1990) (ed.), *The New Learning and Telecommunications*

Technologies: Their Potential Applications in Education (Springfield, Ill.: Charles C. Thomas).

Henry, G. M., and Zerwekh, R. A. (1994), 'Human Factors in CALL Software Design: Examples from the Creation of Multimedia Dictionary Software for Thai and Indonesian', in *Proceedings of the CALICO '94 Annual Symposium*, 14–18 Mar. (Durham, NC: CALICO).

Hertz, R. M. (1987), *Computers in the Language Classroom* (Menlo Park, Calif.: Addison-Wesley).

Hewer, S. (1989), *Making the Most of IT Skills* (London: CILT).

Higgins, J. (1982), 'The Grammarland Principle', *Bulletin Pedagogique*, 80–1/44–5: 49–53.

——(1983), 'Can Computers Teach?' *CALICO Journal*, 1/2: 4–6.

——(1984), 'Learning with Computers', in *Teaching and the Teacher: proceedings of the Bologna Conference*, Apr. (Bologna: Modern English Publications).

——(1985), 'Should Teachers Learn to Program?' in Brumfit *et al.* (1985).

——(1986a) (ed.), *Computer-Assisted Language Learning: Special Issue of System*, 14/2.

——(1986b), 'The Computer and Grammar Teaching', in Leech and Candlin (1986).

——(1988), 'Power to the Pupils: Computer Software in Language Teaching', in Das (1988).

——(1989), *Eclipse Software Manual* (Bristol: Bristol University).

——and Johns, T. (1984), *Computers in Language Learning* (London: Collins).

——and Wallace, R. (1989), 'Hopalong: A Computer Reading Pacer', *System*, 17/3: 389–99.

Hillier, V. (1990), 'Integrating a Computer Lab into an ESL Classroom', *CAELL Journal*, 1/2: 23–4.

Hiraga, M. K., and Fujii, Y. (1994), 'Teaching English from Australia to Japan via Interactive Videoconference Systems', in Jung and Vanderplank (1994).

Hirschheim, R., Smithson, S., and Whitehouse, D. (1990), *Microcomputers and the Humanities: Survey and Recommendations* (New York: Horwood).

Hirvela, A. (1989), 'The Case against CAI: A Reply to John Higgins', *System*, 17/1: 61–5.

Hockey, S. (1987), 'A Historical Perspective', in Rahtz (1987).

Hoffman, R. (1994), 'Powerful, Personal: Electronic Mail and the L2 Writing Process', *ReCALL*, 6/2: 53–62.

Hofmeister, A. and Maggs, A. (1984), *Microcomputer Applications in Education and Training*, Australian Edn. (Sydney: Holt, Rinehart, and Winston).

Holmes, G. (1984*a*), 'Creating CAL Courseware: Some Possibilities', in Wyatt (1984*a*).

——(1984*b*), 'The Computer and Limitations', *Foreign Language Annals*, 17/4: 413–14.

Hooper, R. (1977), 'An Introduction to the National Development Programme in Computer-Assisted Language Learning', *British Journal of Educational Technology*, 8/3: 165–75.

Hope, G. R., Taylor, H. F., and Pusack, J. P. (1984), *Using Computers in Teaching Foreign Languages* (Englewood Cliffs, NJ: Prentice Hall Regents).

Howatt, A. P. R. (1984), *The History of English Language Teaching* (Oxford: Oxford University Press).

Hubbard, P. (1988*a*), 'An Integrated Framework for CALL Courseware Evaluation', *CALICO Journal*, 6/2: 51–74.

——(1988*b*), 'Language Teaching Approaches, the Evaluation of CALL Software, and Design Implications', in Smith (1988).

——(1988*c*), 'Two Steps toward a New Methodology for CALL', *CALL Digest*, 4/2: 7–8.

——(1990), 'Exploring Text Reconstruction Activities on Computers', *CAELL Journal*, 1/2: 2–4.

——(1992), 'A Methodological Framework for CALL Courseware Development', in Pennington and Stevens (1992).

——(1996), 'Elements of CALL Methodology: Development, Evaluation, and Implementation', in Pennington (1996).

Hutchins, W. J. (1986), *Machine Translation: Past, Present, Future* (Chichester: Horwood).

Hutchinson, T. (1987), 'What's underneath? An Interactive View of Materials Evaluation', in Sheldon (1987).

Ingraham, B. D. (1993), 'Advanced CALL Environments (ACE) and the Languages Curriculum', in Gimeno-Sanz (1993).

——(1995), 'Some Applications of Contemporary Information Technology to the Teaching of Language and Literature', *Literary and Linguistic Computing*, 10/1: 27–32.

——Chanier, T., and Emery, C. R. (1994), 'Language Training for Various Purposes in Several Languages on a Common Hypermedia Framework', *Computers in Education*, 23, 1/2: 107–15.

——and Emery, C. R. (1991), '"France Interactive": A Hypermedia Approach to Language Training', *Educational and Training Technology International*, 25/4: 321–33.

————(1993), 'The CAMILLE Project', *ReCALL*, 9: 26.

Jamieson, J., and Chapelle, C. (1988), 'Using CALL Effectively: What do we Need to Know about Students?' *System*, 16/2: 151–62.

Jennings, C. (1995), 'Enriching the Distance Language Learning Experience through Telematics and Multimedia: A Case Study', *ReCALL*, 7/1: 26–33.

Johns, T. (1986), 'Micro-Concord: A Language Learner's Research Tool', *System*, 14/2: 151–62.

——(1988), 'Whence and Whither Classroom Concordancing?' in Bongaerts, T., Haan, P. de, Lobbe, S., and Wekker, H. (eds.), *Computers in English Language Learning* (Dordrecht, Holland: Foris).

——(1990*a*), 'Should you be Persuaded: Two Examples of Data-Driven Learning Materials', in Johns and King (1990).

——(1990*b*), 'From Print-Out to Handout: Grammar and Vocabulary Teaching in the Context of Data-Driven Learning', in Johns and King (1990).

——and King, P. (1990) (eds.), *Classroom Concordancing, English Language Research Journal*, iv (University of Birmingham, Birmingham).

Johnson, D. (1985), 'Using Computers to Promote the Development of English as a Second Language', a report to the Carnegie Corporation.

Jonassen, D. H. (1985), 'Interactive Lesson Designs: A Taxonomy', *Educational Technology*, 25/6: 7–17.

——(1988) (ed.), *Instructional Designs for Microcomputer Courseware* (Hillsdale, NJ: Lawrence Erlbaum).

——(1989), 'Mapping the Structure of Research and Theory in Instructional Systems Technology', *Educational Technology*, 29/5: 7–10.

Jones, C. (1986), 'It's not so Much the Program, More What you do with it: The Importance of Methodology in CALL', *System*, 14/2: 171–8.

——(1988), 'Bottom up', *Muesli News*, 12.

——and Fortescue, S. (1987), *Using Computers in the Language Classroom* (Cheshire: Longman).

Jones, C. M. (1996), 'The Oral Language Archive (OLA): Computer Assisted Language Learning', 9/2–3:235–50.

Jones, F. (1991), 'Mickey-Mouse and the State of the Art: Program Sophistication and Classroom Methodology in Communicative CALL', *System*, 19/1–2: 1–13.

Jones, G. (1986), 'Computer Simulations in Language Teaching', *System*, 14/2: 179–86.

Jones, R. (1995), 'TICCIT and CLIPS: The Early Years', *CALICO Journal*, 12/4: 84–96.

Jordan, G. (1988), 'Designing and Exploiting CALL Programs in the Classroom', *System*, 16/2: 141–50.

Jung, H., and Vanderplank, R. (1994) (eds.), *Barriers and Bridges: Media Technology in Language Learning*, Proceedings of the 1993 CETall Symposium on the Occasion of the 10th AILA World Congress in Amsterdam (Frankfurt: Peter Lang).

Jung, U. (1988*a*) (ed.), *Computers in Applied Linguistics and Language Teaching* (Frankfurt: Peter Lang).

——(1988*b*), *An International Bibliography of Computer-Assisted Language Learning with Annotations in German* (Frankfurt: Peter Lang).

——(1989), 'CALLing around the World', in Kecskés and Agócs (1989*b*).

——(1994), 'Experiential Learning: What Educational Technology can Contribute', in Jung and Vanderplank (1994).

Kalaja, P., and Leppänen, S. (1994), 'Computer Conferencing: A Forum for Written Interaction', in Jung and Vanderplank (1994).

Karovsky, P. (1989), 'Educational Technology's Metaphors', *British Journal of Educational Technology*, 20/3: 157–63.

Karttunen, F. (1986), 'A Linguist Looks at Computer-Assisted Instruction', in Freudenstein, R., and James, C. V. (eds.), *Confidence Through Competence in Modern Language Learning* (London: CILT).

Kearsley, G. (1987) (ed.), *Artificial Intelligence and Instruction: Application and Methods* (Reading, Mass.: Addison-Wesley).

——(1988), 'Authoring Systems for Intelligent Tutoring Systems on Personal Computers', in Jonassen (1988).

——Hunter, B., and Seidel, J. R. (1983), 'Two Decades of Computer-Based Instruction Projects: What have we Learned?' *T.H.E. Journal*, 10/3: 90–3.

Kecskés, I. (1988), 'Computer Programs to Develop both Accuracy and Fluency', *System*, 16/1: 29–35.

——and Agócs, L. (1989*a*) (eds.), *New Tendencies in Computer-Assisted Language Learning* (Kossuth University, Debrecen).

—— ——(1989*b*), 'Expressing the Same Piece of Information using Different Elements of Language: A Text-Based System', *CALICO Journal*, 7/1: 53–65.

Keith, C. J., and Lafford, P. A. (1989), 'Designing Software for Vocational Language Programs: An Overview of the Development Process', in Pennington (1989*b*).

Keller, L., and Preece, J. (1990) (eds.), *Human-Computer Interaction* (UK: Prentice-Hall International).

Kelly, M. G. (1994), 'Telecommunications, Data Gathering, and Problem Solving', *The Computing Teacher*, Apr.: 23–6.

Kemble, I. R. (1991), 'Lexicography', in Brierley and Kemble (1991).

Kemmis, S., Atkin, R., and Wright, E. (1977), *How Do Students Learn?* Working papers on computer-assisted language learning, Uncal Evaluation Studies (Norwich: University of East Anglia).

Kemp, J. E. (1985), *The Instructional Design Process* (New York: Harper and Row).

Kenner, R. (1988*a*), 'Adding Videodisc Control to CAI Authoring Systems: A Software Customizing Methodology', *Journal of Educational Techniques and Technologies*, 21/2–3: 55–7.

——(1988*b*), 'What is a Good Authoring System', *CALL Digest*, 4/5: 1–2.

Kenning, M.-M. and Kenning, M. J. (1983), *An Introduction to Computer-Assisted Language Teaching* (Oxford: Oxford University Press).

—— —— (1986), *A Vous la France!* (London: BBC Publications).

—— —— (1990), *Computers and Language Learning: Current Theory and Practice* (New York: Horwood).

Kidd, M. (1990), 'The LEXI-CAL Authoring System for Vocabulary Acquisition', in Craven *et al.* (1990).

Klobusicky-Mailänder, E. (1990), 'Telecommunications Simulation: Europe 1992', *ReCALL*, 2: 12–15.

Kohn, K. (1994), 'Distributive Language Learning in a Computer-Based Multilingual Communication Environment', in Jung and Vanderplank (1994).

Kramsch, C., Morgenstern, D., and Murray, J. (1985), 'An Overview of the MIT Athena Language Learning Project', *CALICO Journal*, June: 31–4.

Krol, E. (1994), *The Whole Internet User's Guide and Catalog* (Sebastapol, Calif.: O'Reilly and Associates, Inc.).

Kroonenberg, N. (1994/5), 'Developing Communicative and Thinking Skills via Electronic Mail', *TESOL Journal*, 4/2: 24–7.

Kuhn, T. (1970), *The Structure of Scientific Revolutions* (Chicago: The University of Chicago Press).

Labrie, G., and Singh, L. P. S. (1991), 'Parsing, Error Diagnostics and Instruction in a French Tutor', *CALICO Journal*, 8/2: 9–26.

Lambert, S., and Sallis, J. (1987) (eds.), *CD-I and Interactive Videodisc Technology* (Indianapolis: Macmillan).

Lampe, D. (1988), 'Athena Muse: Hypermedia in Action', *The MIT Report*, Feb.

Lampert, D. (1993) (ed.), *The Stack Exchange: Educational Hypermedia for the Apple II and Macintosh* (Tampa, Fla.: Techware Corporation).

Larsen-Freeman, D. (1986), *Techniques and Principles in Language Teaching* (Oxford: Oxford University Press).

—— (1987), 'Recent Innovations in Language Teaching Methodology', *Annals, AAPSS* 490: 51–69.

—— and Long, M. H. (1991), *An Introduction to Second Language Acquisition Research* (London: Longman).

Last, R. W. (1987), 'Artificial Intelligence—The Way Forward for CALL?' in Chesters, G. (ed.), *The Use of Computers in the Teaching of Language and Languages* (Bath: Computers in Teaching Initiative Support Service).

—— (1989), *Artificial Intelligence Techniques in Language Learning* (Chichester: Horwood).

—— and King, P. K. (1979), 'The Design and Implementation of a Computer-Assisted Learning Package for Modern Language Teaching:

A Research Progress Report', *British Journal of Educational Technology*, 10/3: 194–7.

Laurel, B. (1990), *The Art of Human–Computer Interface Design* (Reading, Mass.: Addison-Wesley).

Laurillard, D. (1987) (ed.), *Interactive Media: Working Methods and Practical Applications* (Chichester: Horwood).

——(1991), 'Principles for Computer-Based Software Design for Language Learning', *CALL*, 4/3: 141–52.

Lawler, R. W., and Yazdani, M. (1987) (eds.), *Artificial Intelligence and Education, Volume 1: Learning Environments and Tutoring Systems* (Norwood, NJ: Ablex Publishing Corporation).

Lawrason, R. (1988/9), 'Language Lab Technology and the Instructional Design Process: Fashionable Fad or Pedagogical Tool?' *Journal of Educational Techniques and Technologies*, 21/4: 31–8.

Lee, T. (1991), 'Low-Tech, High-Tech and Mid-Tech in CALL', in Milton, J. C., and Tong, K. S. T. (eds.), *Text Analysis in Computer-Assisted Language Learning* (Hong Kong: City Poytechnic).

Leech, G. (1986), 'Automatic Grammatical Analysis and its Educational Applications', in Leech and Candlin (1986).

——and Candlin, C. N. (1986) (eds.), *Computers in English Language Teaching and Research* (Cheshire: Longman).

Legenhausen, L., and Wolff, D. (1987), 'Issues in CALL', in Legenhausen and Wolff (1989*b*).

——— (1989*a*), 'Evaluating Software: The Dusseldorf CALL Project', *CALL Digest*, 5/1: 7–9.

——— (1989*b*) (eds.), *Computer-Assisted Language Learning and Innovative EFL Methodology* (Oxford: Intellect Books).

——— (1990), 'CALL in Use—Use of CALL: Evaluating CALL Software', *System*, 18/1: 1–14.

——— (1991), 'Storyboard and Communicative Language Learning: Results of the Düsseldorf CALL Project', in Swartz and Yazdani (1991).

Leppänen, S., and Kalaja, P. (1995), 'Experimenting with Computer Conferencing in English for Academic Purposes', *ELT Journal*, 49/1: 26–36.

Levin, L. S., Evans, D. A., and Gates, D. M. (1991), 'The Alice System: A Workbench for Learning and Using Language', *CALICO Journal*, 8/2: 27–56.

Levy, M. (1989), 'Determining Content and Approach for an MA in Computer-Enhanced Language Learning', *Proceedings*, 1989 ASCILITE Conference, Bond University, Gold Coast.

——(1990*a*), 'A Rationale for the Design of an MA in Computer Enhanced Language Learning', Computers-in-Education Edition of *Education*, summer: 446–52.

Levy, M. (1990*b*), 'Concordances and their Integration into a Word Processing Environment for Language Learners', *System*, 18/2: 177–88.

——(1992), 'Integrating CALL into a Writing Course', *CAELL Journal*, 3/1: 17–27.

——(1994*a*), 'The Role of the Computer in CALL: The Tutor and the Tool', paper presented at the APITITE 1994 Conference, Brisbane, 28 June–2 July 1994, *Proceedings*: 781–6.

——(1994*b*), 'Designing the User Interface: The Snowy River Project', paper presented at the CALICO Conference, Flagstaff, Arizona, 14–18 March 1994, *Proceedings*: 148–53.

——(1994*c*), 'CALL Materials Development Survey Report', *Computer Assisted Language Learning*, 7/2: 175–89.

——(forthcoming *a*), 'A Rationale for Teacher Education and CALL: The Holistic View and its Implications', *Computers and the Humanities*.

——(forthcoming *b*), 'Theory-Driven CALL and the Development Process', *Computer Assisted Language Learning*.

——(forthcoming *c*), 'Annotated Bibliography of CALL', *Annoted Bibliography of English Studies* (The Netherlands: Swets and Zeitlinger).

——and Farrugia, D. (1988), *Computers and Language Teaching: Analysis, Research and Reviews* (Melbourne: TAFE Victoria).

——and Garton, J. (1994), 'Adapting a Grammar Checker for Learner Writers', *ReCALL*, 6/2: 3–8.

——and Green, A. (1995), 'CALL Bibliography for Postgraduate Study', *System*, 23/1: 87–106.

Lian, A.-P. (1988), 'Distributed Learning Environments and Computer-Enhanced Language Learning (CELL)' in Dekkers, J., Griffin, H., and Kempf, N. (eds.), *Computer Technology serves Distance Education* (Rockhampton: Capricornia Institute).

——(1991), 'What is CALL Software?' *On-CALL*, 5/4: 2–8.

——(1992), 'Intelligence in CALL', in Pennington and Stevens (1992).

——and Levy, M. (1991), 'An Australian Perspective on Computer-Enhanced Language Learning: The Bond University Context', *Interactive Learning International*, 7: 165–74.

——Thornquist, L., and Thornquist, L. (1987), 'Computer-Based Technology in Language Learning: Beyond the Walls of the Traditional Classroom', *Journal of Educational Techniques and Technologies*, 20/2: 24–31.

Liddell, P. (1993) (ed.), *CALL: Theory and Application: Proceedings of CCALL2/CCELAO2, The Second Canadian CALL Conference*, British Columbia: University of Victoria, 30 Apr.–2 May 1993.

Liou, H.-C. (1994), 'Practical Considerations for Multimedia Courseware Development: An EFL IVD Experience', *CALICO Journal*, 11/3: 47–74.

Lippert, R. (1989), 'Expert Systems: Tutors, Tools, and Tutees', *Journal of Computer-Based Instruction*, 16/1: 11–19.

Little, D., and Davis, E. (1986), 'Interactive Video for Language Learning: The Autotutor Project', *System*, 14/1: 29–34.

Long, M. H. (1988), 'Instructed InterLanguage Development', in Beebe, L. M. (ed.), *Issues in Second Language Acquisition* (New York: Newbury House).

——(1990), 'Task, Group, and Task-Group Interactions', in Anivan (1990).

Loritz, D. (1995), 'The Adolescence of CALL', *CALICO Journal*, 12/4: 47–56.

Lutz, J. A. (1987), 'A Study of Professional and Experienced Writers Revising and Editing at the Computer and with Pen and Paper', *Research in the Teaching of English*, 21: 398–421.

Lyons, J. (1970) (ed.), *New Horizons in Linguistics* (Harmondsworth: Penguin).

McAleese, R. (1993a) (ed.), *Hypertext: Theory into Practice* (Oxford: Intellect).

——(1993b), 'Navigation and Browsing in Hypertext', in McAleese (1993a).

McCarty, W. (1993), 'Language, Learning and the Computer: Desultory Postprandial Investigations', in Liddell (1993).

——(1995), 'Cannot without Process of Speech be Told: Learning from the Failures of Computational Modelling', paper presented at the EUROCALL Conference, 6–9 Sept., Valencia, Spain.

Mackay, W. E. (1988), 'Tutoring, Information Databases, and Iterative Design', in Jonassen (1988).

Mackie, R. R., and Christensen, P. R. (1967), 'Translation and Application of Psychological Research', Technical Report 716–1, Santa Barbara Research Park, Human Factors Research Inc., Goleta, California.

McKnight, C., Dillon, A., and Richardson, J. (1991), *Hypertext in Context* (Cambridge: Cambridge University Press).

McLaughlin, B. (1987), *Theories of Second Language Acquisition* (London: Edward Arnold).

——(1990), 'Restructuring', *Applied Linguistics*, 11/2: 113–28.

——Rossman, R., and McLeod, B. (1983), 'Second Language Learning: An Information-Processing Perspective', *Language Learning*, 33: 135–58.

McNab, A. (1991), 'CALL Resources: Electronic Retrieval of Information', *ReCALL*, 4: 4–9.

Mah, D. (1990), 'Designing an Interactive Videodisc: Applying Theory to Technology', in Brindley, G. (ed.), *Second Language Curriculum in Action* (Sydney: NCELTR).

Markosian, L. Z., and Ager, T. A. (1983), 'Applications of Parsing Theory to Computer-Assisted Instruction', *System*, 11/1: 65–77.

Marty, F. (1981), 'Reflections on the Use of Computers in Second Language Acquisition—1', *System*, 9/2: 85–98.

——(1982), 'Reflections on the Use of Computers in Second Language Acquisition—2', *System*, 10/1: 1–11.

Matthews, C. (1991), *Intelligent CALL (ICALL) Bibliography* (University of East Anglia, Norwich).

——(1994), 'Intelligent Computer-Assisted Language Learning as Cognitive Science: The Choice of Syntactic Frameworks for Language Tutoring', *Journal of Artificial Intelligence in Education*, 5/4: 533–56.

Mayhew, D. J. (1992), *Principles and Guidelines in Software User Interface Design* (Englewood Cliffs, NJ: Prentice Hall).

Meister, D. (1991), *Psychology of System Design* (Amsterdam: Elsevier).

Melby, A. (1996), 'Machine Translation and Other Translation Technologies', in Grabe, W. (ed.), *Annual Review of Applied Linguistics: Technology and Language*, 16 (Cambridge: Cambridge University Press).

Merriam, S. B., and Simpson, E. L. (1984), *A Guide to Research for Educators and Trainers of Adults* (Malabar, Fla.: Krieger).

Merrill, M. D. (1978), 'Hierarchical and Information Processing Task Analysis: A Comparison', *Journal of Instructional Development*, 1/2: 35–40.

——(1980a), 'Analysis of a Procedural Task', *NSPI Journal*, 19/2: 11–15, 26.

——(1980b), 'Learner Control in Computer-Based Learning', *Computers and Education*, 77: 77–95.

——(1983), 'Component Display Theory', in Reigeluth (1983a).

——(1988), 'Applying Component Display Theory to the Design of Courseware', in Jonassen (1988).

——Schneider, E. W., and Fletcher, K. A. (1980), *TICCIT* (Englewood Cliffs, NJ: Educational Technology Publications).

Meskill, C. (1991), 'A Systematic Approach to the Design of Interactive Videodisc Courseware', in Bush *et al.* (1991).

Mitterer, J., Marini, Z., MacRae, D., and Joe, D. (1990), 'Computer-Aided Language Learning: Hypermedia and Direct-Manipulation Interfaces', in Craven *et al.* (1990).

Molla, S., Sanders, A. F., and Sanders, R. H. (1988), 'Artificial Intelligence in a German Adventure Game: Spion in PROLOG', *CALICO Journal*, 6/1: 9–24.

Monk, A., Wright, P., Haber, J., and Davenport, L. (1993), *Improving your Human-Computer Interface, A Practical Technique* (Hemel Hempstead: Prentice Hall).

Moonen, J., and Stanchev, I. (1993), 'Educational Interactive Systems Research: Instrumentation and Implementation', *Computers in Education*, 21/1–2: 163–72.

Morgenstern, D. (1986), 'Simulation, Interactive Fiction and Language Learning: Aspects of the MIT Project', *Bulletin de l'ACLA/Bulletin of the CAAL (Canadian Association of Applied Linguistics)*, 8/2: 22–33.

Moskowitz, G. (1978), *Caring and Sharing in the Foreign Language Class* (Rowley, Mass.: Newbury House).

Mulford, G. W. (1989), 'Semantic Processing for Communicative Exercises in Foreign Language Learning', *Computers and the Humanities*, 23/1: 31–44.

Murison-Bowie, S. (1993), 'TESOL Technology: Imposition or Opportunity', *TESOL Journal*, 3/1: 6–8.

Murphy, R. T., and Appel, L. R. (1978), *Evaluation of the PLATO IV Computer-Based Education System in the Community College: Final Report* (Princeton, NJ: Educational Testing Service).

Murray, J. (1987), 'Humanists in an Institute of Technology: How Foreign Languages are Reshaping Workstation Computing at MIT', *Academic Computing*, Sept.: 34–8.

——Morgenstern, D., and Furstenberg, G. (1989), 'The Athena Language Learning Project: Design Issues for the Next Generation of Computer-Based Language Learning Tools', in Smith (1989).

Naiman, N., Fröhlich, M., Stern, H., and Todesco, A. (1978), *The Good Language Learner* (Toronto: Ontario Institute for Studies in Education).

Nakajima, K. (1988), 'On Developing Hypercard Stacks for the Study of Chinese Characters: Kanjicard', *CALICO Journal*, 6/2: 75–88.

——(1990), 'Developing Hypercard Stacks for the Study of Japanese Ideographic Scripts', in Craven *et al.* (1990).

Neisser, U. (1967), *Cognitive Psychology* (New York: Appleton-Century-Crofts).

Nelson, T. H. (1967), 'Getting it out of our System', in Schechter, G. (ed.), *Information Retrieval: A Critical Review* (Washington: Thompson Books).

——(1981), *Literary Machines* (Swathmore, Pa.: Nelson).

Neuwirth, C. M. (1989), 'Intelligent Tutoring Systems: Exploring Issues in Learning and Teaching Writing', *Computers and the Humanities*, 23/1: 45–57.

——(1992), 'Computers and Composition Studies: Articulating a Pattern of Discovery', in Hawisher and LeBlanc (1992).

——Kaufer, D. S., Kelm, G., and Gillespie, T. (1988), 'The Comments Program: Computer Support for Response to Writing', in *CECE Technical Report No. 2* (Pittsburgh: Carnegie Mellon University).

Ng, K. L. E., and Olivier, W. (1987), 'Computer-Assisted Language Learning: An Investigation on some Design and Implementation Issues', *System*, 15/1: 1–17.

Noblitt, J. S., and Bland, S. K. (1989), 'Tracking the Learner in Computer-Aided Language Learning', in Freed, B. (ed.), *Proceedings for the Conference entitled 'Foreign Language Acquisition and the Classroom'* (Philadelphia: University of Pennsylvania).

Nunan, D. (1988*a*), *Syllabus Design* (Oxford: Oxford University Press).

——(1988*b*), *The Learner-Centred Curriculum* (Cambridge: Cambridge University Press).

——(1989*a*), *Designing Tasks for the Communicative Classroom* (Cambridge: Cambridge University Press).

——(1989*b*), 'Second Language Teacher Education: Present Trends and Future Prospects', in Candlin and McNamara (1989).

——(1990), 'An Empirically Based Methodology in the Nineties', in Anivan (1990).

Nyns, R. (1989), 'Is Intelligent Computer-Assisted Learning Possible?' *System*, 17/1: 35–48.

O'Malley, M., and Chamot, A. (1990), *Learning Strategies in Second Language Acquisition* (Cambridge: Cambridge University Press).

Oren, T. (1990), 'Cognitive Load in Hypermedia: Designing for the Exploratory Learner', in Ambron, S., and Hooper, K. (eds.), *Learning with Interactive Multimedia: Using Multimedia Tools in Education* (Washington: Microsoft Press).

O'Shea, T., and Self, J. (1983), *Learning and Teaching with Computers* (London: Harvester Press).

Osguthorpe, R. T., and Zhou, L. (1989), 'Instructional Science: What is it and Where did it Come from?' *Educational Technology*, 29/6: 7–17.

Otto, F. (1989), 'Special CALICO Programs and Activities: The CALICO Computer Use Survey', *CALICO Journal*, 7/2: 3–12.

Otto, S. (1989), 'The Language Laboratory in the Computer Age', in Smith (1989).

Otto, S. K., and Pusack, J. P. (1990), 'A Cross-Section of Perspectives on Video in Language Teaching', *IALL Journal of Language Learning Technologies*, 23/1: 7–8.

Oxford, R. L. (1993), 'Intelligent Computers for Learning Languages: The View for Language Acquisition and Instructional Methodology', *CALL* 6/2: 173–88.

Papert, S. (1980), 'New Cultures from New Technologies', *Byte* 5: 230–40.

——(1982), *Mindstorms* (London: Harvester Press).

Paramskas, D. M. (1989), 'CLEF: Computer-Assisted Learning Exercises for French', in Smith (1989).

——(1993), 'Computer-Assisted Language Learning (CALL): Increasingly

Integrated into an ever more Electronic World', *The Canadian Modern Language Review*, 50/1: 124–43.

——(1995), 'Meanwhile, up North: The Beginnings of CALL in Canada', *CALICO Journal*, 12/4: 97–105.

Pederson, K. M. (1988), 'Research on CALL', in Smith (1988).

Pennington, M. C. (1989a), 'Applications of Computers in the Development of Speaking and Listening Proficiency', in Pennington (1989b).

——(1989b) (ed.), *Teaching Languages with Computers: The State of the Art* (La Jolla, Calif.: Athelstan).

——(1990), 'Computer-Assisted Analysis of English Dialect and Interlanguage Prosodics: Applications to Research and Training', in Dunkel (1990a).

——(1991a), 'The Road Ahead: A Forward-Looking View of Computers in Language Learning', *Computer-Assisted Language Learning*, 4/1: 3–19.

——(1991b), 'Positive and Negative Potentials of Word Processing for ESL Writers', *System*, 19/3: 267–75.

——(1993), 'Exploring the Potential of Word Processing for Non-Native Writers', *Computers and the Humanities*, 27: 149–63.

——(1995), 'Writing the Natural Way: On Computer', paper presented at the Exeter CALL Conference, 10–12 Sept., Exeter, UK.

——(ed.) (1996), *The Power of CALL* (Houston: Athelstan).

——(forthcoming), *The Computer and the Non-Native Writer: A Natural Partnership* (Creskill, NJ: Hampton Press).

——and Stevens, V. (1992) (eds.), *Computers in Applied Linguistics: An International Perspective* (Avon: Multilingual Matters).

Phillips, M. (1983), 'Intelligent CALL and the QWERTY Phenomenon: A Rationale', paper presented at the 16th annual meeting of the British Association of Applied Linguistics, Leicester Polytechnic.

——(1985a), 'Logical Possibilities and Classroom Scenarios for the Development of CALL', in Brumfit *et al.* (1985).

——(1985b), 'Educational Technology in the Next Decade: An ELT Perspective', in Brumfit *et al.* (1985).

——(1986), 'CALL in its Educational Context', in Leech and Candlin (1986).

——(1987), 'Potential Paradigms and Possible Problems for CALL', *System*, 15/3: 275–87.

——(1988), 'Dear Muesli', *Muesli News*, Apr.: 15–16.

Pica, T. (1994), 'Questions from the Language Classroom: Research Perspectives', *TESOL Quarterly*, 28/1: 49–79.

Pierce, J. R. (1966), *Language and Machines: Computers in Translation and Linguistics*, a report by the ALPAC, National Academy of Sciences and the National Research Council, Washington.

Pope, T. (1990), 'Language Parsing with Special Reference to German', in Craven *et al.* (1990).

Preece, J., and Keller, L. (1990) (eds.), *Human-Computer Interaction* (Cambridge: Cambridge University Press).

Prescott, S. (1995), 'Best Practice in CALL: Technique not Technology', paper presented at the 8th Annual ELICOS Association Conference, 14–16 Sept., Esplanade Hotel, Freemantle, Australia.

Price, K. (1987), 'The Use of Technology: Varying the Medium in Language Teaching', in Rivers (1987).

Pusack, J. (1983), 'Answer-Processing and Error Correction in Foreign Language CAI', *System*, 11/1: 53–64.

——(1988), 'Problems and Prospects in Foreign Language Computing', in Smith (1988).

Rahtz, S. (1987) (ed.), *Information Technology in the Humanities: Tools, Techniques and Applications* (Chichester: Horwood).

Reeves, T. C. (1992), 'Effective Dimensions of Interactive Learning Systems', Keynote address prepared for the Information Technology for Training and Education Conference (ITTE 1992), 29 Sept.–2 Oct., The University of Queensland, Brisbane, Australia.

——(1993), 'Evaluating Interactive Multimedia', in Gayeski (1993).

——and Harmon, S. W. (1993), 'Systematic Evaluation Procedures for Instructional Hypermedia/Multimedia', paper presented at the Annual Meeting of the American Educational Research Association, 14 Apr., Atlanta, Georgia, USA.

Reigeluth, C. (1983*a*) (ed.), *Instructional-design Theories and Models: An Overview of their Current Status* (Hillsdale, NJ: Lawrence Erlbaum).

——(1983*b*), 'Instructional Design: What is it and Why is it?' in Reigeluth (1983*a*).

——and Schwartz, E. (1989), 'An Instructional Theory for the Design of Computer-Based Simulations', *Journal of Computer-Based Instruction*, 16/1: 1–10.

Rézeau, J. (1987), 'CALL and the Integrated Professional Package FRAMEWORK^TM', workshop presented at Third International CALL Conference, Delft.

Rheinhold, H. (1991), *Virtual Reality* (London: Mandarin).

Richards, J. C. (1987), 'Beyond Methods: Alternative Approaches to Instructional Design in Language Teaching', *Prospect*, 2/1: 11–30.

——and Rodgers, T. S. (1982), 'Method: Approach, Design and Procedure', *TESOL Quarterly*, 16/2: 153–68.

————(1986), *Approaches and Methods in Language Teaching* (Cambridge: Cambridge University Press).

Richardson, C. P., and Scinicariello, S. G. (1989), 'Television Technology in the Foreign Language Classroom', in Smith (1989).

Rivers, W. (1981), *Teaching Foreign Language Skills*, 2nd edn. (Chicago: University of Chicago Press).

——(1987) (ed.), *Interactive Language Teaching* (Cambridge: Cambridge University Press).

Robb, T. (1995), 'The Student Lists for Intercultural Exchange and Language Practice', paper presented at the EUROCALL Conference, 6–9 Sept., Valencia, Spain.

Robinson, G. (1991), 'Effective Feedback Strategies in CALL: Learning Theory and Empirical Research', in Dunkel (1991*a*).

——Underwood, J., Rivers, W., Hernandez, J., Rudisill, C., and Enseñat, C. (1985), *Computer-Assisted Instruction in Foreign Language Education: A Comparison of the Effectiveness of Different Methodologies and Different Forms of Error Correction* (San Francisco: Centre for Language and Crosscultural Skills).

Roblyer, M. D. (1988), 'Fundamental Problems and Principles of Designing Effective Courseware', in Jonassen (1988).

——(1989), 'The Impact of Microcomputer-Based Instruction on Teaching and Learning: A Review of Recent Research', ED 315 063.

Rowe, A. A. (1990), 'Language Discovery Environments', *Journal of Interactive Instruction Development*, Spring: 3–7.

Rüschoff, B. (1984), 'The Integration of CALL Materials into the Overall Curriculum', *CALICO Journal*, 1/4: 26–8.

——(1988), 'Self-Directed Learning and New Technologies: Computers as Language Learning Tools', in Das (1988).

——(1993), 'Language Learning and Information Technology: State of the Art', Keynote address CALICO 1992 International Symposium 'Bridges', Maastricht Valkenburg, The Netherlands, *CALICO Journal*, 10/3: 5–17.

Rutter, D. R. (1984), *Looking and Seeing: The Role of Visual Communication in Social Interaction* (Chichester: Wiley).

St John, E., and Cash, D. (1995*a*), 'Language Learning via Email: Demonstrable Success with German', paper presented at the Exeter CALL Conference, 10–12 Sept., Exeter, UK.

—— ——(1995*b*), 'German Language Learning via Email: A Case Study', *ReCALL*, 7/2: 47–51.

Salvendy, G., and Smith, M. J. (1993), *Human-Computer Interaction: Software and Hardware Interfaces* (Amsterdam: Elsevier).

Sampson, G. (1986), 'Transition Networks for Computer-Assisted Language Learning', in Leech and Candlin (1986).

Sanders, A. F., and Sanders, R. H. (1989), 'Syntactic Parsing: A Survey', *Computers and the Humanities*, 23/1: 13–30.

Sanders, R. H., and Sanders, A. F. (1995), 'History of an AI Spy Game: Spion', *CALICO Journal*, 12/4: 114–27.

Sauer, E. (1994), 'Creative Collaboration Online', *The Computing Teacher*, Apr.: 38–40.

Sayers, D. (1993), 'Distance Team Teaching and Computer Learning Networks', *TESOL Journal*, 3/1: 19–23.

Savignon, S. (1972), *Communicative Competence: An Experiment in Foreign Language Teaching* (Philadelphia: Centre for Curriculum Development).

——(1983), *Communicative Competence: Theory and Classroom Practice* (Reading, Mass.: Addison-Wesley).

Scandura, J. (1983), 'Instructional Strategies based on the Structural Learning Theory', in Reigeluth (1983*a*).

Scarborough, D. (1988), 'Survey Review: Software for English Language Teaching', *ELT Journal*, 41/2: 119–25.

Schaefermeyer, S. (1990), 'Standards for Instructional Computing Software Design and Development', *Educational Technology*, 30/6: 9–15.

Schneider, E. W., and Bennion, J. L. (1984), 'Veni, Vidi, Vici, Via Videodisc: A Simulator for Instructional Conversations', in Wyatt (1984*a*).

Schoen, H., and Hunt, T. (1977), 'The Effect of Technology on Instruction: The Literature of the Last 20 Years', *AEDS Journal*, 10: 68–82.

Scott, M., Johns, T., and Murison-Bowie, S. (1993), *MicroConcord* (Oxford: Oxford University Press).

Seels, B. (1989), 'The Instructional Design Movement in Educational Technology', *Educational Technology*, 29/5: 11–15.

Self, J. (1985), *Microcomputers in Education* (London: Harvester Press).

——(1988) (ed.), *Artificial Intelligence and Human Learning* (London: Chapman and Hall Computing).

Sheldon, L. E. (1987) (ed.), *ELT Textbooks and Materials: Problems in Evaluation and Development*, ELT Documents: 126 (London: Modern English Publications and the British Council).

——(1988), 'Evaluation ELT Textbooks and Materials', *English Language Teaching Journal*, 42/4: 237–46.

Sherman, B., and Judkins, P. (1992), *Glimpses of Heaven, Visions of Hell: Virtual Reality and its Implications* (London: Hodder and Stoughton).

Shneiderman, B. (1987), *Designing the User Interface: Strategies for Effective Human-Computer Interaction* (Reading, Mass.: Addison-Wesley).

Shuell, T. J. (1986), 'Cognitive Conceptions of Learning', *Review of Educational Research*, 56/4: 411–36.

Sinclair, J. M. (1986), 'Basic Computer Processing of Long Texts', in Leech and Candlin (1986).

——(1987) (ed.), *Looking Up* (London: Collins ELT).

——(1988) (ed.), *Collins COBUILD English Language Dictionary* (Collins Publishers and the University of Birmingham).

Sinyor, R. (1990), 'The Applicability of Parsing to the Learning of Italian', in Craven *et al.* (1990).

Skinner, B. F. (1954), 'The Science of Learning and the Art of Teaching', *Harvard Educational Review*, 24: 86–97.

——(1957), *Verbal Behaviour* (New York: Appleton-Century-Crofts).

Smarte, G., and Reinhardt, A. (1990), '1975–1990: 15 years of Bits, Bytes, and other Great Moments', *Byte*, Sept.: 369–400.

Smith, S., and Sherwood, B. (1976), 'Educational Uses of the PLATO Computer System', *Science*, 192: 344–52.

Smith, W. F. (1988) (ed.), *Modern Media in Foreign Language Education: Theory and Implementation* (Lincolnwood: Illinois: National Textbook Company).

——(1989) (ed.), *Modern Media in Foreign Language Education: Applications and Projects* (Lincolnwood: Illinois: National Textbook Company).

Spolsky, B. (1989), *Conditions for Second Language Learning* (Oxford: Oxford University Press).

Stern, H. H. (1983), *Fundamental Concepts of Language Teaching* (Oxford: Oxford University Press).

Stevens, V. (1983), 'English Lessons on PLATO: Review', *TESOL Quarterly*, 17/2: 293–300.

——(1989), 'A Direction for CALL: From Behaviouristic to Humanistic Courseware', in Pennington (1989*b*).

——(1991), 'Concordance-Based Vocabulary Exercises: A Variable Alternative to Gap-Fillers', in Johns, T., and King, P. (eds.), *Special issue of English Language Research Journal* (Birmingham: University of Birmingham).

——Sussex, R., and Tuman, W. V. (1986), *A Bibliography of Computer-Aided Language Learning* (New York: AMS Press).

Stillings, N. A., Feinstein, M. H., Garfield, J. L., Rissland, E. L., Rosenbaum, D. A., Weisler, S. E., and Baker-Ward, L. (1987), *Cognitive Science: An Introduction* (Cambridge, Mass.: The MIT Press).

Stolurow, L. M., and Cubillos, E. M. (1983), *Needs and Development Opportunities for Educational Software for Foreign Language Instruction in Schools*, ED 242 204, University of Iowa.

Sullivan, N. (1993), 'Teaching Writing on a Computer Network', *TESOL Journal*, 3/1: 34–6.

Sussex, R. D. (1989), 'Issues in Computer-Aided Language Learning: Towards an Expert Systems Learning Environment', in Candlin and McNamara (1989).

——(1990), 'On the Role of Computers in Language Learning', in Peters, P. (ed.), *Frontiers of Style: Proceedings from Style Council 88*, University of Melbourne, Nov. 1988. The Dictionary Research Centre, Macquarie University.

Sussex, R. D. (1991), 'Author Languages, Authoring Systems and their Relation to the Changing Focus of Computer-Aided Language Learning', *System*, 19/1: 15–27.

——(1995), 'The Epistemology of CALL', paper presented at the Exeter CALL Conference, 10–12 Sept., Exeter, UK.

——and Cumming, G. D. (1989), 'A Lexical Toolkit for Language Learning: Providing Intelligent Help and Guidance', in Bishop, G., and Baker, J. (eds.), *Proceedings, ASCILITE-89*. Bond University, Gold Coast.

—— ——(1990), 'Intelligent Tools and Lexical Support for the Language Learner: Providing Advice at Task and Discussion Levels', in McDougall, A., and Dowling, C. (eds.), *Computers in Education* (North-Holland: Elsevier Science Publishers B.V.).

——and White, P. (1996), 'Electronic Networking in Applied Linguistics', *Annual Review of Applied Linguistics: Technology and Language*, 16.

Swartz, M. L., and Russell, D. M. (1989), 'FL-IDE: Hypertext for Structuring a Conceptual Design for Computer-Assisted Language Learning', *Instructional Science*, 18/1: 5–26.

——and Yazdani, M. (1991) (eds.), *Intelligent Tutoring Systems for Foreign Language Learning: The Bridge to International Communication* (Berlin: Springer-Verlag).

——Kostyla, S. J., Hanfling, S., and Holland, V. M. (1990), 'Preliminary Assessment of a Foreign Language Learning Environment', *Computer-Assisted Language Learning*, 1/1: 51–64.

Taylor, R. P. (1980) (ed.), *The Computer in the School: Tutor, Tool, Tutee*, Teacher's College, Columbia University (New York: Teacher's College Press, New York).

Teichmann, V. (1994), 'An Interdisciplinary Project Orientation using Telecommunications Media in Foreign Language Teaching', in Jung and Vanderplank (1994).

Tella, S. (1991), *Introducing International Communications Networks and Electronic Mail into Foreign Language Classrooms*, Research Report No. 95 (Helsinki: University of Helsinki, Department of Teacher Education).

——(1992a), *Boys, Girls and E-Mail: A Case Study in Finnish Senior Secondary Schools*, Research Report No. 110 (Helsinki: University of Helsinki, Department of Teacher Education).

——(1992b), *Talking Shop Via E-Mail: A Thematic and Linguistc Analysis of Electronic Mail Communication*, Research Report No. 99 (Helsinki: University of Helsinki, Department of Teacher Education).

Tennyson, R. D. (1990a), 'A Proposed Cognitive Paradigm of Learning for Educational Technology', *Educational Technology*, 30/6: 16–19.

——(1990*b*), 'Integrated Instructional Design Theory: Advancements from Cognitive Science and Instructional Technology', *Educational Technology*, 30/7: 9–15.

Thomas, W., and Thomas, C. (1982), 'Needed: A Visual Language for Program Design', *Educational and Industrial Television*, June: 50–1.

Thornbury, S. (1991), 'Metaphors we Work By: EFL and its Metaphors', *English Language Teaching Journal*, 45/3: 193–9.

Tribble, C. (1990*a*), 'Concordancing in an EAP Writing Program', *CAELL Journal*, 1/2: 10–15.

——(1990*b*), 'Small Scale Corpora in ELT', *CAELL Journal*, 1/4: 13–17.

——and Jones, G. (1990), *Concordances in the Classroom* (London: Longman).

Turner, J., and Pohio, V. (1995), 'Using Text-Based Virtual Reality in the Language Classroom—A Narrative', paper presented at the 8th Annual ELICOS Association Conference, 14–16 Sept., Esplanade Hotel, Freemantle, Australia.

Underwood, J. (1984), *Linguistics, Computers and the Language Teacher* (Rowley, Mass.: Newbury House).

——(1988*a*), 'Artificial Intelligence and CALL', in Smith (1988).

——(1988*b*), 'Language Learning and Hypermedia', *ADFL Bulletin* (Association of Departments of Foreign Languages, Modern Language Association) 19/3: 13–17.

——(1989*a*), 'Hypercard and Interactive Video', *CALICO Journal*, 6/3: 7–20.

——(1989*b*), 'Hypermedia: Where we Are and Where we Aren't', *CALICO Journal*, 6/4: 23–6.

——(1989*c*), 'On the Edge: Intelligent CALL in the 1990s', *Computers in the Humanities*, 23/1: 71–84.

——(1991), 'Interactive Video as Hypermedia', in Bush *et al.* (1991).

Van Ek, J. A. (1984), *A Study of the Fundamental Vocabulary for Japanese Language Teaching* (Tokyo: The National Language Research Institute).

Van Elsen, E., Van Deun, K., and Decoo, W. (1991), 'Wordchip: The Application of External Versatility to an English Lexical CALL Program', *System*, 19/4: 401–17.

Verano, M. (1987), 'Achievement and Retention in Spanish presented via Videodisc in Linear, Segmented, and Interactive Modes', unpublished Ph.D. dissertation (Austin: University of Texas).

Walsh, A. E. (1992), 'Programming QuickTime', *Dr. Dobb's Journal*, July: 76–105.

Wang, Y. M. (1993), 'E-Mail Dialogue Journaling in an ESL Reading and Writing Classroom', unpublished doctoral dissertation (Eugene: University of Oregon).

Ward, R. D. (1989), 'Some Uses of Natural Language Interfaces in

Computer-Assisted Language Learning', *Instructional Science*, 18/1: 45–62.

Warschauer, M. (1995), *E-Mail for English Teaching* (Alexandria, Va.: TESOL Inc.).

Weible, D. (1988), 'Towards a Media-Specific Methodology for CALL', in Smith (1988).

Weiman, L., and Moran, T. (1992), 'Newton: A Step Toward the Future', *MacWorld*, Aug.: 129–31.

Weischedel, R. M., Voge, W. M., and James, M. (1978), 'An Artificial Intelligence Approach to Language Instruction', *Artificial Intelligence*, 10: 225–40.

Weizenbaum, J. (1984), *Computer Power and Human Reason* (Harmondsworth, Middlesex: Penguin).

Wenden, A., and Rubin, J. (1987), *Learner Strategies in Language Learning* (New York: Prentice Hall).

Wenger, E. (1987), *Artificial Intelligence and Tutoring Systems* (Los Altos, Calif.: Morgan Kaufmann Publishers).

White, R. (1988), *The ELT Curriculum: Design, Innovation and Management* (Oxford: Blackwell).

Widdowson, H. G. (1978), *Teaching Language as Communication* (Oxford: Oxford University Press).

Wilkins, D. A. (1972), 'The Linguistic and Situational Content of the Common Core in a Unit/Credit System', Strasbourg: Council of Europe MS.

Willis, J., and Willis, D. (1988), *Collins CoBUILD English Course* (London: Collins ELT).

Windeatt, S. (1986), 'Observing CALL in Action', in Leech and Candlin (1986).

Winograd, T., and Flores, F. (1986), *Understanding Computers and Cognition* (Reading, Mass.: Addison-Wesley).

Wittrock, M. C. (1979), 'The Cognitive Movement in Instruction', *Educational Researcher*, 8/2: 5–11.

Wresch, W. (1984) (ed.), *The Computer in Composition Instruction* (National Council of Teachers of English, USA).

Wright, T. (1987), *Roles of Teachers and Learners* (Oxford: Oxford University Press).

Wyatt, D. H. (1983), 'Three Major Approaches to Developing Computer-Assisted Language Learning Materials for Microcomputers', *CALICO Journal*, 1/2: 34–8.

——(1984a) (ed.), *Computer-Assisted Language Instruction: Special Issue of System* (Oxford: Pergamon).

——(1984b), 'Computer-Assisted Language Instruction: Present State and Future Prospects', in Wyatt (1984a).

——(1984*c*), *Computers and ESL* (Englewood Cliffs, NJ: Prentice Hall).

——(1988), 'Applying Pedagogical Principles to CALL Courseware Development', in Smith (1988).

Yazdani, M. (1984), *New Horizons in Educational Computing* (Chichester: Horwood).

——(1991*a*), 'The LINGER Project: An Artificial Intelligence Approach to Second Language Tutoring', *CALL*, 4/2: 107–16.

——(1991*b*), 'LINGERing on!: Towards an Intelligent Language Tutoring Environment', *AISB Quarterly*, 77: 14–21.

——(1993) (ed.), *Multilingual Multimedia* (Oxford: Intellect).

——and Cameron, K. (1989) (eds.), *Computer-Assisted Language Learning: Special Issue of Instructional Science*, 18/1 (Dordrecht: Kluwer).

Yildiz, R., and Atkins, M. (1993), 'Evaluating Multimedia Applications', *Computers in Education*, 21/1–2: 133–9.

Author index

Subject index